TIBET

ASSAM

SADIYA

BOOROO R.

Deenjoy
Chabwa
Tingri

SUBANSIRI R.

DEESANG NUDDY R.

DIKHOO R.

ASSAM COY.
HQ 1839
Nazeerah

NEAMATI

BISNATH

TEZPUR

BURHAMPOOTER R.

DHANSIRI R.

JORE HAUT

SINGRI

KALANG R.

GAUHATI

Hills inhabited by Naga hill tribes.

SYLHET

SURMA R.

CACHAR

SILCHAR

MANIPUR

KUSIYARA R.

MEGHNA R.

BHAIRAB

DACCA

CHANDPUR

BARISAL

BURMA

CHITTAGONG

GAL

Legend:

- - - - - International boundries.

——— River steamer route to Assam 1839–1856

— — — River steamer route to Assam 1856 onw'ds
" " " " Cachar 1863 "

- - - - Seasonal steamer service routes.

▬ First tea tracts worked in 1838: Chabwa, Deenjoy, Tingri and others in this jungle area.

▨ Tracts of indigenous tea found growing in forest – first pioneering area.

▩ Scattered tracts of indigenous tea. First tea garden opened in 1856.

▦ Darjeeling. First garden opened in 1857
Terai " " " " 1862
Dooars " " " " 1874

SCALE   0   Miles   50   100

The Pioneers

To
The Pioneers

(Photo c1868, courtesy Royal Geographical Society.)

The tea industry of today owes much to these men. To travel into the unknown, to wild and inhospitable countries, took guts, endurance, and the spirit of adventure. The pioneers had these qualities in abundance. They opened out fever-infested jungle under impossible conditions, with many dying in the process.

The Pioneers

1825–1900

The Early British Tea and Coffee Planters and Their Way of Life

John Weatherstone

Quiller Press

FRONT JACKET:

OVAL INSET
Tiger. (Photograph by Michael Lyster, courtesy World Wildlife Fund.)
TOP LEFT
Tea planter, Darjeeling, 1860s. (Courtesy Royal Geographical Society.)
TOP RIGHT
'First timers', North-East India, c1863. (Courtesy Royal Geographical Society.)
BOTTOM LEFT
Log-cabin life, Ceylon, 1881.
BOTTOM RIGHT
One of the few – a planter's wife, Ceylon, c1880.

BACK JACKET:

ABOVE
Pioneers, Selim tea garden, Terai. (Photo 1868, courtesy Royal Geographical Society.)
BELOW
A christmas card from Papa, 1875. (From a pen and wash drawing.)

The illustrations, except where individually acknowledged,
are from the authors own collection.

First Published 1986
by Quiller Press Ltd
50 Albemarle Street
London W1X 4BD

Designed by Tina Dutton
Jacket designed by John Weatherstone
Production in association with
Book Production Consultants, Cambridge.
Typeset by The Burlington Press (Cambridge) Ltd.,
Foxton, Cambridge.
Printed and bound by The Burlington Press (Cambridge) Ltd.,
Foxton, Cambridge.

Contents

PLUCKING · TEA · ON
BUNYAN · ESTATE, CEYLON

Preface

Little is known about the early British planters who started the great tea planting industry back in the year 1836 in the wilds of North-East Assam, nor of their compatriots who, in 1825, opened the first coffee (now tea) estates in Ceylon.

In 1869 a leaf disease appeared on the coffee bushes throughout the estates in Ceylon, and within twenty years 250,000 acres of coffee had been uprooted and the land replanted with tea. During this period hundreds of coffee estates were abandoned, and their owners left the country to return to Great Britain, as ruined men. Others stayed on, the struggle and fight commenced yet again, and from the ashes of the burnt coffee bushes there arose the tea industry of Ceylon.

Only those who have lived in the tropics, close to nature and far away from civilization, may understand what daily trials and hardships faced the men who, in the early part of the 19th century, went out to completely unknown parts to claim the jungle from the wild animals. The felling of countless thousands of acres of primeval forest was only the start for those we shall call 'the pioneers'.

The 150th anniversary of the commencement of the great British tea industry in the wilds of the North-East Frontier is as good a time as any to chronicle the life and times of the pioneer planters. It is a story of British enterprise, courage and endurance, backed by capital investment.

The first planters in upper Assam, unlike the soldier in his cantonment, generally lived alone. Left to his own devices the planter had an equally dangerous life to that of the soldier; the dangers coming not only from periodic attacks by fierce hill tribesmen, but also from his encounters with every sort of wild animal. While opening out jungle he had to contend with the malaria-carrying mosquito – the smallest, but perhaps the deadliest enemy, from which he could never long escape. It was not unusual for a planter to be marooned for months on end during the rains, unable to reach even his close neighbour, which in the conditions of the time might have meant anything up to 20 miles of dense jungle.

In spite of disease and the extremely lonely and independent life led by all the early planters, they were not unhappy men; their whole existence was one of self-reliance. The British Empire was forged by such as these. Man is at his best when he has a challenge to overcome, and so it was with the pioneer planters – and where they went, others followed.

The modern day planter merely takes over a firmly established agricultural business, or estate, which in most cases has been in existence for well over a hundred years. His comfortable bungalow, complete with every modern convenience – electric light, piped water, fridge, and today, of all things, television – is already waiting for him, as is everything else from the tea bushes to the estate hospital. He does not have to go out into the unknown, wild, untrodden forests and bivouac under tropical rain for months on end, with but the scantiest of provisions – for all that was accomplished for him long ago.

The nationalization of all the British-owned estates in Ceylon took place in 1975; today, after close on 150 years, the British planter has disappeared from the landscape of India and Ceylon, and the tea estates in those countries are now managed by the Indians and Ceylonese.

Although a certain amount of background statistics relating to the tea and coffee enterprise are necessary, this book is mainly about the pioneers, the men themselves, and their way of life. Having digested some of these statistics, it will be easier to understand the achievements of these men. It is therefore necessary to include the first chapter, which leads us on to the British involvement, and the pioneers. The last chapter is included because, coming towards the end of the era of the British planter, my own experiences, sadly short though they were, might be of interest to some.

Throughout India and Ceylon, vast areas of inaccessible, fever-ridden jungle rang to the sound of the woodman's axe, and the crash of trees. As the axemen made ever-increasing progress against the tall silent sentinels of the forest, man followed and thriving communities grew up wherever a tea or coffee estate was opened; the wildlife fled before the axe, or was shot.

There was wholesale slaughter of animals for the pot and, especially, for sport. The shooting of tigers drastically reduced their numbers and elephants, once abundant in Ceylon, are now relatively scarce. In the 1840s a single sportsman, Major Rogers, is credited with having slain 1400 elephants, while Ceylon's great roadmaker, Major Skinner, is said to have killed half that number – just two men accounting for over 2000 elephants. All animals are doomed unless we do something to protect them and their habitat and curtail the greed of the poacher.

During the great pioneering period of the tea and coffee industries in both India and Ceylon, between the years 1825 and 1900, close on one million acres of jungle were felled and tea and coffee planted in their place. Today, the tropical rain forests of the world are being laid low at a frightening rate, not by the axe, but by giant bulldozers. The deforestation of vast areas of dense tropical jungle in Brazilian Amazonia, parts of central Africa and South-East Asia for logging, cattle grazing, and oil-palm plantations – not forgetting the slash-and-burn technique that has been carried on by natives for centuries – is fast producing a situation of great ecological danger to our planet. We have come a long way since the pioneers.

Having come so near to the jaws of a man-eater in my younger days – as recounted in the Appendix, when the presence of my parent's dog saved my life and forfeited his, I cannot but feel an odd sense of gratitude, not only towards the dog – for neither of us could help being in the tiger's path – but to fate, which plays a part in the lives of us all.

The writing of this book has been for me both a hobby and a labour of love, for I must admit that I have a great admiration for the pioneer planters, and would have counted myself lucky to have been one.

I would like to express my thanks and appreciation to all those in the many museums who have helped me in my researches with their expert advice. In particular the Royal Commonwealth Society who have been good enough to publicise this book to many of their members; for this I am most grateful. My thanks to the Honorary Secretary of the Koi Hai Directory, Mrs Cathie Campbell, also to R.J. Barber, Honorary Secretary of the Ceylon Association, for being so good as to send to all ex-planter members – by way of the 'jungle telegraph' – a synopsis of this work in the quarterly bulletin. My thanks to the Assam Company – the pioneer tea company of India – in whose London Offices I was allowed to explore its extensive collection of old photographs under the friendly eye of F.R. Wilson, himself a planter with the Company for many years.

I am also indebted to Messrs Davidson & Co. Ltd. for allowing me to use some of their early photographs, which come from the past Chairman's booklet *The Sirocco Story* by E.D. MaGuire, MA. I would also like to record my appreciation of the kindness shown by Dr. B. Banerjee, Director of the Tea Research Association, in allowing my wife and myself to stay as guests at the Tocklai Experimental Station at Jorhat, Assam. Although armed with special permits, this made easier our travels throughout the tea districts in the restricted area of upper Assam. I am more than grateful to Sir Percival Griffiths for being good enough to read the manuscript, and make suggestions where necessary. Special thanks to Margaret and Charles Palmer, friends for many years and planters in Malaya and Ceylon, for being good enough to read those chapters in the manuscript relating to Ceylon. Lastly, to my wife Carolyn, for her fortitude during our sometimes unnerving travels in the hill districts around Darjeeling and Sikkim, when on one occasion – owing to a landslip – one of the wheels of our jeep floated in thin air over an almost sheer 3000 foot drop. Also, for the photographs she took while in India and Ceylon, some of which illustrate this book.

It is often hard to track down the whereabouts of old photographs, one needs to approach the task with the zest of a collector, or with the mind of a detective. Many of the illustrations come from my own collection, which has been formed over a period of many years. In some cases, for want of such early material, watercolour pictures have been done depicting the early stages in the tea and coffee industries in Assam and Ceylon. I have tried to put into the mind of the artist the scene that is to be illustrated, with only the written reports of early pioneers to go upon, but sometimes the requirements of the author and the tastes of the artist are at variance.

Travelling in the tea regions of India today, one cannot but be saddened by the state of some of the cemeteries in which the tombstones of the pioneers lie. At Nazira cemetery in upper Assam, there was only a single monument to be seen standing amongst inpenetrable undergrowth and tree saplings, and that was only visible because of its great height. The rest of the tombstones lay unseen and forgotten beneath the tangle of undergrowth. It would be heartening to think that the tea companies cared sufficiently to arrange to put this sad state of affairs right, wherever it is possible.

With regard to the early formative years of the tea industry in Assam, which was solely in the hands of the Assam Company, I have made use of that fine work *A History of the Assam Company* by H.A. Antrobus, which, having read from cover to cover, leaves me only too aware of my own shortcomings in this book.

One may detect many inconsistencies in the spelling of both Indian and Sinhalese names. These are chiefly due to the names of towns, rivers or estates changing from those which are shown on the maps, and in the many quotations – where the original spelling has been maintained – to a more modern spelling of the name.

Had it not been for the support so generously given by Lipton Limited in the first place, to help with the very high costs in printing such a well illustrated book, the story of The Pioneers might never have been told. It has been a pleasure to have worked with Claude Godwin, Chairman of Lipton Tea Services, and his colleagues – and Jeremy Greenwood, my publisher.

Finally, there are the words used by an old and much admired pioneer planter from north-east India, which I, too, would like to use:

> 'I expect to pass through this
> World but once, any good therefore
> that I can do, or any kindness
> that I can show to any fellow
> creature, let me do it now. Let
> me not defer or neglect it, for I
> shall not pass this way again.'

Foreword
by Sir Percival Griffiths

Now that great corporations dominate the world of commerce, it is only too easy to forget that in the 19th century the British commercial empire was built up, in the main, by sturdy individualists. In those days, high taxation and the Welfare State had not damped down the spirit of enterprise and many British young men were ready to risk everything in the hope of making a fortune. Some of them achieved their ambition but for many the reward was failure or death.

Nowhere can the struggles of the pioneers be more clearly seen than in the great tea and coffee plantations. Mr. Weatherstone has written a vivid account of the lives of the early planters and of the courage and determination with which they overcame the many obstacles which confronted them. They lived lonely lives, far from kith and kin, in most cases without the company of wives and children, and they put up with physical hardships which seem almost incredible to us today. Undaunted by those vicissitudes, they cleared vast areas of primeval jungle, they constructed roads, and they built boats, and so laid the foundations of two great industries which contribute much today to the economies of India and Ceylon. All this is in danger of being forgotten and Mr. Weatherstone does well to remind us of it, not in cold statistical terms, but by means of personal narratives.

Today plantation conditions have changed out of all recognition and the difficulties which the planter has to face are altogether different in character from those with which his predecessors coped. It is to be hoped that Mr. Weatherstone will continue his study of these matters and give us a sequel dealing with the life of the modern planter.

In the meantime, the record set forth in this interesting book should encourage those British young people in whom the spirit of enterprise still lives.

P. J. Griffiths

December 1985

OUR FIRST TEA COMES FROM CHINA

CHAPTER I

BREAKING BULK ON BOARD A TEA SHIP
LONDON DOCKS 1877

Our First Tea Comes from China

The first tea to come to Britain was brought from China by the British East India Company which had a complete monopoly of the Chinese trade up until the year 1833.

Its ships, large, strongly built merchantmen of between 1100 and 1500 tons, were nearly all built of teak. Next came what were known as the clippers, which had a far more graceful line than the heavy but strongly armed merchantmen. By the 1860s, the design of the clippers had progressively reached a very high standard and, in 1863, their construction changed slightly once again to that of wooden planking on an iron frame. The composite form of construction, as it was called, was used in the 1860s on such tea clippers as *Cutty Sark, Taiping, Lahloo,* and *Norman Court,* as well as on many other famous sailing ships.

In the early days of European trade in the East, piracy was a force to be reckoned with. Therefore all ships were heavily armed, as with the

PREVIOUS PAGE
Tea chests being unloaded from the 'Louden Castle' at London docks in the year 1877. In the vast holds of the ship were 40,000 packages of tea amounting to two million pounds in weight. Broker's clerks – dressed in top hats – can be seen taking random samples out of some of the tea chests, after which they would hurry away with their samples to the offices of the tea merchants. The seamen, a mixture of Chinamen and Lascars, are down in the holds of the ship, lifting the heavy tea chests ready for winching ashore, while others busy themselves under the watchful eye of a ship's officer. (From a drawing in 'The Illustrated London News'.)
LEFT
A Chinese tea plucker. (From a drawing published in 'The Illustrated London News' in 1857.)

*Taking on cargo in eastern waters.
(Engraving 1873, courtesy Mansell
Collection.)*

Indiamen and, to a lesser extent, the clippers, which always carried a
good number of pistols and muskets in arms racks, generally housed in
the saloon.

Only one of these once famous tea clippers remains to be seen today,
restored to her original condition: *Cutty Sark* now lies in dry dock at
Greenwich. Built at Dumbarton on the Clyde in 1869 at a cost of
£16,150, she was intended for the China tea trade but, being constructed towards the end of the clipper ship era, she only made eight
voyages as a tea ship, mostly from Shanghai and Woosung. It was on
one of these passages that she raced against another equally famous
tea clipper, *Thermopylae*. These two once great rivals were loading tea
alongside each other on June 17th, just a little over a hundred years
ago, in preparation for the great race of 1872.

Thermopylae loaded 1,196,000 pounds of tea. *Cutty Sark* loaded
1,303,000 pounds of tea.

The freight rates – £3-10-0 per ton carried – earned each ship close on
£2000 for that one passage. Having stowed away their cargoes of tea,
the two ships sailed on the same tide, and during their passage down
the South China Sea were never more than a mile apart. It was only
after passing through Sunda Strait that strong trade winds began to
favour *Cutty Sark* in the Indian Ocean and, after three days sailing, she
was thought to have been 500 miles ahead of *Thermopylae*. Disaster
then struck *Cutty Sark* when her rudder was lost and, although a jury
rudder was immediately fixed, she finally arrrived back in London
with her cargo of tea a week after *Thermopylae*.

Freight rates for tea depended upon a ship's reputation – her track

record of speed of passage and safe deliveries; at one time rates rose as high as £8 a ton. Such famous tea clippers as *Ariel*, *Taiping*, *Thermopylae* and *Cutty Sark* could always command the top rates as they were known to be fast and safe; that is, as safe as a sailing ship could be at that time.

However, the beginning of the end was in sight for the clipper ships. The cutting and opening of the Suez Canal in 1869 caused an immediate drop in the tea carried by the clippers, the days of which were in any case numbered because of the new steamers. Some of the Glen Line steamers, using the new route through the Suez Canal, could do the passage in a matter of 44 days, as against the 100 days or more taken by the faster clippers, battling their way around the Cape of Good Hope.

The clippers, on their outward passages, usually carried cargoes of raw materials and goods manufactured in Britain. Between the arrival dates of the tea ships at ports such as Shanghai and Hong Kong, and the loading of the first teas of the season, they would be mainly employed in the eastern coastal trade, carrying cargoes of rice. After trading up and down the coasts, the clippers would make their way to the tea ports in plenty of time to receive their cargoes of tea.

LEFT
'The Cutty Sark'. She sailed in the China tea trade between 1870 and 1877, after which she carried general cargoes until 1883, when she was put to the Australian wool trade. She had an enormous sail area of 32,000 square feet, and her fastest passage from China (Shanghai) to England – 107 days – was made in 1871, with a full load of tea. (An oil painting by Tudgay, 1872, courtesy Cutty Sark Society.)

ABOVE
The stowage of tea chests on board 'The Cutty Sark'. (Courtesy 'Yachting World'.)

BELOW
The opening of the Suez Canal. The view is that seen looking southwards towards Ismailia; to the left is the Sinai desert, while to the right is the valley of the Nile. A large dredging machine is seen moored in the immediate foreground, whilst the small steam launch with covered awning and flags fore and aft coming up in the opposite direction to the larger steamships, is the postal boat on its way up to Port Said. By the late 1870s, the steamers had succeeded in capturing the tea trade simply because they could pass through the canal, whereas the clipper ships had to do the longer route around South Africa. (Drawing 1869 'Illustrated London News' courtesy British Library.)

RIGHT
'The Glenartney' was just one of the many fast screw steamers owned by the Glen Line. This ship was first home with the new teas of the 1874 season, and her time for the passage from Woosung to the London docks via the Suez Canal was 44 days, which included stops to take on coal. (1874, from 'The Illustrated London News'.)

Before the arrival of the season's first crop of tea at the pagoda anchorage Foochow, there would often be as many as a dozen fine tea clippers lying at their moorings. The crack clippers began to arrive towards the latter half of April; their crews would immediately go to work getting everything ship-shape, ready for the tea chests and the four months' race home.

There was always great competition between the owners and the captains of the fast sailing ships employed in the China tea trade for the honour of bringing home to the port of London the first teas of the season, which were always of the best quality. Every year the ship that landed the first China teas of the new season at London docks received a premium of ten shillings per ton of tea.

In the great race of 1866, no less than sixteen famous tea clippers were assembled at the pagoda anchorage, waiting for the first teas of the new season to come down the Min River from the tea growing provinces. Three of the clippers, *Ariel, Taiping and Serica*, completed loading, and all left on the same tide; after a passage half-way round the world, all three arrived on the same tide. The premium of ten shillings a ton, and the special prize of £100, was divided between *Ariel* and *Taiping* as joint winners. As to *Serica*, well, she was a very close third, getting into the dock a few hours later.

During the 1870s, there were between 35 and 40 sailing ships engaged in the tea trade, each one carrying cargoes averaging just over a million pounds. The standard duration of a passage from China to the London docks via the Cape of Good Hope was about 130 days, but some of the faster clippers did the voyage in under 90 days.

In China, the tea was first plucked in the mild and temperate season of spring, when the tea bushes throw out new leaf after the long cold winter. The first 'flush', or leaf, of the season was generally plucked towards the end of April, and from this young and tender leaf the very best grades of tea were made. This was the reason for the presence of all the clipper ships lying at their moorings.

After the first spring 'flush' had been taken, three further pluckings followed at intervals of roughly five weeks, and the season ended with the last leaf being taken in September, after which all plucking was

BELOW
Tea plantations in the black-tea district of China. (Courtesy British Library.)
BELOW RIGHT
Loading tea into tea junks at Tscen-tang for transportation down river to the tea stores at ports such as Canton, Macao and Foochow, where it was then loaded onto the waiting clippers. (Courtesy British Library.)

RIGHT
The leaf coming in from the fields was first placed in wide shallow baskets and then exposed to wind and sun for several hours for 'withering'. After foot rolling, it was spread on thin iron plates over stoves and then roasted to make the finished product: tea. (Courtesy British Library.)

stopped for lack of leaf until the following season. During the growing season, the later crops from the fields were of a coarser leaf and consequently made a poorer quality tea.

During the early years of the trade, the tea was loaded at the ports of Canton, Macao and Shanghai; in later years these were replaced to a large extent by Foochow.

Generally, the first tea came down the Min River in sampans and junks to the pagoda anchorage at Foochow towards the latter half of May. It was then taken on board the waiting clippers and stowed away carefully by Chinese stevedores, who worked day and night until the vessels were fully loaded. The chests of tea were packed closely with wood and matting dunnage, so that the cargo would remain 'tight' throughout the long and dangerous voyage to England. Sailing ships often encountered typhoons during their passage through the China Seas, and every year one or more vanished without trace. During the five or six days of loading and stowing some million pounds of tea, there would be little sleep for anyone on board until the hatches were battened down and the ship cast off.

The end of May and the beginning of June saw the first of the ▷

The English mercantile agent's special mission is that of tasting, pricing, and buying the teas suitable for the British market. He is seen here on board a steam ship approaching the end of his long voyage out to China. 'The Illustrated London News' published these sketches in 1888.

Next we see him on the morning of his first day in China, aroused at six o'clock by a native servant boy, who brings a cup of the refreshing beverage to his bedside, and who has already filled his bath with cold water.

Upon commencing work a little later in the morning, he is to be seen in conference with a plump and spectacled Chinese vendor of teas whose samples are tasted, but not swallowed, from the cups of the steaming infusion. He offers a moderate price and, after much haggling, a final price is agreed upon.

The chests are supposed to contain a certain weight of tea and, when sold, are brought to be weighed in the presence of the buyer.

This scene shows the method by which the tea chests are transported to the wharfside, where they are then loaded onto tea lighters to be taken out to the ship lying at anchor.

Finally, we see our friend burning the midnight oil, hard at work in his office on the eve of the ship's departure to England. He sits writing to his employers in London. So ends the sketch on a tea taster's life and work in China.

ABOVE
Native tea gardens – where the Chinese drink their tea. (Sketch from 'The Illustrated London News', 1863. Courtesy British Library.)

RIGHT
Could this be the origin of the dance, the cha cha, in a tea chest? In the Chinese language the word 'cha' means tea. (Courtesy British Library.)

clippers depart from the tea ports in China. The first teas of the season started to arrive at the London docks in the early part of September, building up in quantity each month until the end of October, when the market in Mincing Lane was at its busiest. Tea did however continue to arrive in London up until December and January, depending upon how late it was received and loaded at the ports in China. By the late 1870s most of the tea clippers had been forced out of the China tea trade by the steamers, which could do the passage from China some 70 days quicker than the clippers.

The unloading of the tea clippers and the warehousing of their cargoes along the wharves of the East and West India Docks always provided a scene of great activity. All the China tea discharged from the sailing ships and steamers – as well as the tea that, by the early 1840s, had started to arrive from India and, by the early 1870s, from Ceylon – was received and prepared for the London market by the dock companies. In 1844, 2000 labourers were employed in the London docks on any one day, handling cargoes of tea, coffee, tobacco, cotton, sugar and wines and spirits.

Enormous quantities of tea were brought into the docks each year. Between 1834 and 1836, the St Katherine's Dock Company almost monopolised the tea trade, having bought the Cutler Street warehouse from the East India Company upon the latter's cessation of commercial activities.

The 'bulking' of the tea that was brought ashore was one of a dock company's tasks. The new Indian and Ceylon teas that were starting to arrive on the market in ever increasing quantities were nearly always bulked immediately after weighing by the customs men and the dock ▷

ABOVE
View of South West India Dock.
(Courtesy National Maritime Museum.)
LEFT
Unloading tea at East India Dock. ('The Illustrated London News', 1867.) And carting tea at the London docks. (Courtesy National Maritime Museum, 1889.)
RIGHT
'Bulking' being carried out with wooden spades at a tea warehouse. A warehouse floor in the 1870s would be walked on with boots that had very likely trodden in horse droppings on the wharfside, thus adding to the flavour of the tea after bulking and refilling. ('The Illustrated London News', 1874.)

W. PARROTT DEL ET LITH

company officials. The reason for bulking Indian and Ceylon teas was the irregularity of the leaf, and the refusal of the tea buyers to accept a tea that was not uniform in quality and appearance throughout. The actual process of bulking was simple: the entire content of a 'break' of tea of one particular grade was taken out of the tea chests and put in a large heap on the warehouse floor, where it was then thoroughly mixed, so that any one pound of tea was the same as any other in quality and size of leaf.

After bulking, the tea chests were refilled, weighed, and nailed down again. This work was carried out by the dock company's men, who were so expert at replacing all the broken parts of the tea chests that it was difficult for the inexperienced eye to detect any difference between an opened and an unopened chest. This bulking in London of teas from India and Ceylon went on until 1884, by which time there was a far greater uniformity in the teas being packed in the tea factories in those countries. A customs concession allowed the exporters to mark the exact weight on every chest, after which only ten per cent of all tea chests were opened to check their weight and content.

By the early 1880s, China's long monopoly of tea exports to all the world was falling rapidly with each successive year as the competition grew from the newly opened tea estates in India and Ceylon. The produce of these two countries was to overtake completely and eclipse all the tea that had ever come out of China. With the increasing population in Great Britain and the Empire drinking more and more tea, a huge market was opening up, and this market was taken by the British.

1887 proved to be the turning point, for it was in that year that, for the first time, Britain imported more tea from India and Ceylon than she did from China. The figures below show the progressive rise in Indian and Ceylon tea imports, and the fall in tea coming from China.

Year	UK imports of China tea	UK imports of Indian tea	UK imports of Ceylon tea
1883	111,780,000	58,000,000	1,000,000 lbs
1884	110,843,000	62,217,000	2,000,000 lbs
1885	113,514,000	65,678,000	3,217,000 lbs
1886	104,226,000	68,420,000	6,245,000 lbs
1887	**90,508,000**	**83,112,000**	**9,941,000 lbs**
1888	80,653,000	86,210,000	18,553,000 lbs
1889	61,100,000	96,000,000	28,500,000 lbs

LEFT
*Weighing tea for export, 1870.
(Courtesy Mansell Collection.)*
RIGHT
Men laden with brick tea for Tibet. One man's load weighs 317 lbs, the other's 298 lbs. Men carried this tea as far as Tachienlu, accomplishing about six miles a day over rough tracks which traversed the mountains at around 5000 feet. The tea was carried in large packages, and the 'bricks' of compressed tea, which were packed inside, were of between six and seven pounds in weight, each one being eight inches in length, and four inches wide. The porters put opium behind their ears to numb the pain caused by the straps and weight. (Photo 1908, courtesy Royal Geographical Society.)

Tea drinkers throughout the world showed their appreciation of the new Indian and Ceylon teas, with the result that, by the end of the 19th century, China's exports of tea had dwindled to a mere fraction of what they had once been. This loss of trade was solely due to the fact that both Indian and Ceylon teas were by then flooding the tea markets of the world.

By the year 1900, a colossal 900,000 acres of inaccessible jungle had been felled, cleared, and planted with tea in both India and Ceylon. This feat was solely the achievement of British enterprise, of the men who went out into unknown parts: the pioneer planters.

The Chinese found it quite impossible to compete with the efficient new plantation system of tea cultivation on the British owned estates. In China, the methods of cultivation and manufacture had remained unchanged for centuries, with little or no capital being ploughed back by the peasant farmers on their small plots of land into systematic planting and machinery. After the loss of much of her once great leaf trade with Britain – and other countries to a lesser extent – China still carried on a quite considerable trade with Russia, mainly in the form of brick teas. Poor quality tea, compressed into solid bricks, had over the centuries been exported to Mongolia, Siberia and Tibet, being carried into those countries by porters.

The discovery of the tea plant growing wild in the remote regions of the Himalayas and in North-East Assam, was to lead to a truly great enterprise in the history of world crop cultivation.

TEA AND ITS EARLY BEGINNINGS IN ASSAM AND OTHER PARTS OF INDIA

CHAPTER II

BRITISH ENTERPRISE: THE NEW TEA INDUSTRY IN THE WILDS OF NORTH-EAST ASSAM AND OTHER PARTS OF INDIA

Tea and its Early Beginnings in Assam and Other Parts of India

The tea plant was first found in India during the late 18th century. It was discovered growing wild at heights of between 2500 and 6000 feet in the northern districts, running from Nepal eastward along the mountainous region and forests of Assam and through to the Chinese provinces of Sechuan and Yunnan where the best China tea was cultivated. There was a similarity of climate and elevation between the tea growing districts in China and those in which the indigenous tea plant was found in North-East India.

As early as 1788, the botanist Sir Joseph Banks had reported to the Director of the Honourable East India Company the possibility that the tea plant could be cultivated in the region bordering the Himalayas, where it was thought to be indigenous. However, nothing was done about the matter for the following 45 years.

Then, in 1823, the East India Company received reports from a Major Robert Bruce stating that the tea plant was to be found growing wild in and around Sadiya, and almost everywhere in the jungles of North-East Assam. He had been shown the tea plants by the Singhpo chiefs. Later, Robert told his brother, Charles Alexander Bruce, when the latter was also in the region, commanding HM gunboat *Diana*.

At first it was not at all clear whether the camellia that grew in the forests was indigenous to the area, nor whether it was the true tea plant. To this day a certain amount of doubt exists as to whether the tea plant was indigenous over much of North and North-East India. However, it would seem from accounts of the time of hundreds of thousands of tea plants of all ages being found over a wide area – a large proportion growing under virgin jungle – that it was indeed indigenous. In many areas compact groups of tea plants were found growing closely together, as though they had been planted, and this occurred both on the plains and in the hills between Assam and Burma.

From time immemorial, natives of the tropical countries of the world have made use of their habitat by felling and burning off small patches of jungle on which they would plant one or two crops in a year before moving on to another part of the jungle to repeat the process. The natives certainly knew of the tea plant and of its value to them, and it is only logical to assume that over the years countless acres of 'jhumed' land had, at different times, been cultivated with the tea plant, even to the extent of planting out young self-sown tea seedlings taken from the surrounding jungle. C.A. Bruce had observed many such small native clearings and, having seen just how quickly the tea plants grew up with fresh growth from the old stumps after being cut down and burned, decided to adopt the same technique in forming his own first small tea clearings. As recently as 1985, while travelling in upper Assam, I was informed by my Assamese driver that tea trees of all sizes could be seen growing wild in the jungle along the Naga border.

PREVIOUS PAGE TOP
Tea planters, Darjeeling area, c1868. (Courtesy Royal Geographical Society.)
PREVIOUS PAGE BOTTOM
Tea pluckers, Assam, c1900. (Courtesy India Office Library.)
BELOW
Sir Joseph Banks. (Courtesy British Library.)

Founding Certificate of the Assam Company, 1839. (Courtesy the Assam Company.)

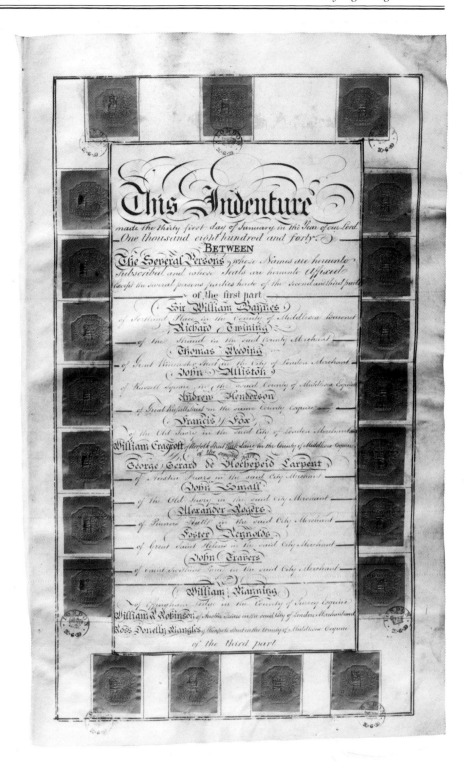

When the East India Company's monopoly of the tea trade with China was abolished by parliament in 1833, the Company turned its attention to India as a possible tea producing area to rival China. In 1834, Lord Bentinck set up a tea committee to investigate the viability of growing tea on a commercial scale in India, with the idea that, should it be found feasible, the Company's experimental nurseries could be handed over to private enterprise for future commercial development. Later that year the tea committee sent one of its members, G.J. Gordon, to China with the object of acquiring as many tea seeds and young plants as could be obtained. He was also instructed to recruit Chinese tea makers, as well as those with a knowledge of the cultivation of the young tea plants: the secrets of tea cultivation and manufacture had naturally been jealously guarded in ▷

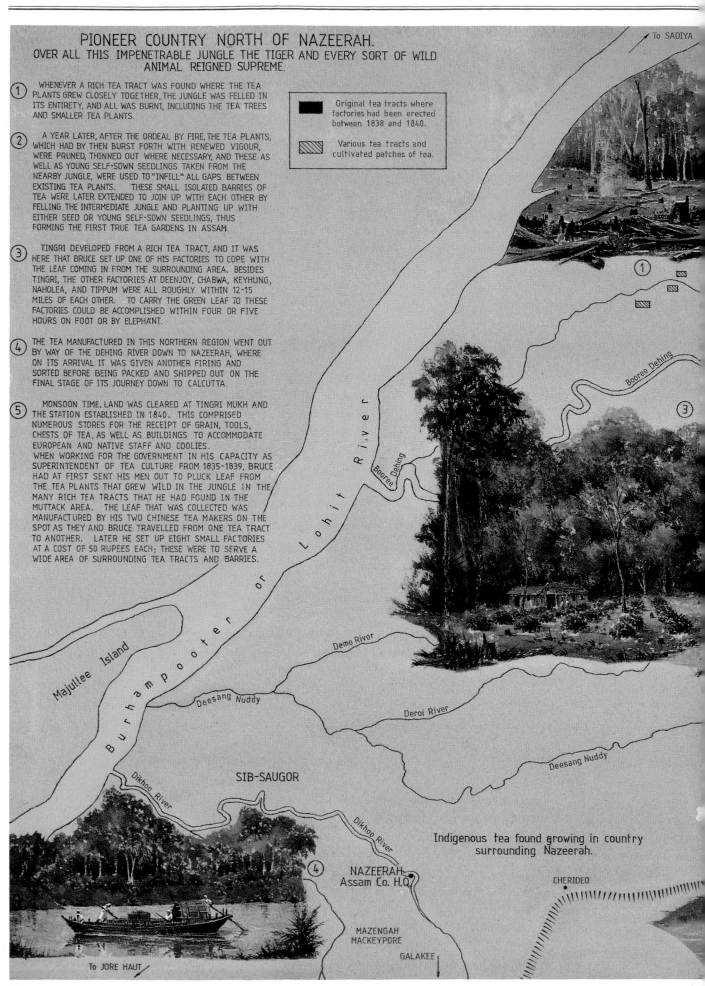

PIONEER COUNTRY NORTH OF NAZEERAH.
OVER ALL THIS IMPENETRABLE JUNGLE THE TIGER AND EVERY SORT OF WILD ANIMAL REIGNED SUPREME.

(1) WHENEVER A RICH TEA TRACT WAS FOUND WHERE THE TEA PLANTS GREW CLOSELY TOGETHER, THE JUNGLE WAS FELLED IN ITS ENTIRETY, AND ALL WAS BURNT, INCLUDING THE TEA TREES AND SMALLER TEA PLANTS.

(2) A YEAR LATER, AFTER THE ORDEAL BY FIRE, THE TEA PLANTS, WHICH HAD BY THEN BURST FORTH WITH RENEWED VIGOUR, WERE PRUNED, THINNED OUT WHERE NECESSARY, AND THESE AS WELL AS YOUNG SELF-SOWN SEEDLINGS TAKEN FROM THE NEARBY JUNGLE, WERE USED TO "INFILL" ALL GAPS BETWEEN EXISTING TEA PLANTS.   THESE SMALL ISOLATED BARRIES OF TEA WERE LATER EXTENDED TO JOIN UP WITH EACH OTHER BY FELLING THE INTERMEDIATE JUNGLE AND PLANTING UP WITH EITHER SEED OR YOUNG SELF-SOWN SEEDLINGS, THUS FORMING THE FIRST TRUE TEA GARDENS IN ASSAM.

(3) TINGRI DEVELOPED FROM A RICH TEA TRACT, AND IT WAS HERE THAT BRUCE SET UP ONE OF HIS FACTORIES TO COPE WITH THE LEAF COMING IN FROM THE SURROUNDING AREA. BESIDES TINGRI, THE OTHER FACTORIES AT DEENJOY, CHABWA, KEYHUNG, NAHOLEA, AND TIPPUM WERE ALL ROUGHLY WITHIN 12-15 MILES OF EACH OTHER.   TO CARRY THE GREEN LEAF TO THESE FACTORIES COULD BE ACCOMPLISHED WITHIN FOUR OR FIVE HOURS ON FOOT OR BY ELEPHANT.

(4) THE TEA MANUFACTURED IN THIS NORTHERN REGION WENT OUT BY WAY OF THE DEHING RIVER DOWN TO NAZEERAH, WHERE ON ITS ARRIVAL IT WAS GIVEN ANOTHER FIRING AND SORTED BEFORE BEING PACKED AND SHIPPED OUT ON THE FINAL STAGE OF ITS JOURNEY DOWN TO CALCUTTA.

(5) MONSOON TIME. LAND WAS CLEARED AT TINGRI MUKH AND THE STATION ESTABLISHED IN 1840. THIS COMPRISED NUMEROUS STORES FOR THE RECEIPT OF GRAIN, TOOLS, CHESTS OF TEA, AS WELL AS BUILDINGS TO ACCOMMODATE EUROPEAN AND NATIVE STAFF AND COOLIES.
WHEN WORKING FOR THE GOVERNMENT IN HIS CAPACITY AS SUPERINTENDENT OF TEA CULTURE FROM 1835-1839, BRUCE HAD AT FIRST SENT HIS MEN OUT TO PLUCK LEAF FROM THE TEA PLANTS THAT GREW WILD IN THE JUNGLE IN THE MANY RICH TEA TRACTS THAT HE HAD FOUND IN THE MUTTACK AREA.   THE LEAF THAT WAS COLLECTED WAS MANUFACTURED BY HIS TWO CHINESE TEA MAKERS ON THE SPOT AS THEY AND BRUCE TRAVELLED FROM ONE TEA TRACT TO ANOTHER.   LATER HE SET UP EIGHT SMALL FACTORIES AT A COST OF 50 RUPEES EACH; THESE WERE TO SERVE A WIDE AREA OF SURROUNDING TEA TRACTS AND BARRIES.

■ Original tea tracts where factories had been erected between 1838 and 1840.

▨ Various tea tracts and cultivated patches of tea.

To SADIYA

Booree Dehing

Lohit River

Booree Dehing

Burhampooter or

Majullee Island

Demo River

Deesang Nuddy

Deroi River

Deesang Nuddy

SIB-SAUGOR

Dikhoo River

Dikhoo River

NAZEERAH Assam Co. H.Q.

Indigenous tea found growing in country surrounding Nazeerah.

CHERIDEO

MAZENGAH MACKEYPORE

GALAKEE

To JORE HAUT

NOTE
This map relates to the pioneering area between the Dikhoo and Dibooroo rivers; see also inside front covers. The watercolour vignettes are not placed in any relation to the map. (Watercolour by S.R. Fever, 1984.)

▷China where, in addition to the many compact tea growing areas, tea was also widely grown by the people on countless small plots.

Six months later a consignment of some 80,000 seeds reached Calcutta, and these were then sent to the botanical gardens in that city for germination. This was a quite remarkable feat on the part of Gordon at a time when Europeans travelling to China stayed mainly in and around the ports, and did not venture into the interior. It was only after Gordon had reached China that conclusive proof was received by the tea committee that the so-called tea plant that had been found growing in Assam was indigenous, and that it was the true tea camellia of commerce. By then it was too late to recall Gordon from China, and in the meantime the China seeds had already been shipped to Calcutta.

In 1835 the first nurseries were set up in North India and Assam. The jungle trees had been felled and the land made ready to receive the young China tea plants that had been germinated 1000 miles away in the botanical gardens in Calcutta. The plants from the original batch of 80,000 seeds were distributed between three trial areas, Assam being alloted 20,000 plants, Kumaon in the North West Province 20,000, and Madras Presidency 2000.

The nurseries set up in the Kumaon were made on land at elevations of between 3000 and 5000 feet, and a large proportion of the young plants fared badly. But from those that survived, many seeds were collected and further nurseries were eventually established.

The ten months old tea seedlings that were bound for Assam left Calcutta on board eight country boats towards the end of 1835. After a protracted journey during which the boats were poled and tracked by gangs of men from the banks, 8000 of the young plants finally reached their destination in good shape – the other 12,000 died. Even those that were eventually established fared badly, for it was not realised at the time that the plants needed to be shaded from the hot sun. Consequently many thousands died; weeds also fought in competition with the small tea plants, and in most cases won.

One can form a better idea of the difficulties involved in getting a convoy of country boats 1000 miles up river to an area near Sadiya if one looks at the map inside the front cover or at the illustration by Daniell on page 66. The route from Calcutta during the late 1830s was a very circuitous one: by government steamer it would either have been by the scores of waterways of the Ganges-Brahmaputra delta known as the Sunderbans or, during the rains, northwards up the Hooghly River into the Bhagirathi and then on to the Ganges, after which the route lay south-eastwards to what is now known as Goalundo, and then northwards on the long journey up to Sadiya. As the country boat drew less water, it could proceed northwards from Calcutta by way of the Bhagirathi at any time of the year.

The man to be entrusted with setting up the nurseries in the wilds of North-East Assam was an ex-Royal Navy lieutenant. C.A. Bruce had first served as a midshipman against the French, later becoming commander of a steam gunboat in upper Assam and, as such, was one of the first Europeans to penetrate the forests in the region of Sadiya. Here he had found the wild tea plants that both his brother and native chiefs had told him about earlier.

Tea of a sort had for many years been made in Assam by the local natives, the leaves being collected from the tea trees that grew wild in the jungle. Bruce, with his invaluable knowledge of the district and the inhabitants, was the ideal man to be appointed Superintendent of Tea Culture in 1835. It was he, and he alone, who gleaned from his first two tea makers, who had been recruited from China, the secrets of tea culture and manufacture that had been practised for hundreds of years by the Chinese people.

Bruce must have worked all the hours of daylight in the jungle, returning each nightfall to his meagre 'basha' or hut where, by the light of a candle, he made copious notes on the ways of cultivating the tea plant and the process of manufacture, which he was slowly learning

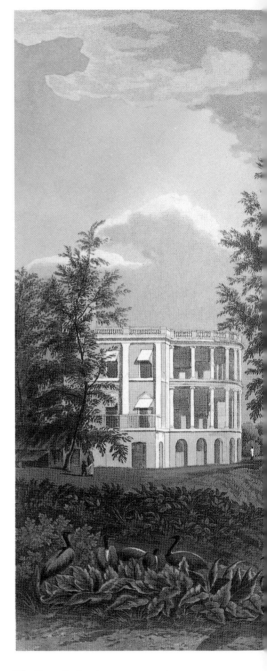

The Botanic Garden House, Calcutta, built in 1795. (Aquatint by J.B. Fraser, 1825, courtesy India Office Library.)

from his Chinese tea makers. Language problems made communication with the latter a long and laborious task; finally the government engaged an interpreter, Dr. Lum Qua, to help him. For four long years he worked in a very remote, wild, and untamed part of the world, which was quite often subject to raids from the various hostile hill tribes.

The Way Forward to the Tea Industry of Today

At the outset of operations, Bruce and his men were kept fully occupied in going from one tea tract to another collecting the leaf from the wild tea plants, just as the natives had done before. These patches of indigenous tea found in the jungle were left growing under the often heavy shade of the trees but were cut down to a height of about three feet from the ground. The young tender shoots that sprang up from the pruned bushes were later plucked, in the words of a young Assam planter, 'free, gratis, and for nothing'. The leaf that was taken was then manufactured into tea by Bruce's Chinese tea-makers at any one of the many small cultivated areas in the Muttack region.

Both before and after the establishment of his first pukka 'tea making houses' at Tingri and Keyhung – where tea boxes were also made – the leaf would arrive for manufacture in a very poor condition and in an advanced state of ferment. It is fair to say that, by today's standards, or even by those of the year 1900, this leaf would have been thrown away as unfit for manufacture. The situation was further complicated by the fact that the Muttack and Singhpo areas, where the tea operation was being carried out, were at that time in a very unsettled state. The local native chiefs had complete control over the sparsely scattered local inhabitants, who were so indolent that starvation alone obliged them either to cultivate their own crops or plunder those of others.

Writing from the jungles at Jaipur in 1839, Bruce was very prophetic: 'I beg to observe that it appears to me, from what little I have seen of it, that machinery might easily be brought to bear; and as Assam is about to become a great tea country, it behoves us to look to this matter.'

That statement was made as Superintendent of Tea Culture, just four years after he had arrived in the jungles of North-East Assam to take up his post. It is likely that the only possible machinery that he could have previously seen was that on the steam gunboat *Diana,* when he was commander of gunboats at Sadiya.

It would seem to anyone who studies the map that it was by no means prudent to have so many patches of tea at such wide distances from each other. However, it was the government's policy to prove that the tea plant could be successfully cultivated over the whole vast province. Indigenous tea was found growing in compact areas throughout the forest region, with the plants tailing off in places and then becoming more numerous again as one pushed through to another rich tea tract in the jungle. Bruce's method for establishing tea as a

The grave of Charles Alexander Bruce (1793-1871) at Tezpur. Pioneer of the tea industry. (Courtesy Inchcape PLC.)

Nathaniel Bagshaw Ward, 1791-1868, a London doctor, standing beside his famous Wardian case. Many useful plants, including rubber, cinchona and tea were transported by sea in Wardian cases. Kew played an important part in the starting of the cinchona and rubber industries. (Quinine was made from the bark of the Cinchona tree.) While on an expedition to South America in the late 1850s, Clements Markham collected and shipped back to Kew a consignment of seeds and young cinchona plants (C. succirubra and C. officinalis) in Wardian cases; these had been collected at some risk to his party, as the local authorities in Peru had disapproved of outsiders making off with their cinchonas. The first trial plantings were made in Ceylon at the Hakgalla Botanic Gardens in 1861. Again Wardian cases were used. (Courtesy Royal Botanic Gardens, Kew.)

Two Historically Important Sites in Upper Assam; Jaipur and Chabwa Estates

About 50 years ago these abandoned China jat tea trees at Jaipur – then already 100 years old – were collar pruned (rejuvenation pruning), since when they have

been plucked as ordinary tea bushes. (Photo 1935, courtesy British Library.)
RIGHT
A part of the same block of original China

tea as that shown (LEFT). Still growing strongly, this half acre block of tea bushes is plucked, on average, 25 rounds a year. (Photo 1985.)

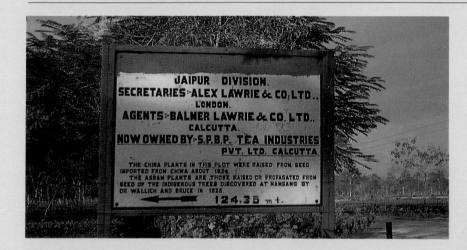

LEFT
The entrance to Jaipur estate. When Bruce came this way 150 years ago, there was heavy tree jungle throughout the whole of the region, with the attendant dangers from wild animals and hill tribesmen. (Photo 1985.)

This photograph shows 100 year old China jat tea growing at Chabwa. These original tea bushes were abandoned 50 years ago, owing to their being pure China jat – the curse of Assam – but, unlike those at Jaipur, these have remained abandoned ever since. (Photo 1935, courtesy British Library.)

RIGHT
Some 50 years later, in 1985, with the help of B. Gope – an entomologist from the Tea Research Association at Tocklai, Jorhat – my wife and I spent a whole morning searching for these original China plants. Two thick tea tree stems, sunlit, are seen between the two figures.

We eventually found them growing as tall trees amidst secondary growth jungle to heights of up to 20 feet. The land on which this original China tea was found no longer belongs to Chabwa, having been handed over to the local villagers under the Land Sealing Act. (Photo 1985.)

commercial proposition was first to send out men to collect the leaves from the countless wild tea plants in the forest and then make tea from them. At the same time he opened out the jungle which contained the best tea tracts – where the tea trees were found growing closely together in their wild state under light forest – thus forming tea clearings and tea barries. All this was done with the help of one European assistant, a small number of Chinese and some local natives.

According to Bruce, the early method of converting a good tea tract into what might be called an open tea clearing or tea barrie, was to cut down the forest trees and undergrowth, leaving the tea plants. These plants or trees – for many grew to a height of 40 feet – were then pruned to three feet from the ground and, with the thick overhead jungle canopy removed and the sunlight let in, the newly pruned tea soon burst forth with new shoots. After a complete area of forest had been felled and the underlying tea trees pruned, the only remaining task was to 'infill' all the gaps. This was done by transplanting two or three year old self-sown seedlings taken from the surrounding jungle, thus building up a compact area of tea bushes.

Alternatively, when a good tract of densely growing tea was found under heavier forestation, the jungle could be felled in its entirety; the fallen trees, including the tea, would, after drying out, be burnt. This was similar to the 'slash and burn' technique employed by the natives. Within a year, the scorched and blackened ground would be covered with fresh light green shoots from the stumps of the old tea trees, and these shoots would then form fine sturdy bushes. Again, the whole clearing would be 'infilled' to six feet by six feet with self-sown seedlings where necessary.

Whether the tea clearing was formed by the selective cutting of trees and gradual opening out of the jungle or by the easier, if harsher method of felling everything and then setting fire to it all including the tea plants, it was nonetheless a formidable undertaking to establish an open cultivated area out in the wilds of Assam at that time. The tea plants were not the only ones that burst forth with a vigorous growth; so too did the shoots from all the jungle tree stumps throughout the clearing, and all these required continual cutting back until they eventually died, and were overgrown by the tea itself.

Regarding the nurseries that had been set up in upper Assam, it was soon found that the China plants *(Camellia sinensis)* did not thrive under local conditions as well as the recently found indigenous type. Therefore, after a false start, all later plantings in Assam were made with the indigenous plant. In later years however, in some of the hill districts such as Darjeeling, and the North-West Provinces, the smaller leafed China plant was successfully cultivated at elevations between 2500 and 6000 feet.

But Gordon's trip to China had not been in vain for, as things were to turn out, the recruitment of the Chinese tea makers and cultivators proved to be invaluable to the enterprise.

The first tea left India for Britain in 1838 on board the sailing ship *Calcutta*. This historic consignment of twelve chests came from the East India Company's tea tracts in Assam and was the direct result of the labours of Bruce and his Chinese tea-makers. The tea was in fact made from the leaves of the indigenous plant, for at that time the China jat seedlings that had been planted out in the new nursery clearings were still very small.

This first break of Assam tea was pronounced by the experts to be satisfactory, and every bit as good as the tea that was coming from China. The first auction of Indian teas caused quite a stir on the market which, until then, had only concerned itself with the tea coming from China. The auction, with its high prices, attracted the attention of certain merchants and businessmen, and this resulted in preliminary steps being taken for the formation of the first tea company in India – the Assam Company – in 1839.

Having over the previous four years ascertained that the cultivation

The family of the man who helped us locate the 150-year old China tea trees, grouped in front of their house. (Photo 1985.)

of the tea plant in India was commercially viable, the government set about handing over its nurseries and experimental lands to private enterprise. Early in 1840 two-thirds of the East India Company's tea lands were handed over to the newly formed Assam Company rent free, for a ten year period. Besides its newly acquired land, the Assam Company also took up leases from the government on certain tracts of jungle which contained tea plants.

The Assam Company now had something tangible to work on – land. European staff were engaged, and heavy country boats built for the transport of the Company's stores up river to Nazira. Following the example of the East India Company, upon opening its operations, the Assam Company recruited yet more Chinese tea makers and cultivators who understood the correct agricultural treatment for the tea plant and the time of the year that the leaf should be plucked.

An essential part of the Assam Company's operations was the establishment of lines of communication – staging posts or stations – all the way up the long river route to its headquarters at Nazira. As the government steamers only came up as far as Gauhati, and then only occasionally, the transport of coolies, stores, foodstuffs and tea between Gauhati, the most important of the Company's stations, and Nazira was by country boat alone. It took twenty to thirty days to do the 200 mile journey from Gauhati up river against the current of the Brahmaputra. Each country boat was tracked from the banks by five men, with those on board assisting by poling. On the return journey from Nazira to Gauhati the time was cut by nearly a half as the boats sailed down with the current of the river, each carrying 150 chests of tea. Travelling by dug-out canoe or small country boat up and down the numerous tributary rivers that intersected the whole vast area of upper Assam could only be attempted during the hours of daylight; at dusk the craft would have to be moored for the night. ▷

The London Commercial Sale Rooms, in Mincing Lane. It was here that the first ever consignment of Indian tea came up for auction on the 10th January, 1839. (Watercolour by Shepherd, courtesy Guildhall Library.)

The Early Stages of the Assam Company's Headquarters at Nazira

THE PLAN

'Inset' relates to the painting, and shows a part of the Nazira station buildings. From the small part shown here of the land and station buildings of the Assam Company's headquarters at Nazira, one can gain an impression of the early working and living conditions of the small community made up of different races whose place of work was the fever infested jungle almost 1000 miles from Calcutta. The making of tea boxes at Nazira was not actually started until 1852*, when a large saw mill (a saw bench with steam engine and boiler as driving power) was brought up from Calcutta. This merely made the job of sawing planks easier and quicker, with the rest of the operation remaining the same. The tea box factory is, however, included in the picture because it gives an indication of the work that was involved when, some three years earlier, C.A. Bruce set up his first tea making houses and supporting tea box making huts in and around the tea tracts at Tingri, Chabwa, Keyhung, and Deenjoy. The area that was given over to crops and to the nursery would, in fact, have occupied far more ground than is shown in this illustration. The scene depicted is of the 1841 period.

*Prior to this date tea box shooks were brought up from Calcutta.

DIKHOO RIVER.

1. Elephants with howdahs strapped to their backs brought in green leaf in sacks, or partially manufactured tea in chests, from the Assam Company's scattered tea barries and tea clearings.

2. In addition to the two factory buildings shown (the main tea making house, as it was called, and the smaller withering shed), the verandah or even the interior rooms of the adjacent planter's bungalow might also have been utilised to wither the green leaf that had been brought in from those tea clearings that were reasonably close to Nazira. In good weather, the leaf might also have been placed in shallow wicker baskets and withered outside in the sun. From the more distant tea barries in the northern division where crude tea making houses had been con-structed, partially manufactured tea was brought into the station in tea chests, and given another firing or two before it was sorted and packed for shipment. The main factory would contain a line of charcoal-burning ovens, over which the tea was dried or fired, and the intense heat from these would find its way out through the thatched roof – there being no chimneys – with the frequent result that the factory was burned to the ground. During the early years, Nazira was the centre of tea manufacture for the company's holdings, which stretched over a wide area of dense jungle for a hundred miles from its most northerly division to the southernmost. In later years, these scattered tea tracts and barries were developed into tea gardens, with each garden or group of gardens having its own tea manufacturing factory. During the early years of the industry, the elephant, the dug-out canoe and the country boat were the only means of travel over this considerable area.

3. Suitable timber for making tea boxes, which had been cut from the surrounding jungle, is seen stacked for seasoning.

4. A sawyer's pit is shown to illustrate one of the methods by which timber was sawn into planks for tea boxes, as well as for building purposes. The thickness of the planking made for rough uneven boxes and was also responsible for the great weight of the early tea boxes.

5. Tea box making factory. Chinese coolies, jhons, were at first recruited direct from China and Malaya, and from those resident in Calcutta.

These men were skilled in making the tea boxes, and their lead canister linings; both were very specialised trades unknown outside China. By 1843, after their secrets had been learned, the Chinese were dispensed with and local labour carried on this work. Maintaining a good supply of sheet lead on site was a crucial factor in the early tea box making days.

6. Timber cutting coolies were employed to cut certain trees from the jungle for tea box making; these were then dragged by elephants to the settlement.

7. Country boats carrying chests of tea were poled down the Dikhoo River to the Brahmaputra, and then down to Gauhati, where they were either off-loaded and stored in the company's godowns until the arrival of a government steamer or, failing that,

the country boats would proceed the whole way down to Calcutta. The return voyage would bring staff, coolies, stores, and would take two-and-a-half to three-and-a-half months, with the craft being sailed, poled and tracked up river against the current, and those travelling on board living off the land as they proceeded each day.

8. European staff bungalows of the superintendent and his assistants differed little in construction from those of the surrounding station buildings, which were all made from local materials. The floors were of hard packed earth, and the thatched roof of 'sun grass' was supported by wood or bamboo uprights and rafters, with mud and ekra walls.

9. Crops such as wheat, barley, flax and, of course, rice occupied a good

The early stages of development of the Assam Company's headquarters at Nazira. (Watercolour by S.R. Fever, 1983.)

proportion of land. Nevertheless, great quantities of rice had to be brought up river by country boat for the support of those working not only at Nazira, but also for those working in the more isolated northern and eastern divisions of the company's holdings.

10. Nursery: an experimental area, and a small nursery containing some 5000 young tea seedlings.

11. The labour force was housed in huts made of split bamboo, with thatched roofs. Similar structures were used to store grain and other necessary commodities.

Gauhati. In this scene of about 1840, a government official is seen talking to a planter in the employ of the Assam Company. These officials, or agents, resided at small towns along the river route to North-East Assam such as Goalpara, Tezpur, Bisnath and Gauhati, and were paid a yearly retainer by the Company to look after its interests. At these places the Company erected storehouses for general provisions as well as accommodation sheds for its European assistants and coolies where they could stay while proceeding on the long journey up river. During 1840, the Assam Company recruited over a hundred Chinese, sending them up river through Gauhati. (Watercolour by S.R. Fever, 1983.)

▷ Having taken over much of the government's trial tea lands, the Assam Company made a request to secure the services of C.A. Bruce; he duly joined the Company in early 1840. Bruce was the ideal choice for, having set up the government nurseries and opened out numerous tea tracts over the previous four years, he was the only person there with knowledge of both the cultivation and the manufacture of tea.

By 1841 the Assam Company had 2638 acres of tea in production, although there were only 457 plants on average to the acre. This acreage was formed by tea tracts or clearings of varying sizes spread over a wide area of dense jungle. The costs of production were enormous. So too were the costs of opening out further jungle containing good tea tracts, and of planting out self-sown seedlings. If sufficient labour was not available for infilling with seedlings, the seeds collected from nearby tea tracts were used to build up an area under cultivation.

A new clearing, or tea barrie, would therefore often be made up of those indigenous tea plants that had been left growing after the felling, of young self-sown seedlings that had been replanted in the area to fill in the gaps, and of seed-at-stake, where seeds had been put down to fill in any gaps there might still be.

Newly formed tea clearings had to be weeded three times a year. There was a great problem in obtaining sufficient labour to carry on the continual battle against the creeping jungle undergrowth, with the result that the smaller tea clearings in many cases were only weeded once a year. This meant that the pluckers could not easily get at the tea plants which were overgrown with creepers, and many such areas were abandoned. In later years, when labour was more plentiful, these clearings were again brought back into bearing.

Tea in the heavy tree jungle would compete like any other tree for sunlight, rising to a height of 40 feet, and having a girth of 18 inches at ground level. When growing in heavy shade, it had dark green leaves similar to those of any Camellia japonica found in England, the two being of the same camellia family.

In 1847, the Horticultural Society sent the botanist Robert Fortune to China to procure more of the best China seeds and young plants. These were destined for the foothills of the Himalayas, the China plant being well suited to these higher regions. Fortune not only learned to speak some Chinese, but also shaved his head and dressed himself in the manner of the people, thus allaying the natural suspicions of the Chinese towards all foreigners. In doing this he managed to travel extensively throughout the tea growing districts, while at the same time obtaining approximately 13,000 tea seeds. He also recruited a great number of Chinese with a knowledge of tea growing and manufacture, explaining that he wished them to accompany him to India where they were to 'teach the poor Hindoos how to cultivate the tea plant'. Although of crucial importance in the starting of the tea industry in Assam a decade earlier, the Chinese recruits were found to be intractable, and more than a nuisance in one way or another. Those that were later recruited by Fortune for North India were no doubt sent packing just as their countrymen had been in Assam, but only after their secrets had been learned by the 'poor Hindoos' – alias the British.

The early planters could not get far without the help of an elephant. The province of Assam was thick with tigers and other wild animals and, even though an elephant only averaged two or three miles an hour, it provided a comparatively safe means of getting around. It could push its way through almost any type of undergrowth and was ideal for fording the numerous rivers and swamps. Moreover, as the jungle was always close at hand, there was little need to feed it: after a day's work and a wash in the nearest river, all one had to do was to lead it to the edge of the jungle, fit malacca-cane hobbles to its forelegs and leave it there for the night. The following day, the mahout merely followed up its unmistakable tracks a short distance into the jungle

A tea box making factory. In general, the use of wood for tea boxes was discontinued by the late 1870s in favour of plywood. (Photo 1870s, courtesy British Library.)

TRANSPORTING TEA IN INDIA. (INDIAN TEA ASSOCIATION)

LEFT
This photograph shows the transport of somewhat unusually shaped tea boxes by porters and ponies from a tea factory. Although the photograph is of the late 1890s, the tea boxes are still obviously made of wood.

RIGHT
It was hard work without the elephant: over two hundred men labour to pull a giant 'tea boiler' to the top of the hill on a tea garden in North-East India. A similar tea boiler is shown on its way to a tea estate in Ceylon. See page 111. (Courtesy India Office Library.)

BELOW
A hoeing gang at work in the tea fields, giving the bushes what was then probably called 'a deep hoe'. (Photo 1870s, possibly taken by S.C. Davidson, the inventor of the famous Sirocco tea drier, when he was planting in Cachar. Courtesy Davidson and Co. Ltd.)

where it had been feeding, and led it back for a bathe in a stream before commencing another day's work. A good sized Indian elephant weighs between four and four-and-a-half tons, its main food being vegetation of one sort or another, but it does also love rice. During the years when the pioneer planters shared the jungle with the wild animals, many a planter's ramshackle rice store was broken into by wild elephants, leaving the entire labour force, and the planter, without anything to eat. When Bruce was working the government tea tracts in 1839, he spent a monthly 18 rupees on feeding four elephants.

European staff who were taken on by the Assam Company during the early 1840s must have lived to a good extent off the land, as the natives did. Assam in those days was a very unhealthy place, and the planters – like all pioneers – lived under no better conditions than the natives.

At the commencement of the Assam Company's operations, local Assamese and neighbouring hill tribesmen were the only source of labour available other than the two or three hundred Chinese that were employed in various capacities. The local natives would only work at certain times of the year and, when it would have interfered with the requirements of their own paddy fields, they could not be engaged at any price. This state of affairs could not be allowed to go on if the expansion of the industry was to proceed at anything more than a snail's pace over such a wide area of inhospitable jungle.

At first, outside labour was recruited from districts in Bengal along the river route up to Assam. Before 1856 government steamers did not proceed any higher than Gauhati and the remaining 200 miles had to be made by country boat. Even during the cold season when the waters of the Brahmaputra were at their lowest, it was still hard going to drag a country boat loaded with provisions and coolies against the current of the river.

During the early years, flat-bottomed barges were always towed behind the steamers. These flats were ideal for carrying garden labour, stores and foodstuffs up river, and tea down river to Calcutta. As soon as the steamer and its flat could proceed as far as Dibrugarh, ie from 1856, the impossible labour situation was eased to some extent. The demand for garden labour, however, continued to grow as the many newcomers to the region, including the first proprietary planters and tea companies, staked their claims to land in the early and mid-1850s.

Much that has been written so far has concerned the Assam Company, simply because it was the only one in the field. In spite of the new arrivals and the formation of many new tea companies during the early 1850s, any tea coming out of Assam up to 1855 was still made on the gardens belonging to the Assam Company.

For those who were already in the Company's employ in those early pioneering days, the urge to take up land on their own account was great. Small embryo tea gardens were appearing everywhere, formed in the manner already mentioned. At first there was a reluctance on the part of planters to open out land which was far removed from the Company's own tea gardens. Many planters, whilst engaged in the service of the Assam Company, took up grants for land in the immediate vicinity of the Company's own gardens, and, while working for, and being paid by, the Company did, at the same time, fell trees on their own land, often using their employer's labour force and tools, not to mention seeds gathered from the Company's own gardens and tea tracts in the jungle. It should be mentioned that, from the outset, the government offered excellent terms to anyone who was prepared to take up land and work it; this applied equally to Europeans and to Indians; applications for land were however not forthcoming from the latter, who may not have felt inclined to venture too far from the more settled parts of India.

It was in the early 1860s that the new tea industry began to attract men of a different kind: speculators, out for a quick profit on land and shares. Applications for land were enormous, and thousands of acres of jungle were felled not only in Assam, but also in the Cachar district. Many of the newcomers, after felling and clearing their patch of jungle, hardly bothered to work up their properties by planting out seedlings or seeds. Not many knew what a tea plant looked like, nor stayed long enough to find out, assuming they had ever visited their holding in the first place. Such land, even with very small and scattered tracts of indigenous tea, would then be sold as a tea garden. The ignorance of the speculators was such that tea gardens would be advertised and bought as consisting of 150 acres of tea when, in countless cases, the full extent of the property ran to no more than half that, much of it being felled jungle with only sparse areas of tea growing on it. These so called tea gardens were bought and sold at highly inflated prices and, every time a garden changed hands, it could only fetch more for its owner. This state of affairs could not go on for long. The crash came in the late 1860s, when the very high prices of the bogus tea gardens dropped as quickly as they had climbed, and those left in possession of gardens on which there was little actual tea growing got out suffering huge losses. By no means all of the tea gardens were involved in the crash; those belonging to the Assam Company and to the Jorehaut Tea Company, founded in 1859, were little affected by this period of wild speculation, except with regard to the labour shortage which had been aggravated by the numbers of new gardens being opened up.

By 1880 the pioneering days of the tea industry in Assam were over. Meanwhile, some 200 miles to the south, tracts of indigenous tea had been found growing over a large area – in particular in the Surma valley in the district of Sylhet and Cachar. Where the indigenous tea plant grew, it was likely that tea could be cultivated on a commercial basis. As in Assam, the same method was followed in establishing the first tea gardens.

Unlike the tea-growing districts in the vast province of Assam,

RIGHT
A view of Darjeeling from the south. It is said that 'close to the spot where this sketch was taken – at an elevation of 11,500 feet – wild tea trees were in blossom just below the fir forest'. The tea gardens in the Darjeeling district were mostly situated slightly below the town itself, which is at 7,400 feet. (1876, from 'The Graphic'.)
BELOW LEFT
A tea plucker in North-East India. (Photo 1900.)
BELOW RIGHT
A fine pair of legs. A garden coolie carrying tea to a railway station on the Darjeeling Himalayan railway. (Photo 1895.)

comprising the middle and upper valleys of the Brahmaputra River, the tea growing areas along the foothills of the Himalayas were all at elevations between 2500 and 6000 feet. In the Darjeeling district, tea cultivation first started in the mid-1850s in a small but compact area around the town of Darjeeling. By 1857, several thousand acres of forest had been felled and cleared, of which 60 or 70 acres had been planted out with tea. Six nurseries had been established, in which a ton of seed had been sown. The China plant, although unsuccessful in its brief trials down on the plains of Assam, was found to be more suited to these higher elevations around Darjeeling and in the North-West Province. With the establishment of tea by the early 1860s in the hills around, and slightly below, the town of Darjeeling, the tea growing district was extended to the Terai, and then eastwards into what is known as the Dooars, where a very large and compact area was eventually opened up.

By far the most remotely situated tea growing area in North India was that in the Kangra valley, also in the foothills of the Himalayas, but some 800 miles to the west of Darjeeling in the North-West Province. Being of a high elevation, this region was also planted with the China jat, with the first tea gardens being opened up near Palampur in the late 1850s. Only a comparatively small acreage was opened to tea in the Kangra and Kulu valleys, which were situated some 200 miles to the south-east of Srinagar. This very northernmost area was found to be too dry, with insufficient rainfall for tea. All the tea from this small

Tab. I.

J.D.H. del. Fitch. lith.

Reeve, Benham & Reeve, imp.

RHODODENDRON DALHOUSIÆ, Hook. fil.

(in its native locality)

BELOW
An excellent view of a tea garden in the Darjeeling district. Tea bushes grown on the steep slopes – immediate foreground – stretch down a further 1500 feet or so to a lower division on the same garden, where factory and garden buildings are seen. Tea pluckers would haul themselves up the slopes by the tea bushes, in this case those of the small-leafed China variety. When tea is grown at the higher altitudes, it is subject to frost and snow, but this has little effect upon the evergreen bushes, which are practically dormant during the winter season. The manager's bungalow – right foreground – nestles within a group of tall trees surrounded by tea, with breathtaking views away to the snow-capped mountains in Sikkim, Bhutan, Tibet and Nepal. (Photo 1920s.)

LEFT
It is in and around Darjeeling that the beautiful straggling shrub Rhododendron Dalhousie is to be found growing up the trunks of large oak trees on the wooded and still dense tropical slopes at between 7000 and 10,000 feet. The shrub is comparatively small, growing only to six or eight feet. Many different varieties of rhododendron extend from Darjeeling eastward to the Mishmis hills above Sadiya in North-East Assam. (Hand-coloured plate by Sir J. Hooker, courtesy India Office Library.)

district, as well as that grown 150 miles to the south-east in Dehra Dun, found its way to the Amritsar market. The illustration gives some idea of the wildness and beauty of the region in and around the Kangra and Kulu valleys.

Some 1500 miles from the Himalayan foothills lay the tea and coffee growing districts of southern India. Although the first tea estates (known as tea gardens in North and North-East India) were opened up in the early 1850s, this region had also been the scene of earlier experiments. A small number of young tea plants of the China jat – from Gordon's original consignment of seeds which had reached Calcutta in January 1835 – had been sent to South India for trial planting in 1835.

As in other parts of North and North-East India, small nurseries were set out and experimental plots of land planted up with the young plants at different elevations and locations. Of the 2000 young China seedlings that had been sent to the Madras Presidency in 1835, the six boxes that were sent up to the Nilgherri hills arrived with no more than 20 of the plants left alive. Those that had been sent to Madras, Mysore and the Coorg suffered much the same fate. It was on small plots of land such as at Ootacamund that government officials and others tended the tea plants in order to see if they could be established and grown on a commercial basis in the many different districts that had been chosen by the government. The 20 plants sent to the Nilgherries prospered and, some four years later, were reported to be growing luxuriously.

However, the commercial cultivation of tea in southern India remained in the background until 1853, when the first tea estate was formed. In this region the tea industry grew up alongside that of coffee, both being commenced at about the same time. The acreage under tea increased slowly, and it was only during the late 1890s that large areas began to be opened to tea.

BELOW
A map showing the tea growing regions in India at the turn of the century.
RIGHT
This drawing of the bridge over the River Ool on the road to Kulu, in the North-West Province, demonstrates the remoteness of the tea gardens in this part of India. It also shows the method of carrying tea chests across frail bridges, along paths and jungle tracks through country *inhabited by tigers, down to the staging post at Palampur, some 30 miles away as the crow flies. The sketch also shows coolies rolling the leaf with hands and wrists; rolling by hand in India was on the way out by the late 1870s, except on some of the small outlying gardens in the northern hill districts. It was replaced by the much quicker and more hygenic method of machine rolling. (Drawing 1883. 'The Graphic'.)*

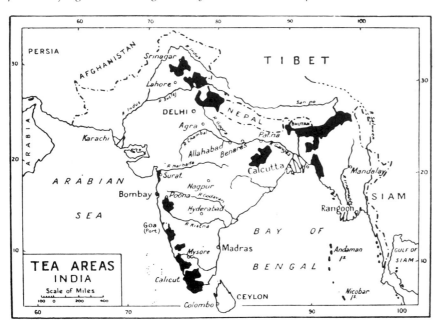

Early Tea Machinery

Machinery was first introduced into North-East India during the late 1860s. Oscar Lindgren, a tea planter in both Assam and Darjeeling from 1877 to 1938, gives us a description of the manufacture of tea in the 1870s, which is of historical interest:

> 'When I first entered tea, leaf rolling by hand was a slow and tedious process, and with a rush of leaf, it was a hard task to get a coolie to roll his maund (80 pounds) of withered leaf. Long tables were arranged around the factory and a space allotted to each rolling coolie . . . the rolled leaf was then made up into balls, and left in that condition to ferment, wet cloths being thrown over the lot to hasten the ferment. The firing was carried out over brick choolas, open fireplaces with charcoal burning at the bottom and wire sieves above, on which the fermented leaf was laid and remained until dried into tea. Sorting tea into different grades was carried out with Chinese bamboo sieves, and pretty tea was made. Plucking was restricted by the manager according to the capabilities of his rolling men in the factory. Sometimes over a hundred men in the factory were necessary for rolling, and a man was in charge of six choolas, to attend to the firing of the tea. The firing started at early dawn and often finished at midnight.'

The use of wet cloths thrown over the fermenting leaf was an excellent and simple idea, as the light was excluded whilst at the same time the temperature was kept low, greatly assisting the process of fermentation. The open charcoal fires over which the fermented leaf was fired or dried into tea were overpowering, especially in a confined space, as

RIGHT
The old method of rolling the leaf: hand and foot rolling. (Photo 1860s, courtesy Davidson and Co. Ltd.)
FAR RIGHT
The rolled leaf spread out for fermentation under wet cloths. (Watercolour c1895.)

was often the case in the early factories or tea making sheds. The firing coolies were often overcome by the intense heat and the stifling atmosphere, thick with pungent charcoal fumes.

Lindgren goes on to describe the Nelson's rolling table, the first of its kind in Assam, as well as the first drying machines ever used:

'The first rolling table introduced into Assam was the so-called 'Nelson'. It was a long table, worked backwards and forwards by a shaft of runners. Two fixed square tables were on top of this movable bottom table, which could be raised and lowered by a long lever attended by a coolie. A bag of strong canvas in which the withered leaf was rammed, was put in between the lower and the top tables, and the bags were rolled until the mass inside was leaf pulp. Sometimes, when time allowed, the rolled leaf was finished by hand on the rolling tables. The amount of broken bags was appalling, but the rolling was effective, if slow, and of a rough treatment.

The next introduction was a 'Kinmond Roller'. The first 'drying machine' was introduced into the upper Assam tea gardens by Davidson; it consisted of a square iron box raised from the ground by brickwork some five feet, having four sets of trays. The heat from

ABOVE LEFT
A tea factory in the Dooars, North-East India. (Photo c1900.)
ABOVE RIGHT
Dwarbund tea estate in Cachar. (Photo 1889, courtesy British Library.)

BELOW LEFT
No.1 'Sirocco' driers in an early factory. (Courtesy Davidson and Co. Ltd.)
BELOW RIGHT
No. 1 'Sirocco' drier. (Courtesy Davidson and Co. Ltd.)

1. *Ging tea garden, Darjeeling.*
2. *Weighing the leaf.*
3. *Plucking the leaf.*
4. *Rolling leaf by hand.*

5. *Withering in the sun.*
6. *Rolling by machinery – early model of Jackson's cross-action roller.*
7. *Hand sorting.*

8. *Sorting by machinery.*
(From sketches made on the spot, published in 'The Graphic', March 1876. Courtesy British Library.)

ABOVE
Davidson & Co. Ltd., Belfast, Northern Ireland. Manufacturers and suppliers of tea machinery for nearly 100 years. Sirocco Engineering Works, 1881. (Courtesy Davidson & Co. Ltd.)
LEFT
Sirocco Works, 1898. (Courtesy Davidson & Co. Ltd.)

a closed in bottom charcoal stove came through the various trays in the drying box to facilitate a draft. It was the idea and commencement of Davidson's 'Up Draft Sirocco' which was patented a few years afterwards.'

Canvas bags were presumably used for packing the withered leaf in order to keep the leaf on the table whilst it was being rolled. With the arrival of the first rolling machines came enormous savings in labour, and the large quantities of leaf from the ever increasing acreages coming into plucking could then be more easily and quickly handled.

The conditions under which tea was manufactured on the tea gardens in the early 1860s bore little or no relation to the term 'manufacture'. The tea makers who had been recruited from China at the outset of the new tea enterprise had brought with them the secrets of how to cultivate the tea plant and make tea from its leaves, but their simple, age old methods involved no machinery of any sort.

The early inventors of tea machinery were, as would be expected, mostly men who were in some way connected with the planting industry. One man, Samuel Davidson, stands out both as an inventor and a planter. He had left Belfast in 1864, at the age of seventeen, travelling with three other local lads bound for India, where they were to become tea planters in the district of Cachar. Within five years two

TOP RIGHT
The transport of chests of tea between river steamer and shore. (Courtesy India Office Library.)
BOTTOM RIGHT
Arrival at Calcutta – a human conveyor belt carries the tea from the transit sheds. (Courtesy India Office Library.)
BELOW LEFT
An historic house-warming party at Ballachera, Cachar. One of the party of young tea planters deserves particular mention, for he is none other than S.C. Davidson (standing fourth from left) who helped to develop the new tea industry in India by the introduction of his tea machinery. (Photo 1868, courtesy British Library.)
BELOW RIGHT
A photograph taken later on in his life, after he had been knighted.

of his three companions had died. Yet, by 1869, Davidson had taken out a patent for his first drying machine, the No. I Sirocco Drier, following it the next year with the patent for a new tea roller. Many new inventions followed over the years, and in 1881 he gave up planting to return to his native Belfast, where he set up his own engineering works.

With the steady increase in the tea acreage throughout India and with the greater efficiency resulting from the newly introduced machinery, the huge amounts of leaf coming in from the fields could be handled quickly and with a fraction of the labour. By the late 1880s, the new tea machinery had been installed on even the most remote of tea gardens.

★　★　★

A completely new industry had been established in a hitherto unexplored and impossible region. The Chinese know-how had been developed by the British, in the first place by guile, and then by the application of science and machinery. The Chinese monopoly of supplying the world with tea had been broken.

Since those first small consignments of the late 1830s, many millions of tons of tea have found their way down the Brahmaputra over the years. And so have millions of tea garden coolies and thousands of planters – all carried by dispatch steamer up and down this magnificent river.

Calcutta is the greatest tea port in the world, from which most of the tea that is grown in India is shipped. The Calcutta tea warehouses at the Kidderpore Docks were known as the 'world's tea caddy'. All the four steamers lying at anchor, have the distinctive black funnels with two broad white bands of the British India Steam Navigation Company – now a subsidiary of the P&O Group.

CHAPTER III

AND THEIR WAY OF LIFE

HE WHO HAS BEEN BITTEN BY A SNAKE WILL
ALWAYS FEAR A COIL OF ROPE

The Pioneer Planters in India

The first British planters to make the journey up to Assam in the early 1840s were drawn from men who were already living and working in Calcutta; young men from Britain were not recruited for the new tea industry until some five or six years later. Like their compatriots in Ceylon, who fifteen years earlier (in 1825) had cleared the first mountain slopes of their primeval jungle to plant coffee, the men lived under conditions of hardship, sometimes equal to and often greater than those in Ceylon.

The tea districts in Assam were even more inaccessible than those in the central hill districts of Ceylon. In the early 1840s it would take approximately ten weeks to get there from Calcutta by paddle-steamer and country boat, and then only during the cold weather season when

PREVIOUS PAGE
First timers, 1863. (Courtesy Royal Geographical Society.)
LEFT
Calcutta, on arrival. (Sketch by S.R. Fever.)
ABOVE
'The bore' or great tidal wave at Calcutta. With the coming of the south-west monsoon, a huge wave occurs for a period of three or four days, during which it races up the River Hooghly. As soon as it is seen approaching, native boatmen in all kinds of craft make for the

centre of the river, which is the only spot where the dangerous wave does not curl over and break. Many native trading craft from inland provinces are lost each year on account of their crew's lack of knowledge of how to ride the wave successfully. (Sketch 'Illustrated London News' 1857, courtesy British Library.)
FOLLOWING PAGE
A view of Calcutta from a point opposite Kidderpore. Tea was put on the sailing ships in the River Hooghly. (Aquatint c1825 by J.B. Fraser, courtesy India Office Library.)

the waters of the Brahmaputra were at their lowest. During the rains, the Great River – as it is known to the people of Assam – became a swirling mass of brown water, sweeping 150 foot jungle trees and whole islands of vegetation along by its strong current.

The first paddle-steamers on the Ganges, the Jumna and the lower reaches of the Brahmaputra during the early 1840s carried masts and were rigged for sail for use when the winds were favourable. These vessels of approximately 300 tons had a very shallow draught, well suited to such rivers where the watercourse was always a mass of sand banks which kept continuously changing from day to day, as did the intricate deeper channels by which the vessels navigated their way along the river.

During the early years of the new tea industry, only the occasional ▷

▷government steamer would proceed up the Brahmaputra as far as Gauhati, while the rest of the journey on to upper Assam – a further 200 miles – would be made by country boat, which was a slow and tedious way of travelling. Often the entire journey from Calcutta to North-East Assam was made by country boat alone, and this would take in the region of three-and-a-half months.

By 1856 government steamers were going up river as far as Dibrugarh. Even after such a voyage, the early pioneer would still have an arduous journey to his tea garden, through tiger infested country either on the back of an elephant, if he were lucky, or on the back of a pony, if he were not.

The opening of Assam to tea owed much to the dispatch steamers of the government and of the river navigation companies which first experimented in this form of transportation on the Ganges and the Brahmaputra. General supplies, provisions and rice were carried up river, and over the years hundreds of thousands of coolies travelled as deck-passengers up to the tea gardens that were being opened up in the great valley of Assam. To many of the coolies and planters going up river to the interior, it was a one way ticket.

By the early 1860s, monthly sailings by paddle-steamers of the India General Steam Navigation Company (IGSNCo) were also being made to Dibrugarh in North-East Assam. Just over a decade later, the demands of the tea gardens for all manner of supplies were such that a weekly service was inaugurated between Calcutta and upper Assam.

The captains of these vessels augmented their salaries by keeping well stocked storerooms in their quarters on board. Provisions of all kinds, such as tins of salmon, cigars, brandy, beer, Hollands gin, cartridges and quinine were kept for sale to passengers as well as to local planters. Those quaint but comfortable paddle-wheelers that came so far up the Great River were part of the planter's way of life.

Apart from a few weeks during the rainy season, the government steamer would not head inland up the Hooghly River from Calcutta, but would proceed down river to a small creek just north of Saugor Island in the Hooghly estuary where it would turn off to negotiate the vast waterways of the Sunderbans. This huge area of mangrove jungle and swamps, inhabited by tiger and alligator, contained thousands of miles of connecting waterways. Some of the smaller ones would lead on for many miles, closely hemmed in by mangroves, only to end up in a creek with no way out. Through all this, the direct route was a little under 200 miles. The steamer route was not clearly defined nor was it marked by buoys; the captains navigated from one known landmark to another if such could be found, and by the simple art of reading the water, its current flow, and its colour.

For the would-be planter, it must have been incredibly pleasant to stretch his legs in a long cane chair on the steamer's upper-deck, while sipping a glass of tolerably cool beer. Certainly, he could be excused for feeling pleased with himself, and life in general and yet it was probably during one of those deeper moments of thought that he came back to the reality of where he was going. He rememberd the Calcutta Agents telling him as he left their offices, 'Once away in the Assam jungles, there is no return for five years.' Of course a statement such as this should, to have been more accurate, have included the three words 'If at all', but luckily for him he did not know that this was often the case, otherwise he would have resigned there and then. It was time to call for something stronger than a beer.

As the early river steamers only proceeded during the hours of daylight, anchoring each nightfall, the voyages were pleasant if prolonged. It was only in later years that paddle-steamers could run during the night, with the aid of powerful searchlights and occasional lamps fixed to poles in the river to indicate the deeper channels and bends along the wide watercourse. During the early years, a variety of events would enliven the passenger's voyage. There was always the possibility of the steamer running aground on one or more of the

This early photograph shows an iron hulled paddle-steamer at anchor on the Brahmaputra. A barge, which was called a flat, was always towed behind the early steamers. In addition to the towing hawsers which ran between the steamer and the flat, there was also a large beam of wood secured between the two vessels by a socket and pin at each end. This beam prevented the barge from colliding with the steamer whenever the latter ran aground, and also acted as a companionway or gangway between the vessels. The accommodation for passengers comprised six to eight single cabins, which opened onto a fairly large saloon up forward; these would also be quarters for the officers. Cargo was stowed in the holds as well as on the after-deck of the barge. The photographer is thought to have been Dr B. Simpson, a tea planter. (Photo c1860, courtesy Royal Geographical Society.)

countless sandbanks that stretched all the way up river. Then, for those who had brought a rifle along, there was always the chance of a shot at wild buffalo on the river banks in the early morning, perhaps even at a crocodile or at the numerous ducks that flew overhead. The old European steamer captains would obligingly always stop the steamer, and put out a dinghy with a couple of Lascars in it to retrieve any game that might fall to a successful shot.

Pilots would come on board and take full charge of the vessel on their particular stretch of river. These men were a law unto themselves in the early years of the steamer companies, for the captains could not possibly pick out and follow all the intricate channels along the river which, in any case, changed constantly. Each pilot would see that all the deeper navigable channels along his particular stretch were marked with poles, and these would be repositioned whenever the main channels changed.

Many a planter would remember in later years with feelings of nostalgia the cry of the leadsman as he stood up by the bow shouting out the depths, 'Ek bau mile na he' – six feet and no bottom or 'all's well as we go'. At times it could be hard to remember one was 500 miles inland on one of the world's great rivers. Each day the ways of the East would impress themselves upon the new traveller. There would be the hordes of coolies travelling as deck-passengers bound for the different tea gardens who, at every landing place, would swarm ashore to buy eggs, vegetables, chickens in crates, as well as the occasional goat which would be carried on board bleating loudly amidst the uproar of excited talk.

In later years, as the European planting population increased, whenever a steamer was expected up river, those planters in need of something special in the way of provisions would leave their tea gardens and make for the various 'ghats' (steamer landing places),

such as those at the towns of Gauhati, Goalpara, Tezpur, Bisnath, and Dibooroo Mukh – which later became known as Dibrugarh. At such places along the river, flats were permanently moored for the receipt of cargo, as well as for the accommodation of travelling planters. These landing places along the river route up to Assam at first consisted of no more than the steamer agent's bungalow and a few huts but, with the expansion of the tea industry, they soon developed into large trading centres.

Any planters on board a steamer would go ashore at the various ghats, where they would often meet up with other planters in the district who had come into town to buy provisions. Frienships in such parts of the world are easily made, and what more natural than to find that the passenger and his newly found friend or old aquaintance had

This fine drawing by the Daniell brothers of the Siccra gulley on the Ganges shows an Indian country craft, such as plied the waters of the Ganges, Jumna, and Brahmaputra rivers from time immemorial. These boats were poled and tracked up-stream against the current when the winds were too light for the use of sail. (Aquatint 1804, courtesy British Library.)

already boarded the steamer for a pleasant evening together before even the last rays of the evening sunlight had dropped behind the jungle horizon.

Apart from going ashore at all the main landing places, and perhaps going off for a shoot, many a pleasant hour could be passed just leaning on the rail looking at the scenery, while always there was the soothing splash of the paddle-wheels going round. When the young planter finally stepped ashore at his destination in upper Assam and made his way to the steamer agent's bungalow – surrounded by nothing more than a few native huts and tall grass – he would have spent a total of nearly six months getting there, including the voyage out from England.

One can conjure up a vision of an old paddle-steamer at anchor, with her night lamps casting a warm glow over her dim outline, surrounded by the noises of the night, the swirl of the water, the occasional drift of laughter and always the sound of sandbanks collapsing with a muffled splash. The men would be leaning against the ship's rail or sitting in wicker chairs on deck, drink in hand, exchanging stories born out of the exigent conditions under which they lived.

In the early years, the Assam Company had sole control of the new tea industry. Upon the acquisition of the East India Company's experimental tea lands and nurseries in 1840, it set about taking on more staff. By the end of that year, some two hundred Chinese had been recruited and sent up to Assam; these consisted of tea makers and those who knew how to cultivate the tea plant. Local labour – when available and willing to work – had also been taken on to work the new tea clearings.

The first European planters started to arrive in the province in the early 1840s. Their main task was to cut down and open out those parts of the jungle in which the indigenous tea plants grew most thickly. A sizeable crop of tea could then be obtained from the tea clearing in the following year. These small tea clearings, often no more than patches of 200 by 400 yards of cleared jungle, were then built up to form tea barries, which in turn became the first tea gardens.

The position was somewhat different in the Himalayan districts where the China jat of tea was successfully introduced and planted out in the field either as seed-at-stake, or young plants taken from the garden's own nursery.

The more productive tea tracts and tea clearings in upper Assam were often situated at considerable distances from each other, and the early planters spent much of their time travelling from one patch of tea to another to supervise the work. The only means of travel was by country boat, by dug-out canoe along the numerous tributary rivers or on the back of an elephant.

As the best tracts of indigenous tea were converted into the first tea gardens, further jungle containing little or no tea was felled, burnt, and the land made ready for planting. They used either self-sown seedlings taken from nearby jungle areas, seed-at-stake (tea seeds gathered in the jungle and planted out directly in the field) or, in later years, young plants taken from the tea garden's own nursery. That was the position as we take up the story of the pioneers – from a slightly more advanced date.

★　★　★

The first-timer's main task on arrival in the jungles of upper Assam, Darjeeling, or the hills of southern India, was to see to the erection of temporary accommodation for himself and his small gang of men.

Oscar Lindgren's description of his arrival in the Sadiya, Dibrugarh, district of North-East Assam, to open out 300 acres of jungle records the conditions under which the planter worked and lived as late as 1877.

'The preliminary arrangements consisted of selecting the area to be

cleared, provisions for certain labour to do the work, and for the provision of forty maunds of tea seed, which was already on the way. My hut had only just been finished before I arrived, and the furniture consisted of boxes. A box served as a table, another as a chair, and a third as a sideboard, and so on. The hut was small, its walls consisted of sun dried thatching grass, fastened to a bamboo frame. A small window and a door made of the same materials. The roof was of large and broad jungle leaves roughly sewn together, and I found it absolutely waterproof. The mud floor was covered with rice sacks, a thoughtful provision of the apothecary (Doctor Babu) to keep the damp from master's feet.

After a rough meal I got to bed comfortably enough, but not so the cook, who made his bed on some boxes which were not too well balanced. A big log fire was kept going throughout the night, for wild beasts seemed to resent this clearing away of their natural home, and without a fire, which all beasts dislike, anything might have happened.'

The men who had arrived in the region nearly 40 years before had even less comforts. Lindgren's hut was only temporary until such time as he had found a more suitable site in his new clearing upon which to build a more permanent structure or bungalow. But with one thing and another the planter often had to make do with his temporary hut for periods of up to a year or more. The huts were generally dingy and damp, and more often than not leaked like sieves from the roof and sides when it rained hard; they had no windows, only wooden shutters, and the mists that hung around the surrounding jungle for weeks on end during monsoon periods drifted right through them.

The pioneers led lonely lives. Frequent ill health, complete isolation, and nothing more than a candle or 'hat batti' (kerosene lamp) to light the long evenings, was the lot of every man concerned in the early stages of opening out the jungle. Apart from curiosity towards the newcomers and their endeavours, the attitude of the local inhabitants was lukewarm and, in some cases, hostile. The lack of suitable labour was a very serious problem for the early pioneers. Local villagers could be recruited, but only in small numbers, nowhere near sufficient for the amount of work that was being undertaken. 'Nagas' from the hill tribes were employed generally for felling the jungle, but all the locals tended to be of an independent nature, and could not be counted on to turn up regularly for work. Labour was also recruited from districts in Bengal that lay along the river route up to Assam. The River Brahmaputra was, from the start, the key to the success of the new tea industry struggling to get established in the remote and distant area of upper Assam. The health of the labour force on any tea garden depended upon adequate food, good drinking water and dry places to live. Quite apart from the more killing diseases, a good 75 per cent of all tea garden coolies had hook-worm, and were generally in a pretty poor condition. Oscar Lindgren goes on to say:

'It was no uncommon thing to have 50 per cent of one's labour force down with malaria, without counting stomach complaints, which are always large items amongst coolies in jungle areas. In addition, wounds from thorns and cuts during clearing operations were naturally numerous. The beginning of the rains gave me an opportunity of planting out 44 acres of cleared land from the nurseries. These nurseries were a constant source of worry, as they were nice and soft, and so were attractive to deer. This night duty added to my other work, resulting in the death of a number of Sambur deer, which were devoured by the coolies, being too coarse for my tongue. The tongues however were a delicacy, and of course I kept the horns as trophies.'

Oscar Lindgren joined the Upper Assam Company in 1877 at the age of ▷

TOP LEFT
This drawing is not precisely connected with the opening out of the jungle, but it does indicate that the wild animals sometimes objected to the presence of the pioneers. (Artist's sketch, 1880.)
BOTTOM LEFT
There is nothing quite like white for reflecting the hot rays of the sun. Darjeeling planter, mid-1860s. (Courtesy Royal Geographical Society.)
BELOW
The photographer had to carry a considerable amount of kit in order to prepare and develop a collodion wet plate glass negative. (Sketch 1876, courtesy British Library.)

1st STAGE

Site of bivouac or first encampment area, c1863. This photograph shows one of the pioneers with a small group of his men. Boxes and sacks containing supplies and possibly tea seed are seen in front of the group, while to the pioneer's right are five most important items – rifles – belonging to the party. The thick jungle on the slopes all around rises menacingly, sheltering under its lofty heights all kinds of wild animals. The men would certainly build a large fire before dark descends. One would suspect that the tent in this particular case was for the use of the British party, while the hut would accommodate the natives. (Courtesy Royal Geographical Society.)

The development of a typical tea garden in the Terai during the 1860s

2nd STAGE

The new tea garden is now some four or five years old. The jungle on the flat area has been felled and has been planted out with tea. A small factory has been built to cope with the leaf coming in from the young tea bushes. Later, as the more hilly parts of the jungle are felled and the timber extracted or burnt, some of these, too, will be planted with tea. (Courtesy Royal Geographical Society.)

3rd STAGE

This photograph, probably taken at the six/seven years stage, shows more or less the same view, but with the addition of a new and larger factory. Much timber has been felled and taken from the slopes behind the factories and habitations of the labour force. This, as well as the timber taken from the tea area, would have been used in the construction of store sheds, bungalows, and factories. (Courtesy Royal Geographical Society.)

TOP RIGHT
The same view 117 years later prompts one to ask the question, what did the British pioneer planters toil, sweat, and die for?
BELOW RIGHT
A part of the long factory foundations, retaining wall and steps, is cleared of undergrowth for my wife to photograph. This tea garden was abandoned about ten years ago, its factory knocked down and most of its old China tea bushes uprooted or left to become overgrown. The adjoining Rohini tea garden has also suffered the same fate, except that its factory is now used for bottling fruit juice. Today, of the 44,000 acres of tea growing in the Darjeeling hill district, some 70 per cent are nearly 90 years old and urgently require uprooting and replanting if the industry is to survive in this region. (Photos 1985.)

All the photographs on these three pages – apart from the one at the top left which is believed to have been taken at nearby Dalingkote – show parts of the Selim tea garden. Considering that photography, like tea, was in its early stages of development, the old photographs are extremely well posed and taken. Although the exact location of the 'tent party' is not known, the picture helps to illustrate the sequence of events during the early stages of opening out jungle to form a new tea garden. After the establishment of a nursery, in this case from China seed, came the felling and burning of the forest. When the young tea seedlings were one-and-a-half years old, they were lifted from the nursery beds and planted out in the newly cleared area; then a further period of about three years would elapse before the tea bushes were ready for plucking. The nucleus of a factory would be built to handle the leaf coming in, and then new factory buildings or extensions could be added when needed. By the end of a decade, the garden would be firmly established and working in full swing.

LEFT
Levelling and marking out the site of the new factory. A small group on the site of the garden's new large tea factory. The foundation trench would appear to be that cut to carry the wall of the factory shown on the opposite page at bottom. Some of the Europeans, with topees removed, appear in the other Selim garden photographs. As these pictures appear to have been taken over a period of a few years, it is just possible that they come from Dr Simpson's camera as he was a tea planter in North-East India during the 1860s. (Photo c1869, courtesy Royal Geographical Society.)

A living community in the jungle . . .

RIGHT
Planters and labour force of the Selim tea garden; the date on the tea chest is 1868. The grades of tea on display are Pekoe and Pekoe Souchong, two of the coarser leaf grades of tea.

Tea was first planted in the Terai district in 1862. Selim was evidently one of the earliest gardens to have been opened in the district, Champta being the first. The view shows cleared forest land on which huts have been erected for housing the labour force.

The purpose of the machine in the foreground of the pictures is not known, but it could have been used in connection with cutting wooden planks to be made into tea boxes. It is obviously the site of sawing operations, which would also include the cutting of timber for buildings and factories.

The markings on the tea chest in the centre of the picture indicate the Chinese origin of the tea, pekoe, and pekoe souchong, and show their respective tare and nett weights;

The small group squatting in a semi-circle on planks are most probably all carpenters and tea box makers.

BOTTOM LEFT
The scene is reset, and this time three planters sit with a small group of women who are demonstrating hand-sorting with the use of Chinese bamboo sieves.

One would be quite wrong to assume that, because the factories on the Selim tea garden are clearly fine strong buildings for the period, the planters' houses would have been similar. In the early pioneering years it was always a case of tea first: money would be forthcoming for new tea clearings, and sometimes for a new factory or extension, or even for pieces of the expensive new tea machinery, but hardly ever was it given for the simple comfort of the planter. (Courtesy Royal Geographical Society.)
BELOW
Portable photographic apparatus. (Sketch 1876, courtesy British Library.)

. . . is prey to many diseases

▷twenty. He finally left the country in 1938, after a remarkable sixty-one years out there, planting mainly in Assam and Darjeeling. The climate must have suited him but, for many others, it meant disease and death. The young European assistants on the new tea gardens would succumb to the unhealthy climate and lack of good food after a year or two; they fell sick with malaria, or black-water fever and, if they were lucky, got out before they became worse and died. All a man could do was to swallow five grains of quinine every other day which, with luck, kept him free of fever.

One such young man, a Yorkshire lad who, attracted by the thought of making his fortune as a tea planter, became an assistant on a tea garden in Assam in the 1870s, wrote:

'Some years ago I was foolish enough to sign an agreement in Glasgow to the effect that I was to serve as an assistant on a tea estate in Assam for four years. A copy of this formidable looking document was presented to me by the head of the firm, free, gratis and for nothing, and it was only natural that, being one of "the parties", I should be sufficiently interested as to attempt to understand the drift of its meaning by perusal. After much wrestling with the mazy intricacies of the legal phraseology, I found I was to lead a strictly moral and sober life; in fact I do believe I agreed to become a total abstainer from all intoxicating liquors whatsoever. However, that is as maybe, and it is sometimes expedient to forget.

When the Assam jungles swallowed me up and claimed me for their own, I was asked by my boss whether I would drink beer or whisky; having a penchant for beer I said so, and drank the health of my new friends and fellow exiles in what I called lager and they pilsner beer. An old planter at the table ventured to hint to me that I should go in for whisky instead of beer in India. I thanked him for his advice, but took due notice that he spoke with a Scotch accent,

The ruins of a planter's bungalow. Built of stone and mortar in the late 1860s, this was sited on the top of one of the hills overlooking the Selim tea factory, and was possibly the home of one of the planters shown in the preceding photographs. A survey map of India dated 1930 shows that the bungalow was still in use at that time, marked as the 'manager's bungalow'. It is thought to have been abandoned sometime between 1940 and 1950. Some of the secondary growth jungle trees and undergrowth were cleared away before the photograph was taken. In the picture, with his helpers, is Rakesh Tandan, whose family now owns the adjoining Rohini tea garden and its converted tea factory, now the Tomp Food Canning Co. Ltd. It is the intention of the present owners to replant their land with hybrid Assam tea. (Photo 1985, courtesy Rakesh Tandan.)

LEFT
This somewhat gruesome photograph, taken in the jungle, shows an 18-20 foot live python strung up by its neck; it has been slit down the middle and its recent meal, a female barking deer, has been removed.

Such a python would always be dangerous if it came out of the jungle and took up residence near the huts where the labour force lived; it would have no difficulty in taking, and swallowing, a child of five to eight years who had perhaps been sent to fetch water from a nearby stream. (Photo 1926, courtesy Royal Commonwealth Society.)

BELOW
A view of a young tea clearing in the Darjeeling district. The felling, burning, and planting have all been accomplished and, in place of the jungle, we look upon a fine clearing of tea bushes. Here and there tall trees – still defiant – stand like sentinels. From a distance, the new clearings look not unlike cemeteries, with thousands of tree stumps bleached white by the hot sun; these, together with the fallen forest giants that lie between the neat rows of tea bushes will have disappeared within a few years while the tea will still be there in four score years or more. The gaps in the tea would later be 'in-filled' with three year old tea plants, as and when the large fallen tree trunks had rotted away. (Photo 1868, courtesy Royal Geogrpahical Society.)

while I am a Yorkshire man myself, and was at that time a believer in our national beverage. A discussion then arose – funny thing that you never hear of a discussion sitting down – and I learned that Assam in the old days drank brandy; got disgusted with it I presume, tried beer, and eventually settled to whisky, as the soundest of the lot; hence the little lecture.'

The tea planting communities were constant prey to wild animals such as tigers, leopards and wolves, as were all the native villages dotted over thousands of square miles of country. These small communities went in daily fear of their lives whenever a tiger turned man-eater appeared in their district. Once a tiger was known to have killed many times in a particular area, entire villages, together with their crops and land would be abandoned; a single man-eater could kill upwards of eighty people over a period of two or three years before being finally shot.

During the 1860s, at the time when much forest land was being opened out to tea, the human mortality rate in all India ranged from 1300 to 2000 victims each year, all from tigers, while the cattle taken and killed by tigers and leopards were quite numberless. There was very little to stop a man-eater from pushing down a door or breaking into a hut to snatch and carry off its victim. Oscar Lindgren himself remarked that, before leaving London, the Secretary of the Upper Assam Company had warned him that 'Assam was a dreadful place for tigers, and to be most careful, as already two of the Company's assistants had been mauled on foot; a very dangerous game, planting'.

The Christening of Tiger Sam is a true story vouched for by an honourable member of the Bengal Club:

'A man-eating tiger had taken heavy toll of life on one of the plantations, carrying off coolies working in the fields. The planter, enraged at the loss, called his two neighbours for a conference. After dinner it was arranged that the three men should sit on the verandah of a disused bungalow and await the tiger which fre-

ABOVE
A planter traces the line of a cart-road on the steep mountainside of a tea garden in the Darjeeling district. (Photo 1860s, courtesy Royal Geographical Society.)
BELOW
The pioneers: a close-up. (Photo 1868, courtesy Royal Geographical Society.)

quently prowled near the building. Something stronger than tea having been drunk at dinner, the three men dozed off in the cool of the evening. Two were suddenly awakened by the calls of the third who, taken by surprise, had been seized by the arm and dragged from the verandah by the tiger they were awaiting. The two planters, realizing the situation, succeeded in shooting the animal. The hero ever after was known by the name of Tiger Sam.'

As the first tea gardens took shape, small communities of men, women and children settled into their new life, living, working, and dying on the newly cleared land, which but a short time before had been fever-ridden jungle. For those living in such surroundings, there were many hazards. Poisonous snakes posed a real threat during the opening out and clearing work. Coolies could inadvertantly tread on or corner a cobra, a banded krait, a tic polonga or a bamboo snake, and die from the bites; while the planters, with their socks, leggings and boots would, in most cases, be more fortunate.

Not all was gloom by any means, even in the midst of such a wild and untamed area; the legends and lays of the planting world shine through. It is perhaps appropriate to illustrate the point by the tale of 'the python and the log', a story vouched for by a tea planter who had the reputation of being one of the biggest liars in Assam:

'Coolies were felling trees in a forest, making a clearance for a tea garden. A monstrous python made its appearance, and the workers rushed from the place. One of the men reported to the planter who came along with his gun; the coolies recovering from their fright, accompanying him. He was shown where the snake had been discovered but, unable to distinguish it amongst the timber, looked for the largest felled tree. Mounting the trunk to secure a better view, he asked that the location of the snake be pointed out. "You are standing on the python, Master" came the reply.'

During the early years in India, the death rate on the gardens was truly grim: cholera, smallpox, dysentery and fever took a heavy toll of both the planters and the natives. They all lived under very rough conditions. To a man who worked seven days a week and lived in a hut in

ABOVE
The death of a man-eater. Note the bullet hole between the eyes. (Photo 1900, courtesy India Office Library.)
LEFT
An assistant's bungalow in Assam. The early planters lived cheek by jowl with the labour force. This building would have had mud and ekra walls with gaps left to act as windows; there was no glass, of course, but the shutters could be propped up by a stick to keep them open. (Photo 1858, courtesy Inchcape PLC.)

which snakes, rats, and all manner of insects held equal rights of possession – and where, for long periods during the monsoon, he could not dry out the clothes he stood up in and slept in – a year would seem like a long time. No wonder that a great number of young planters left after only a year or two, weak with fever, to be replaced by new men out from the British Isles, whose healthy blood was sure to be a great attraction to the hordes of mosquitos from which one could never long escape.

In addition to disease and wild animals, the early planters in Assam had to contend with incursions from the tribes who lived in the hills. There would also be the occasional flare up with the labour force on the garden; over the years many planters were killed by their own coolies.

White women were as scarce as white elephants during the early years. A few managers were married, but rarely an assistant. There was nothing of course to stop a newly arrived assistant (chota sahib) from dreaming of the fair one with chestnut hair and green eyes that he had left behind back in the old country. The young assistant from Yorkshire tells the story of one such lately arrived planter:

'There is one person he writes to every second day, heedless of the fact that his letters will arrive in England in batches of three or four a mail. She looks rather nice in the photograph standing on the what-not, but if you want to rouse the lad, express admiration for the natty frame and astonishment why he does not put a decent photo in it.

Poor Alec writes keenly about his trip home, which he hopes to

get in five or six years. She is going to wait all that time and then come out with him to share the splendours of his bungalow and establishment. Oh, yes. But a day comes when Alec's head gets hot and dizzy, when a cold shiver runs down his spine and there is a queer craving at the back of his throat; his legs ache and his eyes pain him and he turns into bed and gets a real dose of fever. It frightens him; he remembers all the yarns he has been hearing of this man and that man in the district, who suddenly "winked out" – for thus callously do men in tea speak of the death of a neighbour. One would think that Alec would mention his fever in his epistles, but he has more grit than that. Nevertheless his letters take a more doleful turn without his knowing it; the trip home becomes more distant and uncertain; the life of a tea planter has after all its drawbacks, and he explains that the rupee is a fraud and a delusion, and then there are the mosquitos and snakes and things.'

By the 1860s there was another kind of fever gripping all those who were engaged in the tea industry: expansion. Young assistants were engaged by the steadily increasing number of tea companies for the specific purpose of opening out jungle and forming new 'out gardens' or extensions, to the already existing gardens. These blocks of jungle that were to form the out gardens were often situated many miles away from the existing garden and its factory and would be worked by a young assistant under the guidance of the manager or superintendent of the company's tea gardens. He would be left to his own resources and would, in most cases, live completely on his own. His job was to see to the felling of jungle, the establishment of nurseries, the erection of essential buildings and the planting of the cleared land with tea. By the time his out garden had reached a sufficient size, a factory would be built to cope with the leaf coming in from his first plantings. If the

CHOTA SAHIBS OF SORTS

'First, foremost and funniest of all is the 'Chota Sahib' who is in his first year in tea – who counts his time in the country by months as others do by years, and who longs for the day when he can say, like Faither, "I haven't been twenty-five years in the country for nothing, I can tell you;" – nice phrase that, but common, beastly common.

You must have noticed – you probably did it yourself once – that our friend arrives on the garden with all sorts of nice things; a new keeper gun from the Army and Navy, "in a case with implements complete" as the price lists say, a gun which requires a lot of cleaning and talking about; a revolver in an eight shilling leathern holster, "a very hard hitter" he will tell you; any quantity of good English clothes – his drill suits will follow him up from Dutt and Son in a week – including three pairs of knickers with box cloth continuations; two pairs of long boots, and a hunting crop with "To Alec" inscribed on the silver (hall-marked) ring, and you wonder what is the colour of her hair, and feel very disgusted when he mentions the crop as a present from his elder brother.'

out garden was not too distant, his leaf would be carried in sacks by elephant to the company's main factory for manufacture there.

A young lad of seventeen or eighteen, fresh out from school, soon became a man under such conditions. He would live in a small hut within a community of native men, women and children, and surrounded by jungle and wild animals. He might well not see another white face for a fortnight or maybe a month, and at any rate it was not the sort of job a man took if he hankered for the bright lights. His burra-sahib (manager) might visit him to see how things were progressing, and he would occasionally get an invite up to the burra bungalow for tea and drinks, or to stay the night. This of course would be like staying at the Ritz itself, by comparison with his own dwelling. Again we have our unknown Yorkshireman's humorous description of his own manager:

'It would be nonsense to say that the burra-sahib is a fool. He was an assistant himself once, though he seems to forget the fact, and this is the one redeeming point in his favour. There are other good points about him, but none that might be called redeeming. No, I'm wrong there, for he does keep good whisky.

Now the burra-sahib – that is, my burra-sahib – annoys me a good deal. You see he has his notions of how the tila should chall and, unfortunately, I have mine. But a house divided against itself cannot stand, nor can a garden run two dasturs. Rather neat that? If the BS (for short) would only allow me to run the show, why, the proprietors would not know what to do with their profits. However, he does not allow me to run the show, hence the proprietors are quite able to cope with the spending of their measly five per cent dividends. It's this way, see; the boss – 'old faither', we call him – sits in his bungalow and thinks! Did you ever hear of such a thing? We down below, squatting on the tila in the rain, in the sun, in the dumps, in a devil of a bad temper, do the work. When the sun gets

LEFT
A bungalow in the Terai district near Darjeeling. Young 'chota sahibs' enjoying tea with their 'burra sahib' and his wife up at the 'burra bungalow', on one of the few occasions when they could wear their best suits. The inevitable tiger skin is seen stretched out in the foreground. (Photo 1876, courtesy Mansell Collection.)

BELOW
A rope bridge somewhere in N.E. India. (Courtesy Royal Commonwealth Society.)

LEFT
Trollying on the Silligoree Kurseong and Darjeeling Tramway. (Sketch from 'The Graphic', 1880.)

tired and sleepy and the birds begin to wake up and chirrup, 'faither' drives out in his tum-tum round the work, with a face as long as a kodal bait, and at each section grumbles and nags, until our worn-out selves wish him at Jericho. It is hot there, isn't it?'

Then the leaf weighing, which he regularly attends, becomes the nastiest bit of the day's work when it should be the pleasantest, for is it not the end of the 'bela'? Not a woman brings in leaf fit to be seen; poor devils, it is not for want of 'hazri' cutting and 'gallikaroing'. Then a round of the teahouse, and the man there – God help him!

Mark you, now the boss's work is done; he has grumbled, nagged at, and been displeased with every stroke of work performed on the garden that day, work mind you, looked after by efficient assistants – and now we all adjourn by common consent to the factory bungalow, where "Mac" – all engineers, more power to 'em, are called "Mac" – keeps open house.

There, after the third peg, faither opens up a bit and tells of the days long ago; of days of hand-rolling, of real cooly driving, of Lushai scares, and tells also of tales concerning planters only, tales not to be understood by the uninitiated. And so after a 'split' round, the burra-sahib gets into his tum-tum and drives home, and such is the nature of the assistant, that the next peg sees the boss actually toasted, "Not half a bad sort of a chap, socially!"'

On established gardens, the bungalows of the 1880 period were like palaces compared to those in the dark old days. Their appearance was rustic, with thatched roofs; the mud floor of earlier had given way to planks set a little above ground level. The staff list of the Assam Company shows that, while the planters of the 1850s came and went in quick succession (averaging three years), those coming out to Assam in the 1880s stayed on average for eight years, and so conditions improved.

Recreation for the early planters was almost unheard of, for the hardships that were entailed in merely living and surviving were more than enough to fully occupy a man. When the steamy existence and intense work during the rains gave way to the more pleasant cold weather period with its hot and sunny days and cool mornings and evenings, then came a time for recuperation.

For a change of scenery, planters in Assam could make a trip by country boat down the small tributaries that lead into the Great River, where there was always the chance of renewing their aquaintance with a steamer captain, while purchasing some special provisions from his storeroom on board or from the local bazaar. If the planter were recovering from a bad bout of fever, he might take a trip down river on a paddle-steamer, where he could escape the attentions of the mosquitos, feel once again a cool breeze on his face and be offered a change of food and ice-cold drinks.

In later years, groups of planters would get together to form cricket and polo teams. Cricket was the easier to organise, chiefly because the

BELOW
Polo group at Nazira – Assam Company planters and others. (Photo 1893, courtesy Guildhall Library.)

Polo Group at Nazira.

Taken in June 1893

BACK ROW.

THIRD ROW.

SECOND ROW.

FRONT ROW.

Mr Stansbury. Mr Grange. Mr Ardagh. Mr Campbell. F. Winchester. BACK ROW.

Miss Walling. Mr Kind. Mrs Grange. Mr Freelove. Mr Butler. THIRD ROW.

Mr Hulbert. Mr Walling. Mr Freelove. Mr de Laubenque. Mrs J A Thomson. Mr J Thomson. SECOND ROW.

Turnbull. Mr Mildmay. Mr Hulbert. Mr J A Thomson. Mr Severin. FRONT ROW.

ABOVE
A tiger on the lawn of a tea planter's bungalow. The huntsman's trophy, the king of beasts, has been carried back between poles to his bungalow, where he proudly poses for the camera. Beyond the garden fence are the surrounding tea fields. (Photo c1910, courtesy India Office Library.)
TOP LEFT
A dug-out canoe. (Courtesy India Office Library.)
BOTTOM LEFT
Oscar Lindgren, tea planter in Assam and Darjeeling, seen with his mahseer catch in the Teesta valley at the age of 74. (Photo c1930.)

lack of numbers could be made up by the natives who would act as fielders for both sides. Some of the polo teams were coached by the famous Manipuri team, and matches were played against native and European sides.

Hunting was a favourite pastime. The most practical way to go in search of game was to take an experienced native boatman and a shallow dug-out canoe along the tributaries of the Brahmaputra, and penetrate deep into the forest, where pig and deer were plentiful. A dug-out canoe could proceed along the numerous small streams, which were often no more than eight feet wide, and good shooting could be had along either bank by drifting silently downstream with the current with gun at the ready.

The rivers also provided another easy source of food, fish, as well as some good sport fishing for mahseer. The setting of 'night lines' and bamboo traps sunk in the river were both productive ways of obtaining fresh fish for the table. There were all manner of ways of living off the land, providing one knew how. The planters had only to adopt the methods of the natives who had always lived off the land, and game of one sort or another was plentiful everywhere. Many planters would go after big game; bagging a tiger was the ambition of most, but hunting buffalo in the thick cane jungles also provided an exciting, if often dangerous, sport.

During the pioneering years the planter had to get all his supplies carried over long distances to wherever his basha, or bungalow, happened to be. It was often said in India and Ceylon that, if the British planters were ever to leave, all that would remain to mark their many years would be mountains of empty bottles half buried at the rear of their bungalows. According to Edwin Arnold, a planter in southern India in the 1870s, 'even in our hills in every courtyard the beer bottles stood in great heaps, and nobody utilized them except the wasps, which made nests in their necks'.

Today the British planter has disappeared from the scene, but it is very likely that for every single empty bottle, there was also an acre of

fine tea, coffee, cocoa or rubber left for the future generations of today and tomorrow.

Apart from a dog, many planters would also keep a variety of wild pets, which would live in and around the bungalow compound. With the jungle close at hand, a collector – enthusiastically assisted by the coolies who knew they would be rewarded for their efforts – would find in no time at all that he had the beginnings of a small zoo.

Jungle clearance would always result in young animals of different species becoming separated from their parents or abandoned, and many would find their way into the cooking pot, or end up as pets. A stranger to the area, and in particular a town dweller, could be excused for feeling somewhat nervous in the company of many of the planters' pets. There would be monkeys, young bears and wolves, deer, squirrels, hornbills and golden oriels; few would need to be kept in cages and so would have the run of the bungalow, living on the verandah, in the roof, or under the planter's bed. Young leopard cubs, and tiger cubs too, would be added to the menagerie whenever they were found unattended in the jungle, but these – and bears – would later have to be returned to the jungle or crated up and sent off to a more permanent zoo.

In India chickens, however scraggy, and their eggs were much prized items of food. Most bungalow compounds would have a pen in which both the domestic fowl, and its country cousin, the jungle fowl, would be kept. The handsome jungle fowl would have been incubated in the pen under a broody hen from eggs originally found in the jungle. The cost of keeping a dozen or so fowls was not expensive in the days when a planter could obtain them from the local natives for a penny each. Every evening all kinds and sizes of flying insects would

LEFT
The clouded tiger cubs depicted here were raised by the servants of a planter in Assam who had shot the mother. The cubs were taken in as pets when they were only a few days old. (Hand-coloured plate by Joseph Wolf. Courtesy India Office Library.)
BELOW
The red spur-fowl (Galloperdix Spadiceus) is a good game bird, with excellent flesh and very high flavour. It inhabits dense jungle along the top of the Nilgherri hills in southern India. (Hand-coloured plate by John Gould from his 'Birds of Asia', courtesy British Library.)

fly into his living room, attracted by the light, flying remorselessly around his single candle, or hatt batti, until they fell and lay in their hundreds upon the floor beneath. When swept up by the bucketful the following morning, these served to provide a very nourishing diet for the inmates of the poultry house.

The planter's larder would be a pretty meagre one, anything from a rough wooden box with gauze stretched across the front to keep the insects and rats out, to a tin trunk in which a portion of venison would share equal space with the money to pay the labour force. To make up for the lack of storage space in his larder, dried fish would hang from the rafters under the thatched roof. An ice box would have been a boon to the pioneers; many a tasty side of young wild boar or portion of deer would become pretty 'high' before being eaten. Planters would keep a goat or two for milk, and their presence would often result in the visit of a leopard or tiger. Even ship's biscuits were a good standby when there was nothing else to eat; during the early 1840s, consignments of these dry but filling rations were dispatched from Calcutta to the great relief of the planters of the Assam Company at Nazira.

If the planter had a sensible cook-boy, who was thoughtful enough to keep his master's rice in an old sock hanging from a rafter where the rats could not get their teeth into it, he was indeed fortunate. The standard of native cooks was such that many of them did not remain ▷

A HUNTING CHEETA.

TOP LEFT
A planters' club in the Dooars, c1900. (Courtesy British Library.)
BELOW
The manager's bungalow at Chabwa. The first China jat tea was planted out on this garden probably in early 1836. (Courtesy British Library.)

ABOVE
Not exactly a pet, but this tame leopard was kept for the purpose of hunting game. (Photo c1900.)
LEFT
The manager's bungalow, Sam Sing in the Dooars, 1906. (Courtesy British Library.)

Today in Darjeeling there are reminders of the British everywhere: old trains, churches, clubs, guns and old tombstones with many a planter among them

Two marvels of mountain engineering cross each other 132 times on their way up to the town of Darjeeling from the plains below. The construction of the hill cart-road from Siliguri to Darjeeling was started in 1861, and completed in 1869. Lt. Napier of the Royal Engineers, later to become Lord Napier, was in charge of the operation. The construction of the two foot gauge Darjeeling Himalayan Railway was started in 1879, and was extended up to Darjeeling by 1881. (Photo 1985.)

PRESENTED TO

THE
NORTHERN BENGAL
VOLUNTEER RIFLES

BY
LT COL W. LLOYD
COMMANDANT

GUN MADE BY

MAXIM
NORDENFELT

MAXIMS PATENT
1889

GUNS &
AMMUNITIONS
CO LTD

BELOW
The Darjeeling planters' club, now over 100 years old. It is more spacious than it looks, and has every facility to ensure a comfortable rest for the planter while in town. (Photo 1985.)

ABOVE
Maxim gun silhouetted on the balcony of the Darjeeling planters' club. (Photo 1985.)

BELOW
The grave of Thomas Billington Curtis of Tukvar tea estate. Born 15th March 1839, he died in Darjeeling in 1892. (Photo 1985.)

LEFT
In the Darjeeling district only a little of the old, uneconomical tea is being up-rooted today and replanted. Here we see a very small new clearing planted on the Tukvar tea garden in December 1984. (Photo 1985).

RIGHT
The guest house at the Tocklai experimental station of the Tea Research Association, Jorhat, Assam. It is an old colonial style building at which countless planters have stayed while attending lectures and refresher courses. During the Second World War, American servicemen were billeted in the bungalow; there is still a round bullet hole and a crack in the glass front door, reputedly caused by an inebriated soldier. (Photo 1985.)

LEFT
Jaipur estate, Assam. A view of the tea fields directly adjacent to the block of China tea plants put out by C.A. Bruce and his Chinese coolies in 1836. Assamese pluckers carry firewood back to their lines. (Photo 1985.)

Bartchinhull bungalow – morning muster at Robert Elliot's coffee estate in Mysore c1865. (Courtesy India Office Library.)

▷overlong in one spot. Some cooks, however, would seem to a visitor to have been trained at the Ritz, so good were they, were it not known that pure repetition of the same meal over and over again, year after year, had finally made perfect. It was a case of either persevering with one's cook or, for ever taking on new ones. Many a cook has turned up at the bungalow proudly flourishing his chit of reference given by his previous employer: 'This cook is leaving owing to illness – mine.'

The Hill Districts in Southern India

In South India the first tea and coffee estates were opened up during the mid-1850s. The first Europeans to make their way up to the hill districts here were almost entirely British as they had been in North-East India. The tea and coffee districts – however inaccessible – were nevertheless reasonably near to the coastal ports such as Mangalore, Cannanore, Calicut and Cochin. It was at these ports that the first pioneers eventually stepped ashore.

Anyone wishing to seek his fortune as a planter in the hill districts of South India had to sail out from England either to Bombay or to any of the small, then uncharted, ports along the Malabar coast down to Colombo. If disembarking at Bombay, it was then necessary to make arrangements with the native owner of a small coastal craft for a further passage southwards of between 450 and 600 miles to ports such as Mangalore or Calicut, depending upon the final destination.

One of the first men to make the journey up to the jungles of Mysore was Robert Elliot, who opened up his own coffee estate in 1856. He describes his voyage of some nine days from Bombay down the coast to Mangalore:

'I was compelled to take a passage in a patma (native sailing craft) which was proceeding down the western coast with a cargo of salt, which was stowed away in the after-part of the vessel. Over this was a low roofed and thatched house, the flooring of which was composed of strips of split bamboo laid upon the salt. On this I had placed my mattress and bedding. My provisions for the voyage were simple – a coop with some fowls, some tea, sugar, cooking utensils, and other small necessities of life.'

In that same year, 1856, a Scot named William Mackinnon formed the Calcutta and Burmah Steamship Company. Some six years afterwards he established a line of coasting steamers which were to call regularly at all the then little known coastal ports between Karachi and Calcutta, thus opening up a great network of trade around the entire coast of India. It was towards the end of 1862 that the Calcutta and Burmah Steamship Company became the British India Steam Navigation Company.

The early screw steamers of the BISNC were small vessels of between 500 and 600 gross tons, and were rigged for sail. In some of

'Sunday morning found me with kit packed and ready for a forward movement upon the jungle.'

RIGHT
A moonlit ford. The first part of the journey up to the hills in southern India.
BELOW
The palanquin was handy when the going got steeper in the foothills.

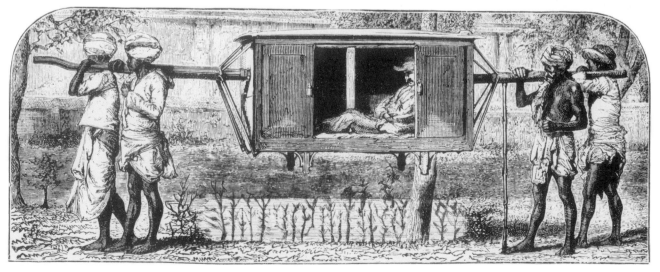

the worst weather imaginable during monsoons, with heavy seas running, these small ships stood off in the open road-stead, taking on their cargoes of tea and coffee from the 'Masoolah boats'. The timely arrival of the coasting steamers solved the early problem of getting the tea and coffee crops out of this particular stretch of the Malabar coast.

The journey from the small ports along the southern part of the Malabar coast up to the tea and coffee districts of the Coorg and Mysore presented little difficulty when compared to the hardships and length of time required to travel up to North-East Assam. From the coastal regions to the foothills the journey was made in a slow bullock cart, which was then swapped for the palanquin, or munchiel, for travelling over the steeper rocky bridle-paths that traversed steeply upwards through tall jungle in the latter part of the journey. Once there, the conditions under which the first planters lived would certainly have been rough, but again nothing like those encountered in Assam.

When opening out completely new areas of jungle, planters would sometimes share a bungalow, going off to work each day at the crack of dawn to their separate areas of land, and returning with their coolies at the end of the day's work. For those who shared, conditions were every bit as primitive as for those who lived alone, as most did. Coffee planter Edwin Arnold gives a graphic description of his first sight of the small clearing in which one such bungalow stood, and of his arrival at the building in which he was to live with the encumbent planter, who was already engaged in opening out new land to coffee in the early 1870s.

'The underwood had been cut down together with a few of the most inconveniently placed trees, and in the rough clearing thus formed (all bristling with stumps and remains of bushes) half a dozen low reed-thatched hovels had grown up a little below an isolated residence, which though of exactly the same construction as the others, seemed a trifle more carefully finished.

Actually there was not much to boast about in my new quarters. The hut was about thirty feet long by about twelve broad, and was divided into two by a chinky partition of palghaut mats. The owner pointed out with great pride that the floor was not the actual surface of the soil, which had been smoothed, and covered with rough sawn boards laid side by side on it. The construction of the hut itself was very primitive, as I took in at a glance. Four strong forked poles had been driven in at the corners, and young saplings roughly lopped and trimmed had been placed upon them. Upon these the roof had been constructed, with a very steep pitch to throw off the heavy monsoon rainfall, and had been thickly thatched with pale yellow lemon-grass from the neighbouring hillside. Yet though the roof was substantial enough, the sides of the hut were frail fragility itself. A few stout stakes had been driven in at equal distances, and to these palghaut mats were fastened, with split rattan creeper; yet as there was only a single thickness of matting, daylight came in at a hundred places, and the green and yellow stains down the inside showed that they made no pretence at being watertight. My friend assured me that when it began to rain in a few days time, we should find the place perfectly watertight – with perhaps the exception of one or two places in the walls – and he told me this was a great deal to be thankful for on a new estate, he having lived many a day under little more than an umbrella and a blanket.'

All first timers lived and slept rough, whether in India or in Ceylon – if not under an umbrella, then certainly under the leaves of the talipot palm.

Such were the wet conditions inside most temporary huts that a man's entire wardrobe – kept in a packing case – would, in the first week of the monsoon, become quite unwearable through damp and mould, and the planter might well find himself in a position of having to go out to supervise the field works in his last remaining dry set of clothes, his dinner jacket:

'The rain came down again, and again we got wet through, and as nothing could be dried owing to the saturated condition of the atmosphere, my whole wardrobe emerged from the packing cases, and becoming wet, was in turn hung up to take care of itself around our walls. I changed my hue like a chameleon, and at last began to look anxiously for a break in the clouds in order that I might dry some things, otherwise I should be reduced to the necessity of going weeding in evening dress'.

For a first timer it was a fight against great odds to make progress in any direction. Together with his band of coolies, he fought to fell the virgin jungle in order to carve out a small open clearing in which to make his nursery, and plant the seeds which, one day – if he kept at it – would form the basis of the new estate. He fought disease and the monsoon rains, while wild animals trampled upon his soft seed beds, or ate the young plants that had been set out in the field. It was indeed a ceaseless fight.

It was during the monsoon season that the young seedlings from the nursery would be planted out, and work would go on non-stop, seven days a week, often in torrential downpour. After a long day in the field supervising the planting, soaked through like drowned rats, the planter and his coolies would make their way back to the muster ground for the roll-call after which, draped in their sodden kamblies (blankets), with teeth chattering, the coolies would at last escape to their huts for the night to dry out as best they could. There would be no escape for the weary planter though. His horse would have to be fed, a job he could not trust a native to do for fear that the horse's food would find its way to the coolie lines to be eaten by the horse-feeder

All that a man could expect when opening out jungle for a new estate. Coffee planter Edwin Arnold wrote of his experiences in the early 1870s: 'the rats simply swarmed, and at nights they came forth from their hiding places and ate up everything within their reach; no sooner had I put out the lights and rolled myself up comfortably, than they were pattering all over the bed and, although I kicked vigorously every now and then, it only caused a temporary scare. But they soon returned to the charge, getting so bold that one woke me up by actually sitting on my forehead. There was no mistake about this for I seized him there, and threw him to the other end of the room'. (Pencil drawing. G. Cunningham, 1983.)

and his family. Also, there would always be the sick to be treated as best he could. Finally, upon gaining the inside of his dismal hut, he would count himself lucky if his cook-boy had managed to prepare a meal of some sort and a good fire by which he could dry out a little. Then he would have to deal with the estate correspondence and pay roll before turning in for the night.

A physically tired man needs sleep to recharge his strength but, as Arnold says when he describes his own misfortunes, sleep was often hard to get:

> 'When the rain began to descend in earnest, it found its way through into my sleeping compartment with very little difficulty. It was necessary to act promptly so, springing up, I rolled all the bed things into a mass and covered them with a waterproof. Then opening an umbrella I sat on top in my flannel sleeping suit, and calmly watched my property being flooded. The rain came in everywhere, and soon everything was afloat, while as fast as I lit lamp after lamp, the rain water put them out and left me in darkness. The tempest howled overhead, and the trees rocked and groaned, until every moment I expected one to come crashing through the roof of my deluged hut,'

Here we begin to form a picture of a planter who is on the record as possessing not only a flannel sleeping suit, but also evening dress; the occasions on which he might have worn either would seem to have been limited. It would however be quite untrue to suggest that the early planters did not wear such things as evening dress while roughing it out in the back of beyond. There is the story, in Chapter V, of a certain Ceylon planter living in the back-woods who, when entertaining the occasional guest in his humble bungalow, always insisted that they sat down to dinner in evening dress. This is not so absurd as it might seem, for a dinner jacket, or for that matter any clothes stored for months in a tin trunk, or left hanging in some corner, is undoubtably the better for a little wear now and then. It was however hard on a guest who, arriving on his horse, had understandably not included the necessary evening wear for his stay.

The planter on an estate had to be paymaster, clerk, doctor, judge, surveyor, and keeper of all. His whole life was one of self-reliance. Practically every day he would sit in judgement over the squabbles and wrong-doings committed among his labour force, but without doubt his most distressing duty was that of trying to act the part of a doctor, with little in the way of medicine to help. Most evenings, on finally returning to his hut or bungalow in the gathering dusk, he would find a small forlorn group of sick coolies sitting on his verandah, huddled together in their kamblies, awaiting his arrival: an ulcerous wound would be bandaged, castor oil given or some quinine, and they would depart knowing that their master was doing his best to help them, which was half the battle won.

The mortality rate amongst the coolies was, as Arnold points out, just as grim on the estates in southern India as on the tea gardens in North-East India.

> 'Many cases, however, were past the mending of any earthly doctor, and in one week fourteen coolies died in the "lines" within a stone's throw of my bungalow. They dropped out of the ranks to be buried in the nearest strip of jungle, and nobody knew when they came, or where they were.
>
> The coolie graves in the jungle nearby were at this time growing terribly numerous, and the jungle was becoming thickly marked with the little hillocks which denoted the last resting place of the poor wretches; there were more already there than we had opened acres, and the numbers increased daily.
>
> Many of the graves were made shockingly shallow, and the wild dogs and wolves tore open and partly dismembered the inmates. In

TOP LEFT
The Good Samaritans – the bazaar. ('The Graphic', 1880.)
LEFT
A medical inspection. ('The Graphic', 1880.)
ABOVE
On the way to ... (c1900, courtesy India Office Library.)
BELOW
The Sunday rendezvous. (c1890.)

ABOVE
'Judge of my feelings when I saw crouching on a branch scarcely six feet above my head, so low indeed, I could have poked him with the ferule of my umbrella, a full grown and gleaming eyed pantha. His body was partly hidden by the branch, but his tail hung over one side, and his head looked over the other, and in the deep shade his eyes shone like opals. When our glances met, his lips curled up slowly into a fierce snarl, showing all his white teeth, and I saw his claws grip into the green bark ready for a spring, and instinctively my hand went down to the hunting knife in my belt. For a moment things hung in suspense, and the next second might have pitted his vast strength, great weight, and superior position against my knife and fever wasted muscles. But he kept his place, though his eyes watched every movement; so I judged discretion was in this case the best part of valour and, slowly taking up my umbrella and keeping my eyes full on his, I backed off until the tree was hidden by others, and then took a swift bee-line for my hut to fetch a rifle. But by the time I was armed and back at the tree, the pantha was gone, and I never saw him again.'

Most planters would have had tales similar to Arnold's. (Artist's sketch, 1870.)

fact, I saw things which will not bear describing, and pretty well hardened as I became, my breakfast was often left untasted, and with my gun on my shoulder I wandered away to the open grass hills to freshen myself up by a little sweet air and undefiled nature, after such dreadful sights and experiences.'

After a hard and long day's work in the field, it was both impossible and dangerous for the planter to ride off along the small winding paths which led through patches of jungle to call on a neighbour; consequently it was at week-ends that planters visited each other.

For those who were stuck away in the hill districts of southern India during the years when there were only a handful of British opening up tea and coffee estates over a wide area, there was very little time for leisure. As in other parts of India and Ceylon, a hospitable planter's bungalow would act as a sort of central meeting place – a club house – and, on Sundays, planters who were not too far distant would put on their best clothes and ride over to meet up with their friends, returning to their estates before dusk.

On the more established estates, a Sunday was also a day outing for the coolies, who would often travel many miles through the jungle and down mountain tracks to the nearest bazaars or markets. They too would get ready at an early hour and put on their best clothes for the occasion; the women wore their gaily coloured saris, and were decked out with bangles and trinkets, their sleek black hair shining with the coconut oil they had rubbed in. At the bazaar they could buy all they needed – clothes, chillies, as well as anything from a live goat to a quantity of arrack, a very potent drink with which to drown their sorrows upon their return to the estate.

For the planters with broken health – who were situated near enough to make the journey – a stay of a few weeks at the hill station of Ootacamund at over 6000 feet was something of a necessary luxury. With its cool mountain air, Ooty, as it was generally called, worked wonders for a man, physically and mentally. Memories would come flooding back at the sight of roses and geraniums growing tall in the gardens of all the villas. The green grass of a golf course and the sight of so many of his own countrymen and women walking about were greatly welcome to any man who had spent so long living alone in wilder parts. There was the pleasure of sleeping between sheets, with a blanket on the bed and a fire in the hearth to keep the cold night air at bay. Ooty was the holiday place of all the government officials in the Madras Province of southern India, much as Nuwara Eliya – situated at a slightly lower elevation – was the sanitorium of Ceylon, and it is to that country that we will go to continue the story of the pioneers.

The Nilgherri Hills and Ooty were to the south of India what Simla was to the north: A temporary haven of peace for the fever-sickened British, jaded by the heat of the plains.

LEFT
The Ooty Club – built by Sir William Rumbold in 1832. Originally a hotel, it

became a convalescent home for the army before being converted into a club by a group of army officers in 1842. The rules for the game of snooker were invented here. The club is also seen in the illustration by Barron, as the long low building in the top left hand corner of the picture. (Photo 1985, courtesy Ooty Club.)

ABOVE

A general view of Ootacamund in the Nilgherri hills. For those coming up from the low country, after ascending the plains of Coimbatore, the cooler airs of the Nilgherri hills are like champagne after the heat of the plains. The cold weather or winter period is like autumn in southern France, the mornings and evenings are quite chilly, and yet the sun at midday is pleasantly hot. Our view is that seen upon gaining the plateau at 6000 feet above sea level. The figures in the foreground are the Bringarries, who carry up grain from the low country to the hill station with their small pack-bullocks. The Nilgherries may be considered as the southern termination of the Western Ghauts, which come to an end here with abrupt, almost vertical precipices; the valley of Coimbatore extends down to Cape Cormorin and divides the Nilgherries from the Paulghaut chain. (Aquatint by Barron 1835, courtesy India Office Library.)

Over the years there have been many strange tales and poems connected with the planting profession. Who can tell what is to be believed and what is not? I would strongly suspect that most have a lot more than a glimmer of truth in them. To end this chapter, here are four voices which give us a very good insight into their way of life.

The Assistant

I wish I were a manager
With umpteen quid a year,
What a glorious life with a handsome wife
And never a boss to fear.

With unlimited powers and no fixed hours
And never a care about muster
(To go out at night and come back when it's light
Is an old managerial dastur).

With a bungalow like an old chateau
And a most expensive car,
A blooming toff with all day off
For that is what managers are.

The Manager

I wish they would say 'you can be the V.A.
And keep the whole gang up to scratch',
I've been so long in tea, they couldn't do me,
But would find I was more than their match.

I'd make them obey and grow tea my way,
Especially old so-and-so;
He can't argue the toss if I am the boss,
Which is one thing I'd soon let him know.

To come out in October and talk about 'goeber'
And compost and pruning and such
And find out their dodgings (such with free board and lodgings)
Would suit this tired soul very much.

The Visiting Agent

If I could afford to get on the Board
And smoke my cigar at the table;
With a nice dividend at every year's end
And get forty per cent, if I'm able.

I'm tired of Sylhet, but I'm not too old yet,
And I want a nice house by the sea.
But I must have the cash, for the wife cuts a dash
To make up for the years spent in tea.

If I'm made a director (a profits collector)
I'll see they're kept short in Assam,
I'll live in good style and I'll die worth a pile –
That's the kind of man that I am.

The Director

I wish I could be an assistant in tea
And start my life over again,
You've only two-fifty but needn't be thrifty,
For that's not the way with young men.

The ladies adore you, your life is before you,
You've the nerve and the legs for a horse,
And dance till the dawn and set to with a yawn
And take life as a matter of course.

But I spend my life playing bridge with my wife
And discussing the past with old cronies:
I've got money and gout; and I long to come out
And be young with my debts and my ponies.

(Watercolours by E.H. Fischer, c1900.)

CEYLON TEA, PLANTED ON THE GRAVEYARD OF THE OLD COFFEE ESTATES

CHAPTER IV

JUNGLE-LAND .... GRANTS OF LAND
RICH VIRGIN SOIL .... AT 5s.0. PER ACRE

Captⁿ C O'Brien del J Needham lith.   ST PAUL'S CHURCH, KANDY.   Day & Son Lith^{rs} to The Queen.

IN THE CENTRAL HILL DISTRICTS

Ceylon Tea, Planted on the Graveyard of the Old Coffee Estates

Tea in Ceylon was first planted on a commercial scale in the year 1867, but before we talk about tea, it is necessary to mention coffee, for much of the tea that grows in Ceylon today was in fact planted on the old coffee estates, after the coming of the coffee leaf disease in 1869.

The coffee plant was first introduced into southern India and Ceylon by the Arabs. In Ceylon it thereafter grew wild in the gardens of the natives and was planted around the temples in which its beautifully scented flowers were used for decoration. During the Portuguese occupation of the island from 1505 to 1655, no attempt was made to cultivate the plant but, after the Portuguese were driven out by the Dutch, certain crops, such as cinnamon and, in 1740, coffee, were cultivated. The first coffee plantation, however, was unfortunately opened in the tropical low country, about ten miles inland from Galle, close to Buddegamuwa on the Gindura River. This south-western part of the island, with its tropical climate, was quite unsuitable for coffee, and the attempt was abandoned.

FRONTISPIECE TO CHAPTER
St Paul's Church, Kandy. The foundation stone was laid in 1843, and the church completed in 1852. (Lithograph 1864, from O'Brian's 'Views in Ceylon'.)
PREVIOUS PAGE
A view near Point de Galle. The first coffee was planted in the low country on the banks of the River Gindura. (Aquatint 1809.)
LEFT
The Gampola ferry crossing in the late 1850s. Coffee carts and, later, tea carts, were a prominent feature of the landscape right up until the coming of motor transport. (Engraving, 1859.)

The British superseded the Dutch in the year 1796. They, too, made an attempt at cultivation, but again without success, as may be seen from the following extract written by C. Lewis in 1855:

> 'The first attempts by British speculators to cultivate coffee in Ceylon were made on the banks of the Gindura River, about sixteen miles from Galle. The failure was so signal, that the plants were taken up to put down sugar cane, and these in turn made way for coconut palms'.

From the low country, which had proved unsuccessful as far as coffee was concerned, we must go to the hills in the centre of the island and, in particular, to the Kandy district. Here the climate was found to be most suitable for coffee, and it is in this district that the planting enterprise began in 1825. The first plantation was opened up between Kandy and the small town of Gampola, some thirteen miles distant. By the 1860s, albeit for a short time, Ceylon became the world's largest producer of coffee.

From the day when the planter cleared his first piece of jungle for his nursery to receive the coffee seeds which, when germinated, would form the plants of his future estate, a period of three years would have elapsed before he gathered his maiden crop. The first task was the felling of the forest, usually in 50 or 100 acre blocks; the fallen trees would be left to dry out in the hot sun for about two months, after which the whole clearing would be 'fired'. After a satisfactory 'burn', the ground would be sufficiently cleared and ready for the next operation of 'lining'. A long rope with tags of white cloth at every sixth foot was stretched as close to the burnt forest floor as the blackened stumps of the old forest would permit; wooden pegs, cut from the jungle, were then driven into the ground at every tag. The straight lines of pegs running up and down the hills were themselves six feet apart. After the whole area had been lined, and pegged, a gang of estate coolies would dig holes 18 inches deep by 18 inches wide at every peg, ready for the next operation of planting.

When the rains had set in, the young coffee plants were lifted and planted out into their permanent positions in the field. In their third year the young coffee trees were ready for 'topping' to a uniform height of between three and four-and-a-half feet – depending upon elevation and site – the plants then taking on the form of sturdy bushes, with drooping lateral branches. This was a convenient height at which to pick the berries, and also to prune the bushes after the crop had been taken.

The more dexterous women coffee pickers could gather as much as four bushels of berries a day on land that would yield 450 lbs of clean coffee per acre. The estate task for each picker was two bushels a day, extra pay being given for anything over that amount. Harvesting of the ripe coffee berries took place for only four months of the year, from the beginning of November until the end of February. (Photo 1878.)

In the mid 1860s, the coffee crop from the Peacock Hill estate and others like it in the surrounding districts would have been carried in two bushel sacks on coolies' heads along steep mountain paths and jungle tracks down to a rough cart road, where it would then be loaded into bullock-carts for the long journey down to the coast and Colombo. In earlier years, in the Matale and Gampola districts, and especially on the more isolated plantations up in the Knuckles range of mountains where paths and rough tracks were almost non-existent, much use was made of pack-bullocks to carry the coffee crop into Kandy.

Moormen traders as carriers, owned their own bullocks and carts, and were employed by the estates to carry their coffee and tea. Before the railway line opened, a pair of Indian humped bulls would pull a cart loaded with 120 bushels of coffee from the hill regions down to the port of Colombo, averaging 20 miles a day in good weather. Having discharged their loads, they would set off again for the return journey, loaded with food stuffs and everything that was required by the estates. ▷

Four o'clock

Tis four o'clock a breeze comes down
From where the bushy ridges frown.

The laden bee hums slowly by;
The jungle wakes with eerie cry.

Tis four o'clock dark shadows creep
Along Kal'pahnas ledges steep.

Old Carpen standing near the store
Declares he's sure its long past four.

Tis four o'clock the horn at last
Full loud and long its ringing blast.

With joyful shout and sack on head
Their homeward path the coolies tread.

Weighing the day's pickings – Ettrick coffee estate, Haputele. (Sketch 1881, from 'Scenes in Ceylon' by Hamilton & Fasson.)

EULABES PTILOGENYS.   ACRIDOTHERES MELANOSTERNUS.

ABOVE

Peacock Hill coffee estate – Pussellawa. Here we see a well established estate; on the left is the planter's bungalow, a very respectable building for the mid-1860s. In front of the store are the drying grounds on which the 'parchment' coffee is spread; coolies are seen carrying their loads up the steps of the pulping house, in which the machinery is turned by a water-wheel; in the foreground is a dam by which the water of a small stream may accumulate at night to work the machinery during the day. In the distance is the village of Gampola, and it was to this area, with its surrounding hills, that the first planters made their way in the 1820s. (Lithograph 1864, from O'Brian's 'Views in Ceylon'.)

LEFT

The Ceylon myna. Holdsworth mentions in 1872 that large numbers of the Ceylon myna – Eulabates Ptilogenys – were recorded as killed in the early morning or evening on some of the coffee estates. The birds presumably formed part of the coolies' diet when they were lucky enough to catch them. Although the entries for this fruit-eating species do not specifically mention coffee berries, it is very probable that these birds – like many of the other pests – also took their toll upon the ripening berries. The myna was much sought after as a caged bird, by Kandians and planters alike, because of its talking ability. (Hand-coloured plate from Legge's 'Birds of Ceylon', 1881.)

A part of Rangbodde Pass: looking across from the Wavenden coffee estate to the Rangbodde Falls and beyond to what was then most probably General Fraser's estate 'Rangbodde'. The winding cart-road would carry the bullock carts on their long journey down to the coast, bearing their heavy loads of coffee and, in later years, tea. Many an axle was broken. To the right is a very small chapel, perched on a bold projection of rock, whilst at the extreme right the land slopes steeply away to the valley of Kotmale below. It is interesting to compare this view with that of the photographs on page 109, which were taken nearly twenty years later. (Lithograph 1864, from O'Brian's 'Views in Ceylon'.)

LEFT
Estates would employ a watcher to shoot pests such as monkeys, squirrels, rats and hares. Great damage was caused by the coffee rat – Golunda Ellioti – whose appearance on the coffee estates in the hills around Kandy was first reported in 1847. Whenever there was a scarcity of their normal food, the seeds of the Nilloo plant, they would migrate in vast numbers across the land, and it was a serious problem for the planter when they put in an appearance on his estate. His coffee bushes would be stripped of both young buds and flowers, and such were their numbers that as many as a thousand were reported to have been killed in one day on a single coffee estate. The rats, of some eight or nine inches in length, were much prized by the coolies, who ate them roasted, fried in coconut oil or made into a curry, thus adding valuable meat protein to their normal diet of rice. In fact, the Tamils had a marked preference for working on estates in districts which were subject to the rodents' periodic incursions. (Engraving 1880.)
BELOW
Coffee stores and pulping house. (Sketch 'Illustrated London News' 1872, courtesy British Library.)

Glentilt estate coolies and planters pose for this photograph in front of the coffee store. Generations of Tamil families would grow up on an estate, and in many cases their descendants still form the labour force of that particular estate today, a hundred years later. (Photo c1880, courtesy Royal Commonwealth Society.)

Coffee stores, when cleaned out and decorated, would double up as a 'ballroom', where planters and their wives would dance until the early hours.

▷ For outlying plantations the cost of transportation into Kandy alone amounted to six shillings per hundredweight of clean coffee, while the remainder of the journey from Kandy down to Colombo added a further three shillings – making the total cost approximately nine shillings for ninety miles: as much as the freight cost for some 11,000 miles by sailing ship to England via the Cape.

The early planting district around Gampola was indeed a beautiful one and, after the first plantations had been opened up, other pioneers pushed on through the fertile valley of Pussellawa through which the Mahaweli Ganga flows, into the valley of Kotmale, then on to the slopes above, to Rangbodde itself. Within ten years of the opening of the first coffee plantation, nearly 4000 acres of forest had been felled, cleared and planted around Kandy. The mountain ranges became rapidly covered with small plantations. There was intense activity everywhere; no forest was safe from the woodman's axe, nor was any mountain side without its pall of blue smoke rising from the new clearings.

The Sinhalese villagers who were employed to fell the jungle on contract had an unusual way of carrying out the task when working on steeply sloping land. The method they used is best described in the words of John Capper, who was visiting a new coffee plantation in the hills above Kandy, on which jungle clearing was in progress.

'To me it was a pretty, as well as a novel sight, to watch the felling work in progress. Two axemen to small trees, three and sometimes four to larger ones, their little bright tools flung far back over their shoulders with a sharp flourish, and then with a 'whirr' dug into the heart of the tree with such exactitude and in such excellent time, that the scores of axes flying about me seemed impelled by some mechanical contrivance, sounding but as one or two instruments. I observed that in no instance were the trees cut through, but each one was left with just sufficient of the stem to keep it upright. ▷

TOP LEFT
A typical small coffee estate in the making, during the 1840s. A block of forest has been felled and much of it burnt off; the land has been 'lined and pegged' and it is at this particular stage that we see the 'holing gang' at work amongst the tangled landscape. A mud and wattle hut with a thatched roof was all that a pioneer could expect to live in when opening out a new estate. (Watercolour 1981 by G. Cunningham.)

BOTTOM LEFT
A new, but well established coffee estate. The neat little bungalow is surrounded by a small garden. The out-buildings to the right are the servants' quarters; there would also be a horse stable and a cow shed. Shaded nursery beds can be seen immediately below the bungalow garden and to the bottom right; these are served by a small stream. (Photo 1860s, courtesy BBC Hulton Picture Library.)

ABOVE
Rangbodde coffee estate, situated towards the top of the Pass, sits astride the road which zigzags its way up to the plains above. Our view is looking towards Pussellawa; in the middle of the picture is a line of bullock carts used for transporting coffee. Within ten short years of this photograph being taken, all the coffee bushes had been uprooted and burnt and Rangbodde had become a tea estate. (Photo c1880.)

LEFT
The ascent from Rangbodde starts in earnest winding steeply upwards at a gradient of one in fourteen; over the next twelve miles the road rises 3000 feet to the cool airs of the plains above and to Nuwara Eliya at 6000 feet. The land to the extreme left of the picture – above the slab rock and waterfall – is planted with coffee, which rises to the heights above. Our view is taken on a part of the road shown in the previous photograph. (Photo c1880.)

▷ 'In half an hour the signal was made to halt by blowing a conch shell; obeying the order of the superintendent, I hastened up the hill as fast as my legs would convey me, over rocks and streams, halting at the top, as I saw the whole part do. They were ranged in order, axes in hand on the upper side of the topmost row of cut trees. I got out of their way watching anxiously every moment. All being ready, the manager sounded the conch sharply, two score voices raised a shout that made me start again, forty bright axes gleamed high in the air, then sank deeply into as many trees, which at once yield to the sharp steel, groaned heavily, waved their huge branches to and fro, like drowning giants, then toppled over, and fell with a stunning crash upon the trees below them. These having been cut through previously offered no resistance, but followed the example of their upper neighbours, and fell booming on those underneath.'

Whilst on the subject of new clearings, and timber in particular, a word must be said about the elephant. With an elephant by one's side almost any task could be accomplished, for, like a tank it can tackle any terrain. Right from the early years of the British administration they were used in considerable numbers, being not only plentiful, but also ideal for transporting heavy objects over rough, steep and unchartered terrain. In later years they proved invaluable in carrying the heavier machinery for the new tea factories. Elephants were excellent for all manner of tasks: for the construction of railways, roads, culverts, and approaches to bridges, for the transportation of heavy timber, and for the uprooting of dead and dying coffee bushes. They were hired on the estates at a daily rate, which would depend upon the type of work involved. An elephant gets through about 300 pounds of green fodder-leaves, bamboo and coconut palm leaves – each day but, when working on an estate close to jungle, it would be allowed to wander off, hobbled, into the jungle each night to obtain its own food.

During the early years of the coffee planting enterprise when vast acreages of jungle were being felled, all the tree stumps and fallen trees that remained after the 'burn' would be left to rot on the land and the young coffee plants would be set in between them in rows. In later years, when jungle was felled for planting up with tea, the land was generally cleared more thoroughly of timber and tree stumps – providing the money was there to do so – and for this work the elephant was of great use.

To keep up the numbers of trained working elephants, hunts were organised every two or three years, and great numbers of local villagers took part as it was an exciting sport much looked forward to by everyone. The method of capturing the wild elephant in Ceylon was to errect in the forest a large single enclosure called a 'korahl' (from the Portuguese 'curral', a cattle pen); this was formed by tree trunks sunk in the ground to a depth of about three feet, with cross beams secured and bound together with creepers from the jungle. Any big korahl was sure to attract scores of Europeans from Colombo; merchants, bankers and their wives would gather in parties on the hillsides surrounding the stockade to watch a day's sport. Planters, or KCBs (Knights of the Coffee Berry) would leave their estates for a holiday, often making a long journey, not only to watch, but also to take an active part as beaters.

As many as a thousand men, under the orders of their village headman, would be employed over a period of many weeks in the construction of the korahl stockade, and also while the elephants were surrounded and driven towards the stockade. Surrounding the herds and then driving fifty elephants slowly through many miles of forest required both patience and expert knowledge of the animals' ways. The native beaters, and those that acted as watchmen every night while driving the elephants for weeks on end, often had to go without food for long spells while passing through remote forest areas.

Once the elephants had been driven within the protruding side-

ABOVE
A boiler, made by Marshalls of Gainsborough, Lancashire, on its way to an up-country tea estate after a long sea passage. (Photo 1890s.)
RIGHT
Having been driven for many miles, the elephants have finally arrived outside the entrance to the 'korahl'. They will now be driven into the trap that lies concealed within the trees.

LEFT
The elephant 'korahl' held at Labugamawa for the entertainment of the Princes Albert Victor and George of Wales in 1882. The long thin white poles – straight branches of about ten feet stripped of their bark – being pushed through the stockade are also seen in greater numbers in the photograph below. Whenever the newly trapped elephants seek to charge against the stockade, the enclosing circle of natives shout and poke their staffs through the stockade so as to frighten them away. (Photo 1882 by Skeen & Co.)
BELOW
The temporary huts seen on the left, outside the 'korahl', were used by the natives who kept watch all night around the stockade. The crow's nest platform in the trees was built for the princes and their accompanying party to view the noosing and capture of the elephants inside the stockade. (Photo 1882 by Skeen & Co.)

ABOVE
The 'alarm' was given only when the elephants were within the side wings. A Sinhalese is seen carrying a part of a leaf of the talipot palm, which was used as protection against night-time rains. (Sketch 1864, 'Illustrated London News'.)
BELOW
The beaters surround the wild elephants and gradually drive them towards the stockade. (Photo c1895.)

wings at the entrance to the korahl, at a given signal the surrounding natives would start to make as much noise as possible by shouting, beating tom-toms, and discharging their muskets – thus driving the elephants towards, and finally through, the concealed and inviting escape opening into the korahl. Once inside, great sliding log bars would be drawn across and the opening closed. At the approach of darkness, scores of fires would be lit around the perimeter of the stockade, and kept burning all night.

After a night of exhausting escape attempts by charging about flattening all the undergrowth and small trees, the elephants would become a little more subdued. The following day, pairs of tame elephants – each with mahouts on their shoulders and a 'nooser' seated behind – would be ridden into the stockade amongst the wild ones, allowing the noosers to get to work. Each wild elephant in turn was isolated form the rest of the herd by two tame ones; it was then sandwiched between them, and whenever a wild elephant lifted its foot, a nooser would drop down, and pass his noose under its legs. After both fore and hind legs had been secured in this manner, the animal could be drawn to and tethered between nearby trees with the assistance of the two tame ones. The task of tying and securing some thirty or forty elephants called for considerable agility and skill.

The role of the tame elephants in capturing their wild brothers was as great as that of their mahouts, for without their great strength in pushing, pulling and sandwiching the captives, the task would have been the harder. The tame elephants also had a quietening effect upon the wild ones when working in close proximity to them.

ABOVE
Noosing inside the stockade. (Engraving 1866.)
LEFT
Free no longer: a captive being lead away between two tame elephants. (Photo c1895.)

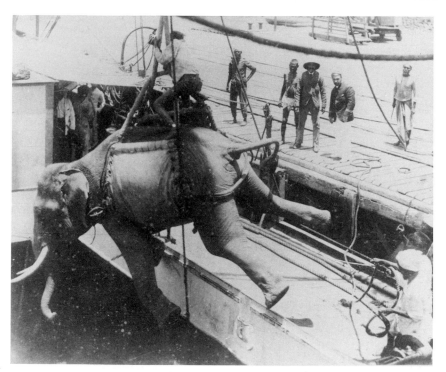

TOP RIGHT
Shipping an elephant. (Photo 1900, courtesy India Office Library.)
BELOW
Elephants on an estate in Kandy. (Photo c1898.)

The captured elephants had to be watered as soon as possible, and the final operation inside the korahl was the slackening of their bonds. With a tame elephant on either side, strong ropes would be passed through the collars of all three elephants, and then they would be led away to the river.

The tame elephants were present at the daily training of the new captives for the first two months until the latter could be ridden by their trainers. A further period of three or four months was usually needed before they could be safely allowed to work, making six months in all from the day of their capture.

Elephants proved invaluable on the coffee estates. As Hilaire Belloc wrote:

'When people call this beast to mind,
They marvel more and more
At such a little tail behind
So large a trunk before.'

The Boom and Fall of Coffee

The rush to secure land in Ceylon was similar to that in Californian and Australian gold rushes of about the same period. Many of the first rough, tough pioneers who had gone out into unknown parts and had opened out the jungle under appalling conditions had disappeared, to be replaced by a new breed of men. Young officers from the East India Company and young men out from England with their own capital were arriving at Point de Galle and Colombo by every sailing ship. Many of these young men became the first proprietary planters who, as superintendents, worked and owned their estates.

The coffee mania reached its climax in 1845, and in that one year alone 19,062 acres of Crown land were bought, mostly for purposes of speculation and not with a view to immediate cultivation. Some two years later there was a substantial drop in coffee prices and a collapse of credit. There were many bankruptcies, and scores of estates changed hands at a twentieth of the original cost. Large areas that had been cleared and planted were simply abandoned and allowed to revert to overgrown scrubland.

After three bad years, confidence returned and exports rose once again. By 1857 a total of 80,950 acres of inaccessible jungle had been felled and the land planted with coffee, and by 1868 the industry had reached its highest peak. Then, in the following year, came a new enemy that, in a matter of twenty years, was to ruin completely the thousands of acres of fine coffee: Hemileia vastatrix, coffee rust.

The coffee leaf disease was first noticed on one or two outlying estates in 1869. At first, small rust-coloured powdery patches would appear on the undersides of the leaves; when these orange blotches became larger, the infected leaves would drop off. After the first leaf fall, the bushes would recover somewhat but, with each successive year, the resistance of the bushes would fall and crop yields would drop until finally the bushes would die leafless. The same disease – with devastating effect – also swept over wide coffee growing areas from East Africa, through southern India, and on to Java.

In 1869, there were approximately 176,000 acres of coffee in cultivation in addition to the small native plantations. The momentum of felling and clearing more and more forests went on unchecked for the next decade, during which time a further 100,000 acres were planted up with coffee. Much of this new land that was opened out was in the hitherto untouched forests from Nuwara Eliya, through Dimbula, Dickoya, and the Adams Peak range which, being between 5000 and 5500 feet, until then had been thought too high and too wet for coffee.

The considerable reduction in coffee yields caused by the leaf fungus was hidden to a large extent by the increase in acreage and by the return of very high prices for coffee on the London market. The planters hoped that the leaf disease would go away – but it did not. Even the new coffee estates had but a very short life, with their owners soon pulling out all the dead and dying coffee bushes that had so rashly been planted a few years before.

From 1869 onwards the coffee blight took its toll. It spread from estate to estate over all the coffee growing districts, destroying upwards of 250,000 acres. By the early 1890s there was but a very small acreage left under coffee. During this period, hundreds of estates lay completely abandoned, many more had little or no crop coming in and no money to pay the labour force. Yet there were others who, whilst facing the ruination of their beloved coffee bushes, grimly prepared to uproot every single bush and to replant – but this time with tea.

The Coffee Men Change to Tea

'Not often is it that men have the heart, when their one great industry is withered, to rear up in a few years another as rich to take its place, and the tea fields of Ceylon are as true a monument to courage as is the lion at Waterloo.'
Conan Doyle

Many of the coffee planters became tea planters almost overnight, once they had steeled themselves to go ahead with the disheartening job of uprooting. By the mid-1890s, nearly all of a quarter of a million acres of coffee that had been planted with such effort and at such great cost, had been uprooted, and the tea camellia planted in its place. Thus began the great Ceylon tea industry.

Both tea seeds of the Assam jat and young tea plants had been sent from the Botanical Gardens in Calcutta to the Peradeniya Botanical Gardens near Kandy in 1839, and small experimental plantings had been carried out over a period of many years. In addition, a handful of the more enterprising coffee planters had cleared the odd half acre and planted it up with tea. The main body of planters, however, had little time for the tea plant, being chiefly concerned in opening out as much land as they possibly could for coffee. The small plots of tea that had been planted out experimentally were almost forgotten for some thirty years in the wake of the coffee mania that had gripped all the planters – but tea did grow. ▷

ABOVE
Galle harbour from the P&O Company's station on Closenberg Island. Galle was a fine natural harbour, and coaling port for vessels of many of the shipping lines. Because of its greater distance from the coffee estates in the central hill districts, it was less favoured than the port of Colombo for the shipment of coffee. (Lithograph 1864, from O'Brians' 'Views in Ceylon'.)

LEFT
Adams Peak (centre on skyline) seen from the Yatteantotta cart-road near Ambogamawa. A large number of coffee estates were opened up in the Ambogamawa district and, by 1857, the 21 independent estates in the area were employing some 6000 coolies. (Lithograph 1864, from O'Brian's 'Views in Ceylon'.)

TOP LEFT
The scene depicted shows dead and dying coffee bushes being uprooted on a coffee estate. The drawing was made for want of an old photograph showing elephants uprooting a part of Ceylon's history.

After the coffee leaf disease struck in 1869, estates saw their yields fall drastically, some interplanted their dying fields of coffee with young tea plants, others, once they had steeled themselves, made a clean sweep and uprooted all. The coffee bushes – 1200 to every acre – were either burnt in the field, used as firewood, or the stems were shipped to England in small quantities, where they were used to make the legs of tea tables.

Our picture shows a typical up-country scene, which was being enacted throughout the whole of the coffee-growing districts during the late 1870s, 1880s and early 1890s. In this space of time, a quarter of a million acres of dead and dying coffee bushes were uprooted, and the land replanted with tea.

Standing in a valley through which runs a river, flanked by towering hills, we see the planter together with his Tamil Kangany, and a Tamil woman; all are dwarfed by their grand surroundings. Two mountain hawk-eagles circle effortlessly above the coffee, where large tree-stumps from the felled forest still stand; others lie where they fell, when the jungle was first opened out.

Many of the proprietary planters, their life's work ruined, sold up and returned to Britain, while the estate coolies returned to their homes in Southern India. There were others who grimly hung on to their land, their labour force in many cases working without pay, and with little food, stood firmly by their employers throughout these difficult times.

The anguish with which the coffee planters faced the prospect of uprooting all their coffee bushes, and starting all over again, can be well imagined, but they did, and out of the ashes rose an entirely new industry – TEA. (Drawing 1982, G. Cunningham.)

LEFT
Laymastotte Estate.
This is one of many 'set-piece' photographs taken on Thomas Lipton's tea estates, showing the dispatch of tea from factory to bullock cart. The tea

drinking public at home in Britain came to think that most of the tea came from Lipton owned estates, while in effect, he owned no more than 5500 of the 380,000 acres of tea in the island. Nevertheless, the name of Lipton has been synonymous with tea ever since. (Photo c1894, courtesy BBC Hulton Picture Library.)

ABOVE TOP
The same tea bushes that James Taylor planted in 1867 seen here 115 years later on Loolecondera tea estate. (Photo 1982.)
ABOVE
The coffee picker with her bag has been replaced by the tea plucker and her basket. (Tinted photo 1890.)

Tea seeds being collected from seed bearers. These blocks of seed bearers were either formed by removing intermediate rows of existing tea bushes to give more space to those left, or by planting up new land so as to keep a distance of 15 ft by 12 ft between the plants. Mature seed bearers range from 12 to 18 feet in height and come into useful bearing after about ten years. (Photo c1890, courtesy Royal Commonwealth Society.)

A nursery of young tea plants established on a flat piece of land from which most of the large jungle tree stumps have been removed. The young plants are shaded from the hot sun by ferns. Above and beyond the nursery, the slope of the hillside shows land that has been cleared sufficiently for planting, while on the right is the jungle boundary. A nursery would preferably be located in a sheltered, wind-free hollow, where there was good soil and an unfailing supply of water from a nearby stream. (Photo c1890, courtesy Royal Commonwealth Society.)

Tea bushes in the foreground, with dead and dying coffee bushes stretching right up the mountainside. When the picture is enlarged, it appears that the rows of coffee bushes on the entire hillside have been underplanted with tea. All that is left of the coffee bushes is their characteristic single main stem running up to about 3 feet in height; these will be cut down or dug out when money and labour are available – as has already been done in the foreground, where the tea alone has been left standing. The planting of tea under and between the dying rows of coffee bushes was the alternative to the clean sweep method. If it was decided to underplant, the dwindling coffee crop could still be gathered while the young tea plants became established; the disadvantage, however, was that the young tea plants would be damaged by the coffee pickers treading on them. (Photo 1870s, courtesy Royal Geographical Society.)

An old coffee store in its new role as a tea factory. Planter and 'kangany' are seen weighing up the green leaf that has been brought in from the fields by the pluckers. To the right of the picture one can see some crudely formed 'tats' on which the green leaf is spread for withering. (Photo c1880, courtesy Chatto & Windus Ltd.)

▷ The first commercially planted tea – on Loolecondera estate in 1867 – had in fact been planted during the coffee boom, just two years before the appearance of the coffee leaf disease. It was indeed fortunate that the tea plant had been found to grow well in the hills of Ceylon. The first recorded shipment of tea came some five years later, in 1872, with two small packages containing 23 pounds, valued at 58 rupees. The first vessel recorded as carrying Ceylon tea to England was the steam-ship *Duke of Argyll*, in the year 1877.

As the ravages of the coffee leaf disease became more widespread throughout the coffee growing districts, more or less everyone was ready to turn to tea. By the early 1880s, the coffee planters' stampede into tea was fast gathering momentum although, at the time, they understood little of the growing and manufacture of tea. Fortunately, the great amount of tea expertise that had been gained over the years in India, first from the tea makers and cultivators recruited from China by the East India Company, then by the Assam Company and others, was freely given to the coffee planters in Ceylon.

In the early years, the big problem was to obtain sufficient tea seed for starting up the new tea estates. In only twenty years, 250,000 acres of old coffee land had been replanted with tea. In addition, a quite considerable acreage of jungle was still being felled every year and planted up first time with tea. One might wonder where all the tea seeds came from as the old coffee land alone would have required approximately one thousand million young tea plants.

To start with, most of the tea seeds were imported from Assam, and to a lesser extent from China, but as the industry got going, tea seed nurseries were established from which seeds were then supplied – at a cost – to estates. As the new tea estates became established, each would reserve a small piece of land for their own seed bearers; the seed

TOP LEFT
Besides the old coffee land that was being replanted, a considerable amount of jungle was also being opened out to tea. Here we see one such new clearing. The planter is superintending the planting out of the young tea plants which have been taken from the nursery. In the tangled landscape it is difficult to see whether the fallen trees have been burnt, as was the practice before the process of lining, pegging, holing, and planting would be carried out, but the tell-tale marks of charcoal on some of the foreground timber tell us that it has. No doubt the wind was insufficient, and a poor burn was the result. A successful burn made things a lot easier, and less costly in the long run. Within a few short years the whole area would become transformed into a soft carpet of light green, covering most of the landscape. The fallen timber would rot quickly under heat and monsoon rains. It was on one such clearing – for coffee – in the year 1867 that William Mackwood, aged twenty, received injuries from which he later died at Gampola. The inscription on his tombstone states: 'He was alighting from his horse on a clearing on Galbodde estate, when he was transfixed by a stake placed to mark out the ground'. He is buried at the Old Garrison Cemetery in Kandy.

The account of his accident comes from J. Penry Lewis's remarkable reference work, 'A list of inscriptions on tombstones and monuments in Ceylon'. (Photo 1880s, courtesy Royal Commonwealth Society.)

ABOVE
Strathallan tea estate, Nawalapitiya. This newly built tea factory has only one withering loft above the main factory floor. The flat piece of land to the right is the nursery, whose specially prepared flat seed beds of fine sandy soil were fertilized with cattle manure. The young tea seed-lings would be sheltered from the sun with 'cadjans' or with ferns. The beds were kept well watered and damp until the plants were about one-and-a-half years old, when they would be ready to be lifted and taken to the new clearings to be planted out, or used to infill vacancies in the already established fields. (Photo c1885.)

BOTTOM LEFT
Plucking gang in a tea field of the 1880s. The young plants were planted out at between 2800 and 3000 per acre. (Photo 1880s.)

from here was usually enough to supply the estate's own need for its new clearings, as and when they were opened. Some estates would also make a profitable business out of selling seed to other estates in the neighbourhood.

During the change-over from coffee to tea, when money was in short supply, a great number of the old coffee stores were converted into 'factories' for tea making. On the new estates which had no old coffee stores, completely new factories were built, and installed with the new tea machinery made by Davidsons of Belfast, Marshalls of Gainsborough, Lancashire, and Tangyes Machine Company, Birmingham.

More land was put under tea during the late 1880s and 1890s than in any other decade after. As the increases in crop production went spiralling upwards, there arose a great need for proper factories to handle the enormous quantities of leaf. With the building of the first true tea factories, came the need for mechanisation.

Manufacture at the turn of the century (photos late 1880's)

TOP LEFT
Weighing up the leaf oufside the factory. (Courtesy Royal Commonwealth Society.)

CENTRE LEFT
Withering. When the leaf came in from the fields, it contained approximately 76 per cent weight of water. Having been weighed, it was carried up to the withering loft(s) to be spread thinly on the 'tats' and left to wither. The tats were wooden structures with loosely woven jute hessian stretched across. Withering allowed the moisture in the leaf to evaporate until the leaf became flaccid and, at the same time, susceptible to a good twist by the rollers in the next phase of manufacture. Depending upon climatic conditions and whether the withering was natural or artificial, by the use of fans which boost warm air – heated by the driers – through the lofts, the green leaf took between 18 and 24 hours to wither. By this time it was ready for the next stage of manufacture: that of rolling.

In the rolling room on the ground floor the noise level would have been deafening – the hollow grinding sound of the gyrating rolling machines, the whirring of the pulley wheels, the slap of the belting and, above all, the deep rythmic thump of the diesel engine. One had to shout to make oneself heard.

BOTTOM LEFT
Rolling. The withered leaf arrived by way of the shutes from the floor(s) above, to be placed in the rollers. In rolling, the leaf is crushed, broken and twisted, so as to break down the leaf cells and release the juices and oils which cover the surface of the leaf. As these juices come into contact with the air, oxidisation takes place and fermentation starts. The roller would rotate in one direction while its unfixed ribbed table base, on which the leaf rested, rotated in the other. When the leaf was sufficiently rolled, it was taken out, golden green in colour, and quite sticky and lumpy. The 'roll' was then put out onto a sloping, fine meshed machine called a roll-breaker which, whilst shaking backwards and forwards at high speed, broke up the lumps, letting the small leaf fall through onto the ground beneath. The large lumps were shaken to the end of the machine. The small leaf that came through the roll-breaker at each sieving was then ready for the next process of manufacture: fermenting. The rest was carried back to the roll-breaker, and the process was repeated three or four times. One rolling machine took the place of several old rolling tables, and did the work of about 60 hand-rolling coolies.

RIGHT
A roll-breaker inside the factory and a rolling machine to the left. (Photo 1900, courtesy Mrs Raffin.)

Fermenting. (For the lack of a suitable photograph, see watercolour drawing on page 53 'fermenting in India'.) It was in the cool, damp, and darkened fermenting room that the leaf, or 'dhool', was spread out on the fermenting beds of smooth polished concrete or cement. The process of fermentation – first started by rolling – now took place and, when the leaf assumed a bright copper colour, it was ready for lifting. Again, the precise time at which the fermentation should be stopped and the fermented leaf removed was crucial, and also depended on weather conditions. However, assuming all the tests had been carried out and the infusions tasted during the withering and again towards the end of the fermenting process, the fermented leaf was ready for lifting for the final stage: firing.

RIGHT
Firing. The fermented leaf was carried to the driers, or firing machines, where it was spread out onto an endless chain of wire trays. These circulated over a continual current of hot air which was drawn up from the stoves below by high pressure fans. Fermentation of the leaf was now arrested. The whole factory became filled with a glorious aroma and the tea, still hot, that emerged from the firing machine was now fully manufactured: it was black, dry, and brittle. One large drying machine – such as the one shown, manufactured by Davidson & Co. – does the work of about 35 coolies working over a line of charcoal-burning ovens. (Courtesy Royal Commonwealth Society.) The tea was now ready to be sorted into the different grades and then stored in large bins until a sufficient quantity had been accumulated for dispatch. From 1000 lbs of green leaf, 230 lbs of made tea is the result. (BELOW LEFT, AND RIGHT)

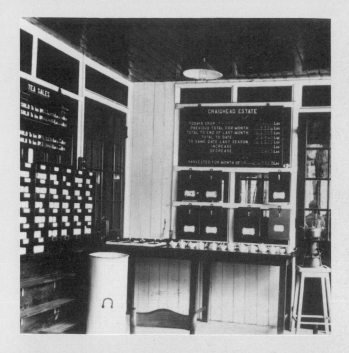

The new 20th century design of tea factory

TOP LEFT
The factory office and tea tasting room. Frequent tasting of teas provides a check on manufacture. A set of white china cups and pots of regulation size were required, together with a copper-bottomed kettle for quick boiling of water and a small balance scale. (Courtesy Royal Botanic Gardens, Kew.)

TOP RIGHT AND LEFT
Two photographs of Craighead factory. The machinery was on the ground floor, with the three upper floors, or lofts, used for withering the green leaf. Any timber that was required for building purposes was taken from new clearings or from estate owned jungle. With three storeys of planked wood throughout the withering lofts, as well as the wooden structure of the tats, a considerable amount of sawn timber was required for building a tea factory the size of Craighead. Excluding the old coffee stores, which in many cases were turned into makeshift tea factories after the collapse of coffee, most of the first true tea factories that were built during the 1880s and 1890s had only one or two withering lofts. The small loft factories soon became overstretched and, from 1900 onwards, many new factories were built with four floors, of which three were for withering. (Courtesy Royal Botanic Gardens, Kew.)

BOTTOM LEFT
Outside the factory on a tea and rubber estate in the southern province in the late 1890s. (Courtesy Mrs Raffin.)

Tea advertisements

A whole series of postcard and newspaper advertisements, using photographs and drawings, was published towards the end of the 19th century by firms such as Liptons and Ridgeways, and what was then known as the Mazawattee Ceylon Tea Company, whose delivery van is shown here.

Liptons' early tea advertisements started to appear towards the end of the 19th century in the UK and America, and helped to increase the company's success so that the name of Lipton soon became synonymous with tea throughout the world.

TOP LEFT PAGE 128
Tamil dockyard workers loading chests of Liptons' teas on to lighters in Colombo docks.

127

Shipping Tea. CEYLON.

LIPTON SERIES.

LIPTON SERIES

POOPRÁSSIE TEA FACTORY, CEYLON.

LIPTON SERIES.

Thomas Lipton came from humble begin-nings. But he had soon left his father's grocery shop in Glasgow behind him and by 1890, his first chain of shops had made him a millionaire. The year 1890 was, for Lipton and many others, the ideal time to buy tea estates, which in many cases were being snapped up at knocked-down prices. The coffee leaf disease had run its course, and most of the old coffee estates had been fully converted into tea. Never-theless, times were hard and money was in short supply for the quite considerable outlay entailed in purchasing the machinery and building new tea factories. But for a millionaire this was no problem. Lipton bought his first tea estates in the Haputele district of Ceylon in 1890. Laymastotte, Monarakande, and Dam-batenne were later followed by the pur-chase of Pooprassie, Bunyan and others, amounting in all to some 5500 acres.

LIPTON SERIES

Muster of Coolies. MONERAMANBE ESTATE CEYLON

PLUCKING TEA ON BUNYAN ESTATE, CEYLON

Loading Elephant. Badella Tea Estate, Ceylon

VIEW ON CEYLON TEA ESTATE. LIPTON SERIES

Tea arriving at foot of Aerial Ropeway, Ceylon. LIPTON SERIES

LIPTON SERIES. VIEW ON CEYLON TEA ESTATE.

LIPTON SERIES.

LIPTON SERIES. Loading Bullock Carts. Dambatenne Factory, Ceylon.

CENTRAL PICTURE PREVIOUS PAGE
Wire shutes were used from the early 1900s until the 1960s to bring the leaf from the fields to the factory. Photo c1900 shows Lipton's Laymastotte factory.
LEFT
A view of Lipton's showpiece, Dambatenne estate. Dambatenne, last of the Lipton owned estates in Ceylon, was handed over to the Ceylon government in 1975, during the period of estate nationalization. (Photo 1966, courtesy Chatto & Windus Ltd.)
(The Dambatenne estate can also be seen CENTRE RIGHT and BOTTOM RIGHT on the previous page. These views are dated 1896.)

BELOW
The old 'up and down' system again seen here on a field of tea that was planted before 1900. This field is still being plucked today, but yields are very poor. Of the 594,000 acres of tea in the country today, a substantial acreage of old uneconomical tea remains, having been planted out before the turn of the century. (Photo 1982.)

ABOVE
Old, though relatively good tea bushes being uprooted on Brownlow state plantation in Maskeliya – these bushes are 75 – 80 years old. When uprooting is completed, the land will be replanted with vegetative propagated tea on the 'contour system' at 6000 to 8000 cuttings per acre. In this case, the bushes are being dug out with the aid of the mumaty, and not pulled out by elephant, which would be much quicker. The replanting programme is of the utmost importance to the future tea industry in the country, and needs to be carried out as quickly as possible. During the years leading up to the nationalization of the predominantly British owned estates, capital was not made available for replanting and other important estate works because of the uncertain future. Consequently, at the time of nationalization, there was much to be done that would otherwise have been carried out long before. (Photo 1982.)

LEFT
A Tamil woman estate worker carries a bundle of hacked and uprooted tea bushes back to her lines, where it will be used as firewood. More old fields with poor yields are seen in the middle distance. (Photo 1982.)

Tamil pluckers tread the steep slopes of Dickoya, in the footsteps of the coffee pickers of 100 years before.

Support for an Army of Workers

By 1900, approximately 380,000 acres of land were under tea. The total labour force required to work this acreage was of gigantic proportions. In the days of coffee, the crop had been seasonal, gathered only between November and April, and therefore there had been regular periods when the pickers would leave the estates to journey to their homes in southern India, returning again at the commencement of the picking season. A small labour force had been kept on for routine works and to run a cattle establishment for the provision of the necessary manure. In the case of tea, however, the 'flush' or leaf keeps coming, and plucking goes on six days a week throughout the whole year. Consequently, enormous quantities of food-stuffs – mainly rice and to a lesser extent flour, sugar, and dried or salted fish – had to be carried up to the estates to feed this huge fully resident army of people, each one of whom consumed a bushel of rice a month. If one then includes young children, and dependents who also lived on the estate but did not work, it will be seen that once started, the planting enterprise led to a veritable hive of activity in the trade of food alone.

At the turn of the century many thousands were also employed on cocoa plantations as well as on the rubber estates that were being opened up at elevations below 1800 feet. In all, it has been estimated that there were well over half a million coolies working on European owned estates in Ceylon by 1900, having exchanged the hardships and unemployment of their native India for a prosperity not otherwise dreamed of by their families back home. The whole planting industry benefited too, as did the country, for without the Tamils, the estates could never have been worked.

LEFT
The field, just showing, at left above a cart-road, is a newly replanted area. This lush green carpet of contour planted VP tea – some two years old – replaced the uprooted original tea left from before the turn of the century, which, in turn, had been planted on old coffee land. The bamboo canes are used not for climbing, but to assist in plucking each bush to a level. (Courtesy National Geographic Society, USA. Photo Raghubir Singh 1979.)

BELOW
Typical tea factory of the 1890 period. (Watercolour by S.R. Fever, 1984.)

The revenue generated on the estates spread far and wide. The cargo steamers of the British India Steam Navigation Company carried on an all-the-year-round trade in the shipment of fish manure from the ports of Mangalore and Cannanore on the Malabar coast down to the port of Colombo, where the manure was dispatched by railway and bullock cart to the tea growing districts for use as fertilizer.

The quantity of rice alone that was required at the turn of the century to feed a total labour force of some half a million souls brought the BISNC, or BI as it was generally called, considerable revenue in freight. BI steamers regularly carried rice from Moulmein in Burma across the Bay of Bengal down to Colombo. Even in 1882, when there had been only 125,000 men and 82,000 women living and working on the coffee and tea eastates, almost 50,000 tons of rice had been shipped into the bustling port of Colombo. There was hardly a single day in the year.

ABOVE
An unusual sight – tea being grown under rubber. (Photo c1900, courtesy Mrs Raffin.)
TOP RIGHT
A new clearing for rubber. In 1876 Henry Wickham collected seeds of Hevea brasiliensis from the jungles of the Amazon which were sent to Kew. Later, after germination, several thousand young rubber plants were shipped out to Ceylon in Wardian cases; these were the start of the great rubber industry, which was to spread to South India, Malaya, and other parts of the East Indies. (Photo c1900, courtesy Mrs Raffin.)

RIGHT
Two sets of coolie lines with the tea factory above and beyond. A double line, such as the one shown in the foreground, would accommodate 12 families. Line rooms were 12 ft by 10 ft, with an overhanging verandah running the complete length to give protection from wind and rain. In the early years there were no latrines on the coffee and tea estates, and pollution of the soil around lines was always a bad health hazard, causing hook-worm. It was only in the year 1917 that the compulsory cutting of latrine pits was introduced. (Photo 1903, courtesy Royal Geographical Society.)

when the distinctive black funnels with broad white bands of a BI cargo steamer could not be seen in the harbour; they were as much a part of the scene as were the crows that hung about the customs sheds by the landing jetty.

The Indian 'deck passenger' trade formed a quite considerable part of the BISN Company's activities from the late 1860s to the 1950s. On some of the large BI steamers, between 3000 and 4000 of these fare-paying 'unberthed' passengers could be carried on the main deck, and 'tween decks. They would squat down in family groups under a canopy provided by the company with all their belongings for the duration of the voyage. They would form a living mass of humanity, eating, sleeping, incessantly talking, and not infrequently dying on the voyage.

Quite apart from the Tamils who made their way to the estates in Ceylon, hundreds of thousands of Tamil and Telegu coolies from the east coast of India left their impoverished land to live and work on the sugar plantations in Mauritius, and in later years on the rubber estates and tin mines in Malaya. Countless thousands of Chinese too, who also worked on the rubber estates in Malaya, were carried by BI vessels as 'deck passengers' between Amoy and Singapore.

Today, if one visits the Seychelles or Mauritius, or in fact any place from the east coast of Africa across the Indian Ocean to Malaya and beyond, one will find the southern Indian, whose great-grandfather like as not arrived there as one of the BI's deck passengers a century ago. The whole vast area was an agricultural hot house, most suitable for growing a variety of plantation crops. Jungle was being opened out everywhere at a terrific pace during the great developing years of the British Empire. The rapid expansion of the planting industry in India,

A typical early BI triple screw coasting steamer, rigged for sail. A part of Colombo harbour looking towards the town. Attendant lighters nestle around the steamers as they discharge and take on cargo. (Photo c1895.)

ABOVE

Kintyre tea estate. If one looks across the field through the gap on the right formed by the line of jungle trees left standing along the banks of the River Maskeliya, one can see the Laxapana coffee estate. (Photo 1894.)

LEFT

Tamil children were allowed to start work on the estates as half-time pluckers or weeders from the age of nine onwards. This 'sinna pulle', or young child, can- *not be more than ten years of age. The infant mortality rate on estates before the turn of the century was in the region of 50 to 60 per cent. (Photo c1895.)*

BELOW

A school on a tea estate. The fully resident labour force on the tea estates meant that there was a need for some simple schooling for the estate children. Therefore every estate would have a small school; under the guidance of one of the Tamil women. (Photo 1900.)

Ceylon, Malaya, and Java had far-reaching effects upon a wide variety of people.

The British India Steam Navigation Company – whose mercantile fleet was once the largest in the world with a total tonnage of just under one million and 158 vessels under its flag – played a very important part during the developing years of the planting industry in India and the colonies.

The pioneer planters did more than merely open out inaccessible, fever-ridden jungle, and establish a thriving new industry where none had been before; with the opening of the tea, coffee, cocoa and rubber estates, there came the need for all manner of other local occupations, such as timber and transport contractors and rice merchants. These latter in turn brought shop-keepers to the area, and small bazaars quickly sprang up to meet the needs of those working on the estates. These bazaars were thriving little communities; the estate workers – far from their native homes in South India – came there for their requirements and for small luxuries such as trinkets, bangles, curry stuffs and clothes. Here too, they could visit various money lenders, have their hair cut or get drunk.

At times the Tamil and his family would travel farther than the local bazaar. From the early days, Adams Peak played an important part in the lives of thousands of coolies working on the estates. Pilgrimages to the Holy Mountain were made, and no self-respecting Tamil would care to admit that he had not journeyed to the Peak – or to Kataragama in the south of the island. During the pilgrimage season a family unit, complete with the smallest child and the aged grandmother, would set out from their estate, travelling on foot for days and sometimes weeks along hot, dusty cart roads towards their final goal. As they drew nearer to the Peak, they would converge with thousands of other pilgrims coming from the different estates. Both those on their way and those returning would rest each night by the road side, or at special rest houses along the pilgrim's route. On a clear night, and from many miles distant, all could see the outline of the Peak against

Pilgrims nearing the summit. (Photo c1900, courtesy Royal Commonwealth Society.)

Ramasamy's children. Each Tamil family living on the estate had many children. (Photo c1900.)

Waiting for the train – going to the coast. 'Simiki poitu varen': 'having gone to the coast, I shall return'. Tamil families would leave their estates to visit relations in their village homes in southern India, and would then return to the estate. (Photo 1890.)

the sky, with hundreds of flaming torches stretched out over the dark landscape, like a thin living chain of fire wending its way up towards the summit.

Many of the more aged pilgrims died by the wayside on the long approach, and yet more came to grief tackling the final ascent of the cone itself. The headstones of some who died long ago can still be seen today beside the path, and many more, without headstones, undoubtably lie close by in the fringe of the jungle.

The climb is extremely steep on the Ratnapura side, and is made at certain parts with the help of iron chains fixed to the almost vertical

rock face. Over the years whole families have been torn from the chains by strong winds, falling to their deaths hundreds of feet below. The very old are carried to the summit by the younger and stronger members of the family. It is bitterly cold upon the summit during the hours of darkness, and the wind is often so strong that the temple shrine itself was shackled down in olden times with strong chains to stop it being blown off the summit. Many thousands make the pilgrimage every year of their lives, Hindus and Buddhists alike.

For the Tamils who travelled to and from the estates during the earlier years of the coffee enterprise, there was no railway to speed them on their way. If they could afford to travel as deck passengers, they would come from Tuticorin by boat down to Colombo for the fare of one shilling per person. They would then make their way on foot along the road up to Kandy and on to their estates – an 80-120 mile walk. Alternatively, they would arrive in the north of the island at Manaar, and then make an appalling journey southwards on foot along a rough route which led into Matale, from where they then had to press on to their estates – in all, some 140-200 miles on foot. Thousands died over the years, especially those travelling by the northern route.

For those travelling as deck passengers between Colombo and Tuticorin, the journey was short, sharp and sweet compared to the north road route. The Reverend W. Urwick, who took passage on one such vessel in the late 1870s, describes his experience:

'A great exodus always follows the gathering of the coffee crop. In the steamer in which we crossed from Colombo to Tuticorin there were about five hundred Tamils, men, women, and children, on board returning to their native land. Many of them crowded the deck all night, and in spite of much roughness from the sailors, seemed patient and light hearted. After a calm starlight night we found our vessel anchored off the flat sandy coast of India, about six miles from the shore. The steamer could not be brought nearer on account of the shallows; and though the sea was calm and billows of ▷

ABOVE
The approach into Kandy. This splendid bridge, built at Peradeniya in 1831, was constructed entirely of satin-wood, without the use of a single nail or bolt in it, the whole of the massive woodwork being merely dovetailed together. The great strength of the stone buttresses and their foundations on each side was undoubtably the key to its long life. The view shows the river flowing under normal dry season conditions.
BELOW
A close-up of the steam engine, with cow-pusher.

RIGHT
The scene of an accident when the line was being pushed through lowland country outside Colombo. Having hit an obstruction, the train and its trucks were thrown off the line and overturned in the rice field that ran alongside. 36 coolies and the European driver of the train were crushed and killed. The trucks seen in the illustration were of the type used both for the transportation of earth, and for the conveyance of coolies working on the railroad. (Drawing 'Illustrated London News' 1865, courtesy British Library.)

FAR LEFT
Kaduganawa Incline – Sensation Rock. (Photo 1885.) This shows the type of steam engine that ran on the Ceylon government railway 100 years ago. The cow-pusher on the front of all engines was a necessity: in 1890, a total of 129 bullocks, buffaloes, and cows were run over, and an even greater number pushed off the tracks. Engine drivers were all British, being found to be more cool-headed than the natives in times of danger.

LEFT
The Prince of Wales during his tour of the island riding the engine while traversing Sensation Rock. (Sketch 1882, courtesy Royal Commonwealth Society.)

BELOW
Journey's end, the port of Colombo. The lines of buildings along the right are the Customs sheds, the other side of which is the harbour itself. (Photo 1890s.)

Colombo harbour, Ceylon, 1888, seen from the old Customs sheds. The 'Tweed' is shown about to sail – on April 8th, 1888 – bound for New York. The beginning of April brings with it the first onset of the south-west monsoon. At first the winds are faint, there are light showers, thunder commences, and the atmosphere broods heavily upon the scene. This is generally referred to as the 'little monsoon', which always comes before the full outbreak of the monsoon. Under a threatening sky, Tamil dockyard workers are seen going about their daily tasks, loading tea chests and other cargo into the numerous lighters moored along the wharfside. The small launch with a tall funnel, more or less in the middle of the picture, was known as a 'jolly boat', and was used for taking passengers from ship to the landing jetty. The construction of the harbour was begun in 1875. It comprises three breakwaters: the south-west arm, the first stone of which was laid by the Prince of Wales in 1882, the north-east and the north-west breakwaters, all of which were finished by 1883. On completion, the harbour had a water area of a square mile which provided safe anchorage for 50 vessels as well as for smaller craft. The quaint old jetty lasted from the 1870s up until the mid-1950s, when it made way for the present harbour facilities. (Oil painting by S.R. Fever, 1974.)

▷ heavy swell chased each other over the sand-banks with a long lazy sweep towards the land. A fleet of heavy native sail boats came out to take the passengers ashore, and in a four-oared boat, after passing Hare Island, we reached the landing stage of Tuticorin in an hour.'

The need for transport, right from the early coffee days, was never really satisfied until the railway was opened to Kandy in 1867. Both Ceylon, and the planting industry, were fortunate in having a very clear-thinking governor, Sir Edward Barnes, as well as some very capable engineers, who pushed the first roads through to serve the planting districts locked away in the hills. A man famous for opening up the interior with good roads was Major Skinner, who arrived in the colony in 1818, at the ripe age of fourteen and, after fifty years of untiring public service to the country, finally retired and left the island in 1869. He was entrusted with the construction of various sections of the road from Colombo to Kandy, including the most difficult eleven miles up through the Kaduganawa Pass. Upon this road, on its completion in 1831, ran the first Royal Mail coach ever started in Asia.

As early as the year 1828, work was started on the Nuwara Eliya road from Gampola, in the heart of the coffee growing district, up to Rangbodde. The building of the satinwood bridge over the Mahaweli Ganga at Peradeniya was commenced in 1830, and completed a year later. During the first phase of the work, 1200 men were employed in laying and filling up the approaches on either side of the river.

Opened in the year 1867 at a cost of £1,285,000, the single broad-gauged line was laid at a great cost of lives. Hundreds of coolies died from fever while working on the lower portion of the line which ran for 50 miles from Colombo through lowland swamps and jungle. Numerous fatal accidents also occurred during the cutting, blasting and excavation work along the most impossible stretch leading up to the top of the Kaduganawa Pass. The thousands of labourers lived in crude temporary shelters pitched along each side of the railroad and, as the line progressed, they moved along with it. So bad were the conditions, with men dying every day and being buried alongside the track, that it was decided to base the entire labour force in Colombo, and truck them out to work each day. British engineers who supervised the work were invalided out, their health broken, and returned to Britain.

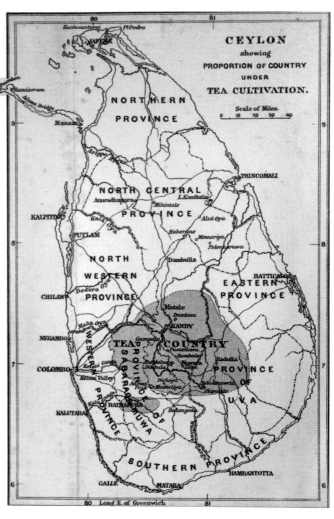

The main tea growing area in the central hill districts. (Map c1900.)

THE PIONEER PLANTERS IN CEYLON

CHAPTER V

AND THEIR WAY OF LIFE

'Now then, just look alive!
The coffee bring, the butter and the bread:
With eggs and pie, and pudding too
The table quickly spread!
Hi, carpen-boots and gaiters quick:
And see they're all well oiled,
My breeches too, of cannomore
Are those eggs nearly boiled?' …

LOG CABIN LIFE IN 1881 – A HUNTING MORNING

The Pioneer Planters in Ceylon

After the opening, in 1825, of the first coffee estate just outside Kandy by the Governor, Sir Edward Barnes, there was a rush by public servants in Colombo to buy land in the central hill districts around Kandy. Those fortunate enough to get in early bought at the then attractive price of 5s per acre, which soon climbed to £1 an acre. The proprietors of jungle and forest land – who knew little or nothing about coffee – then had to set about developing the land they had bought locked 80 miles away in the hills.

It was at this stage that some of the first men to become planters arrived on the scene. The easiest part for those who wished to go out into an unknown tropical country nearly 150 years ago, and stake everything – including perhaps their own lives – was the three months' voyage out. In the 1820s and '30s, sailing ships would put in at Point de Galle, 80 miles to the south of the capital.

Those who were destined to become the pioneers of the new coffee enterprise were an odd mixture of men: some were adventurers out from Britain, while others had seen service in the army in Ceylon and had been bought out by the new land proprietors. These men were engaged as superintendents, put on a fixed salary and then – knowing little or nothing about agriculture, let alone coffee – set off for the unknown interior.

The beginning of the 19th century held tantalising opportunities for the more adventurous; the great British Empire was, in its early years, demanding of all sorts of men.

Considering the population of Scotland in relation to the rest of Britain, a very large proportion of the planters were Scots, many from the area around Aberdeen. They often came from the same village or farming area, and those at home would hear from friends and relations – who were already planting – of the chances that were open to a young man in Ceylon. Whole families became planters, as was the case with James Taylor and his numerous planting relatives. These tough, hard-headed Scots were the real pioneers of Ceylon's early plantations, which were destined to become the tea estates of today. They fought their way through pathless forests, and bivouacked in virgin jungle which, in those days, was full of wild animals.

At the time when the first planters made the journey from Colombo to Kandy, detachments of the British army were encamped in that town. Before the coming of the new road, which was commenced in 1820 and finally completed in 1831, these detachments of artillery had had to manhandle their guns, equipment and provisions through lowland swamps and then through thick jungle every inch of the 74 miles to Kandy, taking in all six weeks.

Before setting off on the journey to the hills, the planter would purchase everything necessary for living and working on the new estate. He would take on a few Tamil coolies, the first of his labour

PREVIOUS PAGE
Log cabin life in 1881. 'A Hunting Morning' shows three planters from the Haputele district preparing for a day out hunting. The planter on the left is about to put on his leech gaiters: these were made of closely woven cloth through which the leeches could not reach the skin. Could those be the leaves of the talipot palm that are seen neatly folded away under the roof? (From 'Scenes in Ceylon' by Hamilton and Fasson.)

ABOVE
Colombo was the harbour from which nearly all the coffee and tea was shipped to Europe. This view is from Mutwall, looking across towards the fort, with the Customs house and open roadstead where the larger sailing ships and steamers used to take on and discharge their cargoes, often with a high surf running when winds beat up from the south-west during the monsoon. Colombo was also the port at which most of the rice was received destined for the Tamil coolies working on the coffee estates in the central hill districts. The tall building to the left of centre is the lighthouse. (Lithograph 1864 from O'Brian's 'Views in Ceylon'.)

force, and buy provisions for his men and himself. Tools and equipment would be needed, mumaties, axes, knives, lining rope, an oil lamp or two and a good supply of matches and candles, as well as a rifle with which to shoot game and to protect himself from wild animals. Also a rudimentry box of first aid materials, even leech gaiters to protect his legs and feet in wet weather from the thousands of leeches that he would undoubably encounter, the bites of which could turn septic very easily. Last but not least, he would buy enough coffee seed to plant 50 acres of land. Finally, when all was ready, the proprietor, his superintendent and a small party of men would move off by bullock cart on their journey to the hills, to the unknown.

The proprietor's problems had only just started, as had the planter's. Having bought some hundred acres from the government which, at the outset of the coffee venture, was no mean amount, the purchaser then faced the daunting task of making that land into a coffee plantation. 5s an acre might seem more than reasonable at first sight, but what in fact he had bought for his £25 was 100 acres of dense jungle 70-80 miles away – to which no roads existed. From then onwards the proprietor had never ending expenses and no income to look for before some four years.

It was only when his superintendent had established a nursery and felled and burnt the first 50 acre block of jungle that the new owner could contemplate the planting out of the cleared land with young coffee plants. And from that day he had another three years to wait before he gathered his maiden crop. By that time he would have spent some £8 an acre to bring his coffee into bearing. And throughout these long years he would have to contend with all kinds of vicissitudes: his nursery beds or clearings could be trampled by elephants, elk, porcupines or wild pigs, his few resident Tamils might decide to leave, his superintendent might become ill and die.

In simple terms, the proprietor, who owned the land (virgin jungle), sat in Colombo and paid, or hoped he could pay, for everything entailed in the opening out of his land, its planting with coffee, and its upkeep until it came into bearing. As to the planter, well, he merely went out and did the rough pioneering in the jungle itself. The former supplied the capital, while the latter had the spirit of adventure.

The journey by bullock cart along the then partly constructed road, up through the Kaduganawa Pass and on to Kandy, would take the small group of men up to nine days in good weather. A few years later, upon the completion of the Kandy road, the planter would set off from Colombo in greater style, in a then unbelievably luxurious form of travel, the Royal Mail coach. The coach started off precisely as the morning gun fired at 5 am in the Colombo Fort. There were between ten and twelve stages along the 74 miles of road up to Kandy, and the coach journey took in the region of five days.

Upon reaching the town of Kandy, the party would probably have stayed the night, purchasing a few further provisions before pushing on, this time by horse and on foot to their ultimate destination on some mountainside within 15 miles of Kandy.

After much travelling, quite often under tropical rain, with ravines and rivers swollen and impassable, the small party would eventually reach the patch of land upon which their future depended in varying degrees. The proprietor, having been shown the extent of his land by a surveyor if he himself had not visited it before, would then return to Colombo, leaving his superintendent to get on with things.

To demarcate and survey tropical jungle was an extremely difficult ▷

TOP RIGHT
The view looking up Chatham Street, Colombo, towards the lighthouse with its fine clock. Where else in the world can a lighthouse be seen in the middle of a town? (Photo 1880.)
BOTTOM RIGHT
The Royal Mail coach. (Photo 1895.)
BOTTOM LEFT
Passing through a native bazaar on the way up country: a hive of activity with many different nationalities to be seen. (1881. From 'Scenes in Ceylon' by Hamilton and Fasson.)
BELOW
James Taylor, born in Scotland in 1835, was the first man to plant tea on a commercial basis in Ceylon in 1867. He is seen here with his cousin Henry Stiven. (Photo Kandy 1864, courtesy Chatto & Windus Ltd.)

ABOVE

In 1815 the British army for the second time fought its way up to and captured Kandy, and thereafter the town was garrisoned by the Ceylon Rifle Regiment. The view is from the hill, a little below the garrison cemetery, looking down on the lake and the Malagawa Temple. A carriage road runs around the margin of the lake. On the opposite side from the town are the monasteries of the priests and, above them, the residence of principal civilians and merchants. After the

opening of the first coffee estates, planters would ride into Kandy every month to obtain provisions and to collect money from the 'Chettes' – Moormen traders – to pay their estate labour force. For those who came from afar and stayed the night at any of the small boarding houses or at the Queen's Hotel, built in 1841 – seen right of centre facing the green – a pleasant stroll around the lake was a welcome change from their lonely estates. (Lithograph 1864, from O'Brian's 'Views in Ceylon'.)

FAR RIGHT

Kaduganawa Pass – looking up. The ascent into the Kandian hills begins at Rambukana, at 290 feet and, from there on, the road winds its tortuous way over the next 13 miles through dense forest and along steep precipices until it reaches the village of Kaduganawa at the top of the Pass. The tall monument was erected in 1832 to commemorate Captain Dawson, who planned and superintended the construction of the road. (Engraving c1860.)

The fulfilment of a prophesy; the rock was pierced and the road taken through

LEFT
*Kaduganawa Pass –
looking down. There
was an ancient prophecy
amongst the Sinhalese
in the Kingdom of
Kandy that, whoever
should pierce the rock
and make a road from
the plains, would receive
the kingdom as his
reward. The Portuguese
and the Dutch failed,
and the prophecy was at
last fulfilled by the
British, who pierced the
rock and built the road.
(Photo c1890.)*

'He assured me that a few leaves of the talipot palm was the only shelter that he possessed for nearly three months and that, too, only during the monsoon.' (Watercolour 1984, by S.R. Fever.)

▷but lucrative job back in the early 19th century, for it was hard enough to get to the area in the first place, and once there, the task of cutting 'sight lines' through virgin jungle prior to survey – generally over steep and rocky terrain – was an even harder task. Trees nearly 150 feet high had to be frequently felled in order to cut good wide lines through the jungle that would not become overgrown and lost to view six months later. The cost of surveying the land was usually charged to the lessee, and much of the land surveyed during the early years was found to be wildly inaccurate when surveyed in later years.

Civilization, with its doctors and shops had by now been left far behind. The new life in the jungle was full of excitement for the young and strong adventurer, with wild elephants, bears and snakes to contend with; at the same time there were plenty of red deer and wild hog to be shot for the table.

One of the first tasks for the planter on arrival at his patch of land was to locate a suitable spot near a stream which would supply good fresh drinking water, and to see to the building of a good set of dry 'lines' – long thatched huts for his Tamils – for, unless they were well cared for and well fed, they would not remain in such remote areas. Next in priority would have been the immediate felling of a small block of jungle for the establishment of his nursery, and the planting of his coffee seeds which, when germinated, would form the basis of his new plantation. Only after these first two important tasks had been carried out would he see to the construction of a hut of some sort for himself.

The Pioneer's First Shelter – The Talipot Palm Leaf

The description by John Capper, himself a coffee planter in the 1850s, of a visit to a new coffee estate in 1840 helps to illustrate the type of construction that passed for the coffee planters hut in the early pioneering days.

> 'The spot we had opened upon was at the entrance of a long valley of great width, on the one side of which lay the young estate to which we were going. Before us were, as my companion informed me, fifty acres of felled jungle in the wildest order; just as the monsters of the forest had fallen so they lay, heap upon heap, crushed and splintered into ten thousand fragments. Struggling on from trunk to trunk, and leading our horses slowly between huge rocks that lay thickly around, we at last got through the 'fall', and came to a part of the forest where the heavy quick click of many axes told us there was a working party busily employed.
>
> In the midst of these busy people I found my planter friend superintending operations in full jungle costume. A sort of wicker helmet was on his head, covered with a long padded white cloth which hung down his back, like a baby's quilt. A shorter jacket and trousers of checked country cloth, immense leech gaiters fitting close inside his roomy canvas boots, and a Chinese paper umbrella made up his singular attire. Passing through a few acres of standing forest and over a stream, we came to a small cleared space well sheltered from the wind, and quite snug in every respect.'

The well chosen and most important plot of land at which the party had arrived was, in fact, the site of the nursery; it was also the site of the planter's own habitation, which was however unrecognisable as such to the visitor. Capper goes on to say:

> 'On learning that we had reached the 'bungalow', I looked about me to discover its locality, but in vain; there was no building to be seen; but presently my host pointed out to me what I had not noticed before – a small low-roofed thatched place, close under a projecting rock, and half hidden by thorny creepers. I imagined this to be his fowl house, or perhaps a receptacle for tools, but was not a little

astonished when I saw my friend beckon me on, and enter at the low dark door. This miserable little cabin could not have been more than twelve feet long by about six feet wide, and as high at the walls. This small place was lessened by heaps of tools, coils of string for 'lining' the ground before planting, sundry boxes and baskets, and one chair. At the far end, if anything could be far in that hole, was a jungle bedstead formed by green stakes driven into the floor and walls, and stretching rope across them. I could not help expressing astonishment at the miserable quarters provided for one who had so important a charge, and such costly an outlay to make. My host however treated the matter very philosophically. Everything, he observed, is good or bad by comparison; indeed he told me that when he had finished putting up this little crib, had moved in his one table and chair and was seated, cigar in mouth, inside the still damp walls, he thought himself the happiest of mortals.'

This then was the planter's home until such time as he could build himself a better hut or log-cabin in which to take refuge from the elements and the wild life. The material used in the construction of such huts was taken from the jungle, just as with the native Sinhalese dwellings. The inside would be much the same as those used by the planters in India, and would have smooth mud plastered floors, with walls either of mud and wattle or timber planking, no windows, and with perhaps a few gunny sacks thrown down on the floor and on the top of the bed to make things more homely.

It is important to realize the prevailing conditions at that time: a hut such as the one described by Capper would indeed seem like a palace to its owner, and all the more so after his previous mode of habitation, which again is best described in the words of the day:

'I was told that his first habitation when commencing up here was suspended over my head. I looked up to the dark dusty roof, and perceived a bundle of what I conceived to be dirty brown paper, or parchment-skin. Perceiving my utter ignorance of the arrangement, he took down the roll, and spread it open outside the door. It turned out to be two or three huge talipot leaves, which he assured me was

Log cabin life: a working day. Always referred to as 'the bungalow' whatever its form, whether a thatched hut or a grand two-storey building. The planter stands arms akimbo surveying the Tamil men and women working in his new clearing. His first small nursery is seen at the left of the picture; the small plants are shaded from the hot sun with cadjans. (1881, from 'Scenes in Ceylon' by Hamilton and Fasson.)

the only shelter he had possessed for nearly three months, and that, too, only during the monsoon.

During one particular night he lay sleeping, supperless, fatigue having overcome hunger, when a great storm of rain and wind arose, and far into the night he was rudely awakened by a sensation of intense cold; looking upwards from his jungle couch he saw a few stars twinkling between flying masses of clouds, the rain falling on him as he lay. A strong gust of wind had swept away the talipot roof, and he had no recourse but to creep in beneath his wretched stick bed, and lie shivering there until the cold morning broke.'

Bivouacking out in jungle bounding with wild animals, snakes, and leeches, swamped by rain, lying at night on wet ground, shivering with cold and perhaps fever with only the steady downpour and swirling mists outside for weeks on end: these were conditions of privation that only men of a true pioneering spirit could overcome, and many died in the process of opening up the coffee estates.

The umbrella, the tent and, in Ceylon, the leaves of the talipot palm, were all used by the first timers for their only shelter in the jungle by the side of the small clearing that they were endeavouring to open out. The order of the day was work, from dawn till dusk.

The New Clearing
The ruthless flames have cleared his lands
No trace remains of green,
When lost in thought our planter stands
And views the sterile scene.
In dreams he sees his coffee spring
Fed by the welcome rains
And berries many a dollar bring
To take him home again.

From the excellent detail shown in the drawing of the interior of a planter's log-cabin (frontispiece to chapter), the folded leaves of the talipot palm are clearly visible suspended from the rafters. In this particular case, they may well have been used to form a more waterproof covering for the cabin. The sketches, and verse above by Hamilton and Fasson are all remarkably accurate in their portrayal of life in Ceylon in the late 1870s. ▷

BELOW LEFT
A part of the talipot leaf. (Woodcut 1681.) Knox says of the talipot palm: 'It is as big and tall as a ship's mast, and very straight, bearing only leaves which are of great use and benefit to this people, one single leaf being so broad and large that it will cover some fifteen or twenty men, and keep them dry when it rains. The leaf being dried is very strong and limber, and most wonderfully made for man's convenience to carry along with them; for although this leaf be thus broad when it is open, yet it will fold close like a lady's fan. It is wonderfully light; they cut them into pieces, and carry them in their hands. The whole leaf spread is round almost like a circle, but being cut in pieces for use, are near like a circle. Soldiers all carry them, for besides the benefit of keeping them dry in case it rain upon the march, these leaves make them tents to lie under in the night'. (From Robert Knox's 'An Historical Relation of the Island of Ceylon' 1681.)
BELOW RIGHT
Talipot leaves used as umbrellas. (Photo 1900.)

Group of palms at the entrance of the Royal Botanic Gardens, Peradeniya. The large tree to the right, on which a man is climbing, is a young talipot palm. During its first ten years, the palm grows only large fan-shaped leaves, but then a trunk or stem begins to form. As the tree ages and climbs forever upwards, it is encircled with closely set rings marking the leaves shed over the preceding years. (1864. From O'Brian's 'Views in Ceylon'.)

▷ We also have the words of Major Skinner, that great maker of Ceylon's roads who, when engaged in the late 1830s in surveying the area known as the Wilderness of the Peak, lived as rough as any of the early coffee men:

> 'For six or seven months in every year I never knew the shelter of a roof from between four or five o'clock in the morning till seven in the evening, and occasionally much later. My wigwam consisted of five sheets of the talipot leaf, stretched together with threads of the same material. Each leaf was about six by four feet; three of these formed two sides and one end, with two others for the roof. This tent of leaves contained my little camp bed, a small camp table, and a chair. I think the talipot leaves used to cost 13½d and generally lasted the working season, which was six months; my lodgings therefore were not expensive!'

There were many ways in which a planter could come to grief during the tough pioneering years. Countless planters have found their last resting places in the small cemeteries of the quaint little churches that are to be seen throughout the hill districts. In the churchyard of St Mark's at Badulla, the headstone of one such planter, who died in 1880, says:

William Bennison Junr.,
of Mausa Estate Hewa Ellia
. . . aged 23 years
This monument is erected by his brother
planters of Madulsima and Hewa Ellia
as a token of their respect for his memory.
He was shot by his Appu during dinner.

Oddly enough, in the churchyard
of Holy Trinity Church, Nuwara
Eliya, there is yet another similar inscription:

Arthur S. Reeves
died March 31st 1891
He was murdered, while at dinner, by his Appu

Boy
Appu

What fatal fascination dinner held for 'appus' one cannot say, but I am reminded that it was during dinner that yet another appu played a devilish trick upon a friend of mine and, in particular, on his guests, which I will tell you about in the next chapter.

'The battle of our life is brief,
The alarm – the struggle – the relief,
Then sleep we side by side.' (Longfellow.)

BELOW LEFT
Christ Church, Dickoya. (Photo 1982.)
BELOW RIGHT
Lindula Church surrounded by tea
bushes. (Photo 1982.)

RIGHT
*'In pious memory of James Taylor of
Loolecondera Estate, Ceylon. The pioneer
of the tea and cinchona enterprise in this
island, who died May 2 1892, aged 57
years.' (Photo 1982.)*

RIGHT
*'In pious memory of James Taylor of
Loolecondera Estate, Ceylon. The pioneer
of the tea and cinchona enterprise in this
island, who died May 2 1892, aged 57
years.' (Photo 1982.)*
BELOW
*What more peaceful final resting place
could one wish for: a kangany's grave
amongst the tea bushes he tended all his
working life. (Photo 1982.)*

The names on the tombstones tell the sad story of the life and death of many a young man who once walked the surrounding mountains amongst the coffee and tea bushes. Now, they lie side by side, many of them pitifully young, cut off in the prime of their manhood by cholera, fever or dysentery. Others, near to death, were brought by fellow planters from their lonely and distant estates into Kandy hotels, where their ultimate fate was little improved by the change.

The old Garrison Cemetery in Kandy is perched on a small oblong patch of land above the lake. When visited in 1982, this cemetery was – unlike most others – in very bad order, overgrown with tall six foot grasses and young tree saplings. Here also are to be seen the sparsely scattered tombstones of many of the early planters. The ground between the tombstones no doubt contains the graves of many more, but today nothing remains of the black headboards and low mounds that once marked the last resting places of some of the first men to plant coffee in Ceylon.

A short distance away, also in the town of Kandy, is the Mahaiyawa Cemetery, which contains the grave of James Taylor. He died on his estate Loolecondera within a few days of developing dysentery. His body was apparently carried from the estate by his coolies along the high twisting road that leads along the mountainside on its way down to Kandy. When Dennis Forrest visited Loolecondera in 1965, he was told of this fact by one of the estate labourers who had, in turn, been told the story many years before by his parents:

'My mother told me of his funeral. Twenty-four men carried him into Kandy, two gangs of twelve taking turns every four miles. It was about eighteen miles the way they went. They started in the morning and got to Kandy at four o'clock in the afternoon. The Sinhalese woman who kept his home came out of the bungalow crying and waving her arms, and would have gone with the funeral, but Mr Gordon prevented her. The kanganies and labourers walked behind the coffin. They called him "sami dore" (master is God).'

ABOVE
The superintendent's bungalow on Loolecondera. The bungalow of today has changed little from the earlier view. (Photo c1935, courtesy British Library.)
LEFT
All that remains of James Taylor's bungalow, built sometime between 1852 and 1856. There is a collapsed pile of stone covered in jungle creepers and an astonishingly well preserved chimney, in front of which the young Scots lad must have sat on many a cold damp night. The position of the fallen stones indicated that there would have been just the one living room. It would appear that the walls of some seven feet or so were constructed of granite stone, which is abundant on the steep slopes of the jungle all around. Coming from Laurencekirk just below Aberdeen, where many of the native Scottish farm buildings were constructed in this way, he would not have been slow to adapt the same method of building his own bungalow. The site is situated some 10-15 yards inside the jungle, just above the open tea fields that fall away down the mountainside below. Also in the picture is the Sinhalese superintendent of Loolecondera estate, L.H. Wickremasinghe. (Photo 1982.)
RIGHT
Opening out. (Drawing by G. Cunningham 1982.)

left to rot. Much activity has been taking place in the surrounding jungle, for new clearing work is in progress. All the jungle trees on the mountainside beyond the coffee have been felled and it is just possible to see that paths have been traced and cut. Compare the size of the natives with that of the broken jungle tree close by, with its huge 'flying buttress' roots. By the edge of the river the Sinhalese ferry-man has his one section of talipot leaf, under which he shelters from the sun or the rain. (Photo 1880.)

Our view of Laxapana coffee estate captures everything of the pioneering way of life led by the early coffee men. There is much in this scene to give a man great hope for the future, to give him the will, the courage, and the determination to tackle anything on earth. He has coffee in bearing, fine new clearings in the surrounding hills, and then there is the towering jungle, teeming with wild animals still to conquer. In the middle of the picture, standing on a path amongst his coffee bushes, is the planter himself, while a short distance beyond is his neat little bungalow, to the left of which appears to be a small enclosure made of bamboo, where he might well have kept a dozen or so fowls to provide him with eggs and meat. The top of the pen appears to be covered with net, or with the young shoots of bamboo,

interlaced, which strongly indicates that fowls were in fact kept inside, for it was in such surroundings that the Ceylon mountain hawk-eagle was most at home, and could often be seen perched on the dead tree stumps which stood in all the new coffee plantations. One can well imagine in such surroundings the attention that would be paid to the planter's poultry house; the fierce civet cat was particularly destructive and even the leopard would take a hen if nothing better was available, and make a right mess of the poultry house in doing so.

It is on such a coffee estate as the one illustrated on the previous page that one can visualize the scene described by an old coffee planter, M.J. Bremer, when he tells of an attack by a leopard on his estate in the year 1875:

'One day a large cheetah, ie. a leopard, appeared amidst the coffee pickers, close to the big bungalow on Tilicoultru estate. The coolies, when picking coffee, start their work in the morning either from an estate pathway or perhaps from the edge of the jungle where the

TOP LEFT
Close to the water's edge, 98-year old tea bushes, once belonging to Kintyre estate, now incorporated in Brownlow state plantation. By looking at the 'stocks' of the tea bushes which stand on old coffee land, there is evidence of much soil erosion on the steep slopes. (Photo 1982.)
BOTTOM LEFT
Two Tamils with many years of faithful service to Brownlow estate between them: R. Selliah, Brownlow office staff and, centre, M. Sivalingam Pillai, who was born on Brownlow estate in 1905, and

became head kangany in 1930 upon the retirement of his father, who had also been head kangany on Kintyre from just before the turn of the century. (Photo 1982.)

ABOVE

This high angle view, taken from the tea fields of Brownlow state plantation, shows (arrowed) the approximate position of the pioneer planter's bungalow on Laxapana coffee estate 100 years ago (previous pages). In 1969, 243 acres of Kintyre tea estate, and much of Laxapana,

were submerged under the waters of the Maskeliya reservoir. The remaining acreage of Kintyre, and that of other estates in the valley left above the waterline, was incorporated into the surrounding tea estates. The Maskeliya valley and the slopes to Adams Peak bear witness as well as anywhere in Ceylon to the fact that the first pioneers were mainly Scots. The names of the early coffee estates surrounding Laxapana were all of a distinctly Scottish flavour – Dalhousie, St Andrews, Moray, Blantyre, Hamilton, Kintyre and Braemar. One of the first

Scotsmen to make his way up to the jungle-clad slopes surrounding Adams Peak was James Fettes Moir who, in 1869, bought 315 acres of land to form Tarf coffee estate. Tarf was later amalgamated into the Brownlow estate. James Moir was just one of a group of 14 Scots – which included his three brothers and two of his cousins, James Taylor of Loolecondera and Henry Stiven of Ancoombra – who all came out to Ceylon from the small town of Laurencekirk and its immediate vicinity in Kincardineshire. (Photo 1982.)

'I really must go and find something to eat'. (Photo c1900.)

coffee rows commence and, without knowing, they must have been driving this cheetah in front of them all the time until it made a dash to escape. The result was that two of the coolies were very severely mauled. A panic ensued, and I was called to the place by the head kangany and hurried up with a friend who was staying at my bungalow, he with a revolver, and I with a gun. We found the coolies wild with fright and excitement, and the two wounded men were shown to us: one of them had his scalp hanging over his forehead, while the other had his arm torn open. There was nothing for it but to appease the coolies, by telling them that we would shoot the brute if he was still there. So the two of us pushed our way through the thick coffee towards the cinchona tree where he was last seen. We advanced cautiously from opposite sides but, although we made a wide circuit, there was no cheetah. A heavy shower stopped further proceedings for an hour, then we again followed the animal's track, but in vain. To reassure the coolies who were still rather scared, the estate jungle into which the cheetah had made his escape was beaten next day by about three hundred coolies, tam-taming and shouting, and by the Dimbula pack of hounds, but without success.'

'We found the coolies wild with fright and excitement, and the two wounded men were shown to us . . . one of them had his scalp hanging over his forehead, while the other had his arm torn open.'

A dead leopard and two 'jungle men'. (Photo c1900.)

The rogue charging. (c1881 from 'Scenes in Ceylon' by Hamilton and Fasson.)

A host of smaller animals, including porcupines, did much damage on the estates at night time. Plagues of rats would, on their migratory paths across the land, give their undivided attention to all the young shoots and blossoms on the coffee bushes, whilst the larger animals would trample and break young plants by the score. The wild hog was also particularly vicious and dangerous and a good sized boar would stand about three feet high and weigh between 300 and 400 pounds – the weight of two large men. In nearly all cases on estates wild hog were shot or the wily old ones were often trapped in pits dug in the ground which were camouflaged across the opening with branches.

Some of the Tamils on the estates would dig their own 'dead-fall' pits both in the jungle and along the estate boundaries, in order to catch pig and deer to supplement their nomal diet of rice. Unfortunately the Tamil huntsman's dogs – as well as those of the planter – often came to grief in the bottom of such pits. Whenever a dog disappeared for longer than a night, it could usually be assumed that it had met its end by being taken by a leopard, caught by a phython or had fallen down a 'dead-fall' pit.

For the sporting planter, the hunting of elk and wild boar with a pack of trained hounds and nothing more than a hunting knife was an exciting, if dangerous pastime. Wild hogs usually travel about in large herds of sows and young boars, the latter leaving the herd when mature. Once they had come upon the quarry, the job of the dogs – if they could dodge the flashing tusks – was to run in and secure a hold, and to hang on to the maddened boar as it rushed about the undergrowth dragging the dogs with it. Once a good dog had seized an animal such as an elk or wild hog, it would never loosen its hold, thus enabling the huntsman, who followed up on foot, a slightly less dangerous approach until he could finally slip into the melee, and thrust home his long-bladed hunting knife. ▷

ABOVE
A melee. (Lithograph c1853, from 'Rifle and Hound' by Baker.)

LEFT
'The bay'. (1881 from 'Scenes in Ceylon' by Hamilton and Fasson.)

BELOW
The elk's leap. The voice of every hound familiar to his ear, the planter treads the hills with anxious pack. (Engraving 1885.)

BOTTOM LEFT
Dead boar and the hounds. (Photo c1900.)

ABOVE
Stalking a herd of elephants. (Lithograph 1853.)

RIGHT
A leopard killed by a cow. Sometimes a cow can be particularly savage when her calf is with her – the picture illustrates a true story of a leopard killed by a cow in Nuwara Eliya in the 1870s. The leopard's entry was made from the thatched roof of the cattle shed onto its quarry. (Engraving c1885.)

BOTTOM RIGHT
Thomas Farr of North Cove estate with his pack of hounds. (Photo 1900.)

▷ Regarding the frequent incursions onto the estates, Colonel Gordon Cumming wrote in 1878:

'The wild hog are the worst enemies we have to contend with – those which enter the estates are generally the large single boars and, as they are ferocious to a degree, especially when surrounded, we run considerable risk in effecting their capture. You can fancy what their strength must be when one rip is sufficient to cut open a horse or a bullock. I have had so many dogs cut to pieces that I have given up keeping them and, in general, I now shoot as many boars as I can.'

The sambur deer, known as the elk in Ceylon, is the largest of all Asiatic deer, and a good sized buck can go anything up to 600 pounds. The animal is found at all elevations from low country jungles up to the mountainous districts at around 6000 feet.

As might be expected, there were many fatal accidents. One young planter, George Balfe Behing, died on February 19th, 1876 at the age of twenty while hunting elk. The entry states:

'He was killed by a sambur, which was at bay in the river somewhere near Elfindale estate. He went to stick it, holding his knife daggerwise. The stag struck him with his fore leg on the arm, and the blow drove the knife into his heart, and he fell dead in the stream. A kangany or coolie only was with him.'

He lies buried in the Mahaiyawa Cemetery in Kandy. It seems from this account that he was out exploring the jungle with one of his Tamils and possibly his dog and, having startled the elk which was lying-up

LEFT
The Ceylon mountain hawk-eagle (Spizaetus Kelaarti). Vincent Legge, the ornithologist, states in his fine work 'The Birds of Ceylon' – from which comes the illustration – that: 'the eagle has its headquarters in wild, isolated and lofty jungles, whence it descends to the neighbouring coffee plantations in search of its prey in the poultry yards of the planters. It is quite powerful enough to be capable of carrying off the largest inmate of the poultry yard and, indeed, could make quick work with a moderately sized lamb or young deer'. (Hand-coloured plate, 1881, from 'Birds of Ceylon' by Legge.)
BELOW
Ceylon jungle fowl (Gallus Lafayettii). (Hand-coloured plate 1881, from 'Birds of Ceylon' by Legge.)

Spotted buck. (Photo c1900.)

during the heat of day, his dog drove it into a pool where, unaided by further trained hounds, he endeavoured to kill it.

Like the elk, the elephant in its wild state is usually a nocturnal feeder and traveller, seeking the cover of the forest an hour or so after dawn and lying -up until just before dusk; both he and the wild buffalo provide more testing game for the skill and courage of the huntsman. The elphant is met with all over Ceylon from the lowland jungles in the Southern Province to the plains in the north and the wilderness of the Peak, where its footprints have been found upon the highest ridges of Adams Peak itself.

While still on the subject of animals, and particularly of elephants, a story must be told. An old coffee and tea planter, Andrew Nicol, was well known to his brother planters for his exploits as a huntsman. At the time of the tale he had been staying at a somewhat isolated rest house, where he had been endeavouring to teach a bemused appu the art of frying sardines in paper. The following is the story as he told it:

Gordon Reeves on the Wattekelle Patanas. (Photo c1900.)

> 'We were bothered with a brute of an elephant at Batticoloa. Jock Cumming had been after him for days, but could not get near him. I was living in a small talipot hut, and at night my servant lay at my feet. One night I was awakened by the shrieks of my appu, and a strange rattling, thumping noise in the roof. With my dim floating light I could just see the huge trunk of an elephant swinging backwards and forwards right above me; his head filled the door way, and he had evidently made up his mind to have a lark with us at his leisure. I mounted to my elbow, slipped my hand below my camp-bed where my rifle lay always ready loaded; steadily and deliberately I took aim and fired. There was a terrific snort, a trumpet, and something like an earthquake. I replaced my rifle, turned on my side, and was asleep again in five minutes; but in the morning a large rogue elephant lay dead in front of our hut!.'

Pay day was always eagerly awaited by the estate labour force, if not by the planter, for whom a hard day lay ahead. This story concerns such a pay day. By way of leading up to this unusual, but true story, it must be mentioned that for the first couple of years of its life the Tamil child runs about the lines naked, the only adornment is a string around its

A small ornament hangs around the infant's waist to avert the evil eye. (Photo c1890.)

waist, and a bead or some such small treasure that hangs down to avert the evil eye.

This particular story concerns a planter who had been suffering from tooth-ache for many a long month. Having at last managed to get away from his remote estate, he rode into Kandy as fast as his good steed would take him, which, with night stops spent at other planters' bungalows, took the best part of three days. In Kandy the next morning a dentist removed the offending tooth, and as it came from a prominent position, it was replaced with a single denture.

Back on the estate he absent-mindedly left for muster without putting in his new denture. Upon returning to his bungalow to rectify the omission, he found that the tooth had vanished. The tooth-glass, in which it had languished all night was still on his bedside table, clean but empty. His house boy, unaccustomed to his master's new denture, had thrown the contents of the glass out of the window. A big search was started around the bungalow compound for the missing tooth, but it could not be found.

One day towards the end of the month found the manager sitting at the pay-table paying out his labour force, who were drawn up in front of him. His conductor, standing to one side of the table with the big check roll, was singing out the names of the coolies fast and furious, while the manager gave each his due at the pay-table. Amongst the many, a plucking Kanakapulle, accompanied by his toddling infant, came up to receive his pay. With eyes nearly popping out of his head the manager shouted "my tooth!" – for there was the missing denture, dangling on a piece of chain in front of the otherwise naked child as a potent object to avert the evil eye!

Planters, as in India, would keep a goat or cow for milk and would go out with a gun for fine venison to supplement their monotonous diet which was mainly roast chicken, or game bird and egg curry, or fried egg and chicken curry, always with plenty of rice; both the chicken and the eggs would come from his poultry yard, and the bird from the jungle. His entire labour force lived on rice and, for most of the year, there would be an adequate supply in his rice store. The rice that was brought up from Colombo by the slow bullock cart and then transported form the nearest cart road to the estate by his coolies was often in a wet condition on arrival, and if that were not so, it still stood a good chance of becoming wet and ruined in the estate rice store itself.

Practically every planter kept a dog, or dogs, mainly for companionship but, also for hunting purposes. Dogs were very much sought after by leopards, and they were frequently taken while sleeping on the bungalow verandah at dusk; many also came to grief in 'dead-fall' pits (as already shown) or whilst out hunting in the jungle. There were also many instances of dogs being pounced upon while following behind their masters along jungle paths.

Most of the estates had at least some of their boundaries adjoining jungle in which pig, red deer, spotted deer, jungle cock and porcupine could be shot, the meat of the latter being very tasty, and not unlike pork. A man who spent his whole life living close to nature would know just when and where to go to shoot a brace of wood pigeon for the pot, or to bag the handsome jungle fowl. Great numbers of these lovely jungle fowl were attracted to the patana lands in the up-country planting districts during the flowering and seeding years of the shrubby plant Strobilanthus nelu. This particular shrub flowers and seeds once only every seven years, and it is then that the jungle fowl, together with hordes of rodents, gorge themselves upon the seeds, becoming to a certain extent intoxicated, and falling as easy prey to the planter's gun, as well as to leopards. Another fine sporting bird which was good to eat was the spur fowl which, according to Legge, 'comes out of the forest early in the morning, and feeds along the edge of the coffee plantations in silence'. The estate coolies would snare it in much the same way as pheasants are snared in Britain, but with a noose of hair.

Apart from going out with gun and dog to secure food for the table, the main recreation of the early planters, both in India and in Ceylon, was to visit one another for a meal and a few drinks, and to talk shop, in other words, that all important topic, coffee or tea. Methods of planting, pruning, manuring, their failures and successes were all discussed at every opportunity, as were the frequent labour troubles. Before planters' clubs came upon the scene, there was no place out in the wilds where a group of exuberant young planters could meet apart from a fellow's bungalow and, because of this, certain bungalows

ABOVE
A coffee planter's wife on horseback. (Photo c1878.)
LEFT
An invitation is accepted and the planter turns out to watch an evening performance of a Tamil 'drama'. (1881 from 'Scenes in Ceylon' Hamilton and Fasson.)
RIGHT
Beckington bungalow: weekend. (Photo 1890, courtesy Royal Commonwealth Society.)

acquired a reputation which has survived to this day. British planters in Ceylon behaved no differently from those in India, and it was not at all uncommon for mounds of empty bottles to be found at the rear of some of the bungalows. It is better that the incriminating evidence comes once again from the pen of an old coffee planter, John Capper:

> 'The small bungalow in which these protracted revels were held has long since disappeared; its site, thickly overgrown with thorny brushwood and lantana, was once sought for by friends of one of the early planters, and was at length discovered by the vast memorial mound of empty bottles piled about the lonely spot.'

Whenever a planter became ill – and this was a frequent occurrence during the early pioneering days – he just stuck it out in his bungalow, and was looked after, in a rude fashion, by his bungalow boy and appu. If he had reasonably close neighbours, they would of course rally round and see him through his illness, doing the best they could to run his estate while he was laid up. It should be remembered that, in the early days, to reach a near neighbour some 12 miles away as the crow flies might well have entailed the best part of a whole day's ride on horseback along mountain paths of 25 miles or so, as all hill paths were notorious for doubling backwards and forwards. Often the estate Tamils would walk many miles to a neighbouring planter's bungalow to bring news of their master's illness, fever or death. The estate labour force – all Tamils from the coastal region of southern India – also contracted many illnesses, especially on estates at the higher altitudes. This posed a great problem for the planter in that he always had a good proportion of his men sick, and unable to work.

After the tough pioneering years, during which hundreds of small coffee estates were carved out of the hitherto unexplored jungle in the central hill districts, a different breed of men started to replace the first-timers. These were men with capital which, if not their own, was that of their fathers. One such young man, Adolphus Folingsby, the son of Sir John Folingsby, Bart, is the subject of the sketch and poem by Hamilton and Fasson. Standing astride a dunghill on his newly acquired coffee estate, he has an easy bearing which does not belie the purposefulness of his outlook – in this case his all but dead coffee

bushes. For a second son, a problem boy with an adventurous spirit, a father could do no better than settle him somewhere in the valley of wildest Assam, the hills of Darjeeling or southern India, or in Ceylon:

The Shuck Estate

Thus Sir John to his offspring did say:

'to shorten my story, I briefly may state
That I wish you to choose a profession.
Let's know your intentions before it's too late,
You've already reached years of discretion.

Don't dream of the Army – you couldn't afford it,
Nor the Church (though you've had good tuition),
You don't know your subject – you've never explored it,
You'd be a most gross imposition.

If you went into trade, you'd be but the tool
Of some dealer in wool, eugh! perhaps tallow;
You can't be a lawyer – you're too great a fool,
Your mind, like your purse, is too shallow.

Planting coffee or tea, or we'll say sugar cane,
From your self-respect could not detract, Sir;
But Lombard Street, or that d...d Mincing Lane,
I cannot abide, that's a fact, Sir!

Sir Jellaby Jingle and Admiral Sneeze
Have each got a son in Ceylon.
If I stand you five thousand, you can, if you please,
Make a fortune. Come say, are you on?'

'Make it six', said the youth. The stern parent replied,
'Five thou; so let's have your decision.
Five thousand will make (so you best quick decide)
In my income a lively incision!'

Having arrived in Colombo, young Adolphus promptly fell in with a complete stranger, who took the opportunity of selling him a shuck (dud) estate away in the hills, with no crop coming in and very little leaf on the coffee bushes.

Perseverance and pluck at length gained their reward,
Leaves appeared and grew greener and thicker!
The Folingsby fortunes might yet be restored,
For 'returns' became larger and quicker.

He called on his neighbours, was cheerful and gay,
Ceased to look like a lamb led to slaughter;
Took a trip to Colombo, where people do say
He spooned Colonel Jigger's fair daughter.

Years fled, and at Folingsby Park as of yore
Sir John sat enjoying his claret;
And, 'but for his brave boy Adolphus' he swore
He'd be drinking 'Old Tom' in a garret!

He felt proud, he assured me with glistening eye
And flushed face 'to be such a son's debtor'.
I feared the old fellow was going to cry
As he handed me over a letter.

A photo fell out. Dark eyes all aglow,
Wavy hair, and a very fine figure;
And, inscribed in blue ink, this legend below,
'Polly Folingsby, née Mary Jigger'.

That Sir John keeps his foxhounds, the joy of his life,
Drag servants and hunters galore;
That Adolphus has won such a duck of a wife,
Is owing alone to – manure!

ABOVE TOP
The 'Shuck' estate (1881 from 'Scenes in Ceylon' by Hamilton and Fasson.)
ABOVE
When in good condition, a rush-bottomed seat is surely the most comfortable of chairs in the East. (Photo 1900.)
TOP RIGHT
Sunday at the club. (Photo 1880.)
RIGHT
Possibly the Rowing Club at Nuwara Eliya. The young ladies, one carrying a megaphone, appear to be about to set off with picnic basket down to the lake. (Photo c1890.)

If one looks at the illustration of a coffee store on pages 106–7, the following story will be the easier to understand for those of us who are unfamiliar with such buildings.

For those who were inclined to a spot of dancing, local hops were arranged on some centrally situated estate where an old coffee store would be cleaned out, decorated, and turned into a ballroom. However, when the incumbent planter had an extra large and palacial bungalow, the dance would be held in the big bungalow itself. At such times the coffee store would be used, not as a ballroom, but as a dormitory to accommodate bachelors, grass widowers, etc. The few women that there might be could freshen up and change from their riding gear into evening dress in the bungalow.

Although one might not think it, a coffee store was a very comfortable and dry place at which to put up, providing one had the foresight to come prepared. One planter who, after long experience, knew the form at such meets, is said to have turned up at the designated estate complete with all that he deemed necessary for the questionable salubrity of a coffee store. He appeared upon the scene riding beside a bullock-cart on which he had loaded a four-poster bedstead, a mattress, a tin bath, a carpet and other essentials to a man's comfort, including a rifle. After the unloading of his cart, his creature comforts were carried by eager Tamils into the coffee store where he pegged out his claim on the ground nearest to the door, on account of the air being fresher there. Just before dusk, having settled in, quite a party developed among the inmates of the store who, having imbibed a little

more than was good for them at such an early hour, then endeavoured to negotiate a change into evening dress. The proud owner of the bedstead, affectionately known as Nobby – on account of the brass knobs on the four corners of the said contraption – proceeded to tank up faster than most, until he became a nuisance. Luckily for everyone it was not long before he passed out, after which a certain calm prevailed while the others gathered themselves for the climb through the coffee to the big bungalow farther up the hillside.

As the ladies had been allotted different bedrooms in the married planter's bungalow, it was necessary that the party be brought to a close at the reasonable hour of four in the morning, so that they could retire to the comfort of their beds in peace. The rest of those present turned out and stumbled down the hillside in the bright moonlight to the coffee store which, being situated in a hollow, was enveloped in a white ground mist to about waist high.

Upon a sudden impulse, a small group formed around Nobby's bed and, with one heave, bed and inmate were lifted and carried outside and unceremoniously dumped in the middle of the flat coffee drying grounds with only a blanket as cover. Back at the coffee store, candles were lit, singing commenced and the party went on until it was quite light. Meanwhile, with the first glimmerings of dawn the apparent corpse on the bed slowly regained consciousness. Finding himself in a cloud, with only the golden knobs of his four-poster bed visible above him, and the singing of many angels coming from close by, he thought he had passed on. It was only when the bungalow staff got on the move that one of the house boys, looking down, was attracted by the four golden orbs catching the rays of the rising sun. Recognising them for what they were – for Nobby had been this way before – the boy hurried down the hill, and walking through the still waist-high mist, presented on a silver salver a cup of hot tea. Nobby, seeing only the top half of the apparition standing before him, wondered a little; the suspicion grew upon him that he had not passed through the Pearly Gates after all and, upon being asked if he would care to partake of a cup of tea, knew that it was only a bad dream, turned over and went to sleep again.

The almost complete absence of any European feminine company during the early years often led a planter to take a pretty Sinhalese girl into his bungalow, and there is no doubt that, under the conditions that prevailed on the isolated plantations, a certain happiness and companionship was achieved by many. With such arrangements, the planter would often find that he would end up by not only looking

One of the few. (Photo c1880.)

A Christmas card 'from Papa'. (Ceylon, 1875.)

RIGHT
The bungalow of C.R. Cruwell, coffee planter on Laymastotte estate, near the Haputele Pass. It is, for the period, a well built if unimaginative structure, of the same style as a coolie line. The buildings to the right and rear are those of the kitchens, servants' quarters, rice store, tool sheds and stable. In 1890 Sir Thomas Lipton bought Laymastotte together with other estates in the Haputele district, including Dambatenne. All the coffee on Laymastotte had, by then, succumbed to the leaf disease, and had been replanted with tea. (Lithograph 1864.)

BELOW
Glorious isolation. A bungalow somewhere in mid or low country. It is no wonder that the planter threw himself into every kind of leisure activity with great energy when he could. (Photo c1890, courtesy Royal Commonwealth Society.)

after his concubine, but her entire family away in the village as well.

In the early days it was a more common practice for the planter to have his concubine live with him in his bungalow, whereas later it was more usual for the Sinhalese girl to live off the estate in her village nearby. If the planter was that way inclined, and by no means all were, it was an unwritten rule that he had nothing to do with any of his own labour force, who were in any case all Tamils. Perhaps this is the right place to tell an old Ceylon planting story.

A young bachelor had invited his sister out to Ceylon to stay with him. The young lady spent a perfectly wonderful first day, being shown over the estate and was impressed with everything, the sweet scent of the temple flowers that hung so close to her window, the lovely garden itself, the evening sunset, but most of all by her brother, whom she had not seen for three years. Even the appu and boys looked smart in their white sarongs and coats. The two retired quite late that night as there had been much to talk about. Her bedroom, next to her brother's, looked out onto a well cut lawn of blue grass. Being tired, she soon fell asleep. Next morning at five o'clock she was awoken by tapping on her bedroom door. She distinctly recognised the appu's unmistakable voice saying, 'Time for Missie to go home, all Missie go home now.'

★ ★ ★

By the early 1890s clubs were being formed and a more sociable sort of life commenced. The married planter was no longer the exception, and many a planter's daughter out on holiday from Britain was assured of meeting droves of eligible batchelors and of soon becoming the wife of one, if she so chose.

Cricket was a popular pastime, and it was not unusual to ride 40 to 50 miles in order to get to a cricket ground. By 1890 there were a dozen cricket grounds in the country. Many of the estates had tennis courts and croquet lawns carved out on a flat piece of land amongst the tea bushes. In the up-country districts there would be the chance of a day at the races, or of playing polo or golf. Fishing could be had with rod and line in the lake at Nuwara Eliya, which by the late 1890s had been stocked with carp and trout.

As early as 1882 the first attempts were made to introduce brown trout into the main stream in Nuwara Eliya. The Ceylon Fishing Club was formed in 1895 and, in that same year, the ova of the rainbow trout were introduced into many of the mountain streams. One of the most remote and untouched areas was on the Horton Plains, some 20 miles from Nuwara Eliya where a good stream provided some of the best rainbow trout that could be taken. In such a setting, in the cooler airs at around 7000 feet, magnificent rhododendron trees flourished in all the hollows around the banks of streams and even on the open grassland. This glorious haven of 'patana' grassland interspersed with belts of heavy jungle was the ideal place for the sportsman.

So after a hard week's work on the estate, the planters at the turn of the century had a bewildering choice of leisure activities: a Saturday evening dance at the club, a variety of sports, shooting, hunting and fishing, with just the possibility of marrying too – things were looking up! But up to the year 1900 there was still a predominance of bachelors. Few white women had had anything to do with the very early pioneering community, or put in an appearance on any of those small remote plantations back in those tough adventurous 1840s, but there were of course exceptions.

The ratio of men to women in the planting districts in the late '70s and early '80s, would not make for much actual dancing, but as Jack and his brother planters well knew, there's more to a dance than dancing!

The Dance at Nuwara Eliya

'There's a dance in New'ralia, Jack – do you hear,
'Twill be a grand spree, as you well can conceive
H.E. and all the big guns will be there,
And Camilla de Snoppington Snooks, I believe.

You'll come?' 'No, I can't, the old mare's cast a shoe,
And the journey's too much, it will precious near kill her
Oh, bother the ball! By the way, what do you
mean by calling Miss Snooks by the name of Camilla?'

'No offence meant, old man, pray do not get riled,
Camilla – beg your pardon – Miss Snoopington Snooks
If you give her the slip will be perfectly wild,
And will spoon someone else in these nice little nooks'.

Twere needless to mention their final decision,
They resolved in Society's vortex to shine
Go prepared, being dressed, with the utmost precision,
To encounter the perils of women and wine.

'This really is pucka, the music's superb;
One turn more, Mrs T. – what, finale already?
Collison, by Jove, Pray your energy curb,
Jack my boy. Is he cocked? I say, steady Jack, steady.

What's wrong with you man?' 'Why it's just this my friend,
I came here to dance, not to watch you perform.
And under the impression I'm out on the bend,
I've taken the champagne department by storm.

I'd dance if I could, but it's out of the question,
When every girl swears she's engaged twenty deep.
A nice state of things. Now (hic) 'scuse the suggestion,
Just sheer off old man, for I'm anxious to sleep.'

'Who is that pretty girl dressed with parsley and eggs?'
'Sore mouth! Goodness gracious, the very best thing
Is – bone dust and Poonac – such beautiful legs,
A medium choke-bore, you should just hear her sing'.

Meanwhile, some who at spooning are quite . . .
Have during the supper retreated to bliss
In some corner they fondly suppose ungettable
To eavesdroppers.

But dancing and spooning and eating and drinking,
Like everything else, must at last have an end,
And hitherto sparkling eyes begin blinking,
As daylight concludes this New'ralia 'bend'.

Dance at Nuwara Eliya. (1881 from 'Scenes in Ceylon' by Hamilton and Fasson.)

*Nuwara Eliya. Like the hill stations of
Simla and Ootacamund in North and
South India, Nuwara Eliya was the hill
station and sanatorium of Ceylon. (From
O'Brian's 'Views in Ceylon', 1864.)*

The Tamby

Whenever a sleek smiling Tamby appears,
I'm always assailed with excusable fears;
For tho' I'm in debt, and the Fiscal's Court's nigh,
I know that the wretch will induce me to buy.
His blarning chat, as his wares he discloses,
Would wheedle out gold from a scion of Moses,
It's no use to say 'I've no money got.'
He says 'that don't matter, don't matter a jot.
Master just look – my pretty things see;
If Master won't buy, don't matter a d--.
Plenty things got it, and all very cheap',
And the rogue smiling blandly piles up a great heap
Of shawls, stockings, rings, slippers and fezzes,
Till the whole of the place in a regular mess is.
To cut my talk short, although I protest,
And laugh at his wares with ironical zest,
In vain my attempts to escape from the deal,
In vain alike silence, abuse, or appeal.

And before he goes off I have taken some socks,
Eight yards of white flannel, an ebony box
And an enamel ring, which I trust isn't glass –
Tho' the gold I must own looks very like brass.
Rupees forty-two he puts in his pocket,
And asks for ten more for a Swani-work locket.
''Tis monstrous', I cry, 'Why, seven's enough!'
But he rolls up his pack in a well acted huff.
'Well, I'll give eight!' 'Then take, Master, take;
That too cheap at ten, but a present I'll make.'
And Salaming he smiles at the consummate ease
With which he has rooked me of fifty Rupees.
'Tis thus that a poor bachelor's pocket is harried,
So imagine what 'tis like when a fellow is married.
A man of the family may sometimes beware,
But a woman just loves to run into the snare.
And here you may see on the opposite page
Allurement, its victim, and impotent rage.

The Tamby. (1881 from 'Scenes in Ceylon' by Hamilton and Fasson.)

TOP RIGHT
A croquet lawn amidst the tea.
(Photo c1897.)
TOP LEFT
A young Tamil golf caddie. (Photo
1900.)
ABOVE
A pioneer gets married. For a wedding or
a funeral, planters would ride from miles
around. This number of men would be
quite considerable in terms of square
miles of tea country. (Photo c1890,
courtesy Royal Commonwealth Society.)

There is no doubt that those planters who were married lived under better conditions than their bachelor friends. The influence of a woman in the home worked wonders for a man's inner self, his comfort, the appearance of his bungalow, and also his own general appearance and way of dress. One might wonder what dress had to do with the life of the pioneers living out in the back of beyond. It would be true to say that the first men to go out and claim the jungle from the wild animals prior to the 1860s had little use for evening dress but, for those who came later, things were different. Ernest Haeckel, who travelled through the planting districts in the early 1880s, had this to say:

'I arrived after sundown at a very remote plantation, and the hospitable master gave me very clearly to understand that he expected me at dinner in black tail-coat and white tie. My sincere ▷

ABOVE
An up-country tea estate bungalow.
(Photo c1900.)

LEFT
The Gymkhana.
'Poor planter, overworked and worn,
Waking to cares and toil each morn;
Reports and paylists cast aside,
and let the d--d old totum slide.'
(Totum = estate.) (1881 from 'Scenes in
Ceylon' by Hamilton & Fasson.)

BELOW FAR LEFT
The interior of the bungalow on Craighead tea estate. The great numbers of rifles and trophies show well the life of the early planters, when game was abundant. Note the walking sticks standing inside the stuffed elephant's feet. It is interesting to compare the interior of this bungalow with that of the log-cabin shown on the frontispiece to this chapter. (Photo c1910, courtesy Royal Botanic Gardens, Kew.)
THIS PAGE
The Grange bungalow – Agra Patanas. (Photos c1910, courtesy Royal Geographical Society.)

▷ regrets and explanation that my light tourist kit for excursion in the mountains could not possible include black evening dress did not prevent my host donning his in my honour, nor his wife – the only other person at table – from appearing in full dinner toilet.'

Each generation of planters found conditions improving. The era of the pioneer planter in Ceylon is generally considered to have lasted as late as 1900. By that year some 380,000 acres of tea had been planted out and land on which the leopard and the elephant, the elk and the wild hog had once roamed had become well established tea estates. The leaves of the talipot palm were no longer used as a shelter, gone too were the mud and wattle huts and log-cabins in which the early pioneers had lived and often died. In their place came the more traditional bungalow, surrounded in most cases by an attractive garden. Those that were situated on up-country estates, at higher elevations, were all built with chimneys for fires, as the nights were often quite cold.

What would those early coffee men have thought, and said, if they could have seen our last picture of the bungalow on Carolina tea estate at the turn of the century: 'The tea don't look too special, but the bungalow do!'

It is doubtful whether we who live in the 20th-century comfort of our homes – with nothing more than a tame cat roaming around in the garden, with instant light at the touch of a switch and water at the turn of a tap – can possibly imagine the lonely and often dangerous life of these first planters whose courage, endurance and fortitude in the face of all adversity made them what they were . . . the pioneers.

TOP
The bungalow on Carolina tea estate. (Photo 1903, courtesy Royal Geographical Society.)
ABOVE
The last of the pioneers. Harry Storey went out to Ceylon in 1887 and became a tea planter in the Matale district. He was a great sportsman. (Photo c1900.)

REMINISCENCES OF MY OWN PLANTING DAYS

APPENDIX

Reminiscences of My Own Planting Days

The year was 1929, and the place was Malaya. Although strictly speaking Malaya does not come within the confines of this book, the tiger affair had to be told, firstly because it happened on a plantation and, secondly, because it may help those readers who live in the concrete jungles of our cities to compare more vividly the hazardous life of a planter with that of a man who journeys to his office on the same train, at the same time, and even in the same carriage every day of his working life.

I was one-and-a-half years old. My father was a rubber planter out there and, at the time when the tiger first put in an appearance, he and my mother had been living on the estate for some three years. I had been born on the estate in the rambling old thatched bungalow; on one side, a strip of jungle came within a stone's throw of the house, whilst all around rubber trees came up to the garden boundary.

Although there were many tigers in the jungle up and down Malaya in the 1920s, they were rarely seen. The first reports from the alarmed estate coolies stated that a tiger had been seen on the fringes of the jungle adjoining the rubber trees. Not unnaturally, some of those whose tapping blocks lay along the estate boundaries became extremely nervous of tapping scores of rubber trees adjacent to the jungle. It was soon after the sightings that the tiger made its first human kill in the district. The victim was a Tamil woman who had been tapping her block of rubber trees on an outlying part of the estate; her partial remains were later found some distance into the jungle.

News travels fast in such circumstances, and my father and the other planters in the district were now on the look-out, for once a tiger has turned man-eater, it loses all fear of humans, and the sooner it is shot, the better it is for all who live in its path.

It is as well to say that humans are not the tiger's natural prey and there is usually some reason that makes it leave its customary hunting ground to frequent the habitations of man. This particular tiger could have received a gun-shot wound, or it could have been old and, being unable to catch its natural prey in the jungle, was seeking easier food. However, in most cases a tiger becomes a man-eater because of an injury of some sort; for instance, if a porcupine's long needle-sharp quills became embedded in the foot-pad or leg of a tiger, it would not be capable of catching its natural prey with such a wound. It is probably fair to say that man could pass quite safely through areas which are inhabited by tigers, unless the animals are cornered inadvertantly in a ravine, or wounded in some way. I can do no better to illustrate this point than recount my uncle's experience of hunting peacock in Siam. He came face to face with a tiger at about 70 feet and, as he was only carrying a twelve-bore shotgun, he turned and beat a very hasty retreat. Having gone but a short distance, he looked back fearfully, only to see the tiger running too – in the opposite direction. By the laws of the jungle he had been reasonably safe and had no need to run, but sometimes that is easier said than done.

To return to the story. A day or so after the woman had been killed, the tiger paid its first visit to my parents' garden, carrying off their one and only goat which had been kept for milking. The goat had spent its nights in a lean-to shed at the back of the bungalow, next to another small shed that housed about a dozen chickens. The next morning the tiger's pug marks were clearly seen on the soft earth nearby. By now everyone on the estate was feeling a little nervous.

Under the bougainvillea tree were the pug marks of the man-eater; it had obviously been watching them.

A few evenings later, my parents and a friend from a neighbouring estate were sitting out on the verandah with their drinks – no doubt talking about the man–eater and its activities – when, in the fast fading light, my father saw, or thought he saw, a movement under a large Bougainvilia tree in the garden. He called for the boy to bring his rifle, but no one saw or heard anything further that night. The following morning at around six my father went across to the spot where he thought he had seen the dark shape and, close to the tree, on the round flower bed amongst the cannas, were the pug marks of the tiger. It had obviously been watching them.

The tiger paid its third visit a night or so later. It entered through the side of the bungalow, passed through a downstairs room, and then mounted the stairs that led to the bedrooms. My parents always slept upstairs on the right side of the house as one looks at the photograph,

PREVIOUS PAGE
The culprit brought to book.
The lightning conductor came in useful once or twice.
RIGHT
Pontian bungalow and garden with bougainvillea tree on left of picture.

Either a baby or the dog would have made a tasty, if small meal for a man-eater. As things turned out, it was the dog.

whilst I was stowed away each night in a cot in the bedroom across the landing. It was the custom of our faithful dog Dunny to spend each night curled up at the entrance to my bedroom, lying just outside the open door on the landing. As I have already mentioned, my age was such that on that particular night I was blissfully unware of the entire proceedings and, as I came to learn later on, so were my parents.

Nothing was known of the tragedy until early next morning, when the boy came upstairs to call my father, as he always did around 5.45 am. On this occasion he burst into their bedroom to say that the tiger's pug marks were clearly to be seen all the way up the stairs and then on to my bedroom, and that Dunny was not there as usual. If Dunny had not

always slept outside my bedroom, the tiger in all probability would have carried me off instead. My parents had heard a noise of some sort during the night, probably a floor-board creaking under the animal's weight, but the cook and the boys who slept at the rear of the bungalow in an adjoining building had heard nothing.

Before the tiger had carried off the rubber tapper, my amah (nanny), a Javanese girl, had taken me for my daily outing in the pram along the cart road that ran through a patch of jungle at the approach to the bungalow. It was just a case of either being in the right place or wrong place when the man-eater first showed up. Countless humans have been taken by tigers up and down Malaya, India and other countries.

I have often wondered why there was no sound from Dunny, who either did not smell or hear the tiger's approach, or if he did, was petrified into silence, or at most a whimper of fright. My uncle who is now 86, and who was also out there planting at the time, can confirm the facts, but cannot add to what I have told you. A dog's life on an estate was often a short one; another of my parents' dogs fell down and died in a 'dead-fall' pit that had been dug in the jungle by some of the estate coolies to catch wild pig, and yet another just disappeared. As to the tiger, it was shot a few days later by another planter some miles away.

There was one other occasion when my parents came very close to a tiger, or to be more precise, the tiger came very close to them. They had been staying on Penang Island for a week end and were driving back to the estate through Ipoh when the incident occurred.

At times the road led through rubber estates and interconnecting jungle. It was while they were travelling along one such jungle stretch of the road that a tiger, which had been standing on the verge, rushed out at the car in much the same way as any pi-dog of the east will dash out at a motor cycle or car when it passes. It ran full tilt towards the car, which was veering off somewhat owing to my father taking as much avoiding action as he could while still staying on the none too wide road. The tiger undoubtably lost some of its momentum during its arc-like approach of the speeding vehicle, but for a few moments it bounded along by the side of the car before making an abortive attempt to jump on board.

My mother, sitting in the front passenger seat, had the best view of the proceedings as it was on her side that the tiger attempted to board. As the whole incident took only a few seconds, she was aware only of the beast running towards the car, and then of a sickening jolt as it landed on the running board and fell off all in the same moment. The car lurched, but sped on until my father pulled in about half a mile down the road to see

One of the women rubber tappers was the tiger's first victim; her tapping block lay along the jungle boundary on an outlying part of the estate.

what damage had been caused. There was no running board left, and there was quite a dent to the door. A few moments after the collision my father had seen the tiger scampering off the road into the jungle, having probably learnt that the fastest thing on wheels yet seen in the jungle was not to be trifled with.

ABOVE
Enormous acreages were being cleared for rubber in the 1920s. My father (left) in a new clearing on Pontian estate, Johore Baru, 1926.
RIGHT
The old V-cut system of tapping. All photographs shown here were taken between 1926 and 1929.

Like my father, uncle and great-uncle before me, I became a planter – and duly went out to Ceylon in the *Chilka* BI cargo passenger vessel leaving Tilbury Docks in November 1950. We travelled via the Suez Canal and I and the other eight passengers on board enjoyed the trip so much that we were quite sad to leave *Chilka* and climb down the companion-way in Colombo, some five weeks later.

Some twenty years on

Young men going out to take up a planting career were usually under contract not to get married during the first tour, a period of roughly five years, which was followed by six months leave back in the UK before returning for the next tour.

The Colombo agents had thoughtfully reserved a room for me at the Grand Oriental Hotel – generally known as the GOH – opposite the jetty, in which I was to stay for three days before setting off for the hills and Kandy. The time was chiefly spent in buying clothes for the estate – half a dozen pairs of khaki shorts, a dozen or so shirts, plenty of long Boy Scout type stockings, bed linen – some sight seeing and a hair cut.

My brief but pleasant stay in the capital being over, I reported once again to the agents, who told me to travel up to Kandy by rail the following morning, where I would be met by the superintendent of the estate to which I was going.

Having completed all that was necessary, I boarded the train at Maradana Station, where crowds of porters surrounded me like flies, all anxious to lift a case or open a carriage door. Before leaving England I had learnt many handy phrases in Tamil from my father and, for an hour or so each day during the voyage out, had tried to improve my vocabulary, consequently a few well chosen phrases did wonders to dispatch the majority of my eager helpers, and left me in command of the situation.

Unlike the first pioneer planters of 125 years before, my journey of four-and-a-half hours up to Kandy was both quick and enjoyable, passing lovely scenery, especially in the vicinity of the Kaduganawa Pass.

The superintendent was the only European on the platform, so it was easy for

LEFT
'M.V. Chilka', British India Steam Navigation Company. (Photo c1950, courtesy P&O.)

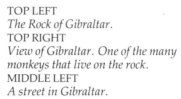

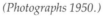

(Photographs 1950.)

TOP LEFT
The Rock of Gibraltar.
TOP RIGHT
View of Gibraltar. One of the many monkeys that live on the rock.
MIDDLE LEFT
A street in Gibraltar.

MIDDLE RIGHT
Marseilles, France; men stop and stare as a pretty girl goes by.
BOTTOM LEFT
Port Said.
BOTTOM RIGHT
Bum-boats alongside our vessel.

us to pick each other out. After my luggage had been loaded into the estate lorry, I found that he had arranged for us to have lunch at the Queen's Hotel with some other planter friends of his, including one old planter who, as my manager reverently told me, had spent his early years coffee planting in the district, which would have made him over eighty.

The estate was situated between Kandy and Matale and, with the manager at the wheel of his car, I had every opportunity

of taking in the lovely scenery all around. As we pulled off the Matale road on to the estate, I got my first look at the tea factory, which was soon lost to sight as we sped steeply upwards along a narrow twisting cart road under old rubber trees. I distinctly remember wondering what would happen if we suddenly met someone else coming down the hill on one of the many sharp bends, but the manager obviously knew his rights as a Grand Prix driver. Although the drive was undeni-

ably exciting it was something of a relief when we swung around our last bend and landed up almost smack in front of the garage.

Every young planter in Ceylon starts his profession by becoming a 'creeper' and I was to spend the next eight months living with the manager as his paying guest in his bungalow. During that time I was expected to learn the rudiments of planting, and of course the language, for it was necessary to learn the ungrammatical language spoken by the estate labour force – colloquial Tamil. The term 'creeper' has been used for those entering the profession since the 1880s, and is probably derived from the fact that one must creep before one walks.

From my top bedroom window of the G.O.H., I could see my old floating home. (1985, Sketch S.R. Fever.)

My working day was a long one, generally from 6 am, until 5 pm with an hour in the bungalow at lunch, but to me it was not long enough. I would walk around the estate visiting all the different field works that were going on and practice upon the coolies my newly learnt Tamil. At certain times of the day and night I would spend a number of hours in the factory, watching the different processes of manufacture; on some days I would accompany the superintendent, walking behind him along the narrow paths between the tea, as he did his rounds of the estate, and during such walks I would gain much knowledge from his long experience.

At all times I treated my manager with the respect that youth pays its elders, always addressing him as Sir, while he called me by my Christian name. We got on very well together and, apart from my early breakfast and departure, we nearly always had lunch and dinner together. After a month or so he allowed me to call him by his Christian name.

The tea factory. (Photo 1951.)

An early start to the working day

The early morning between 5.30 am and 8 am is the loveliest time of the day, the air is sharp and bracing, whilst the sky's glorious colours unfold as the rays of the sun break over the tops of the dark and still brooding mountain masses. Having shaved and breakfasted, and after a hasty scramble up the steep mountainside by way of a short cut through the tea, I would reach the muster ground at about 5.50 am. Muster is held at central points on an estate, such as close to a factory or by a muster shed in which tools are kept. About ten minutes before 6 am, while a late cockerel was still voicing its noisy call from the nearby lines, the coolies, draped in their kamblies, would start to arrive at the muster ground where they would wait in rows. At 6 am sharp they would be sent off to their various tasks for the day. A gang of about 50 pluckers would move off to a particular field for plucking, whilst two small groups of men would be dispatched with their tools to another part of the division to clean out road drains and repair the cart road. It was the beginning of the pruning season: the 45 acre field was being pruned by some eighteen men and a kangany. The weeding gang, with a kangany in charge, would go off to the 94 acre field to continue the never ending battle against weeds.

There are many field works that are carried out at different times of the year, such as mossing and ferning, forking, lopping, manuring, draining, weeding,

and cutting back boundaries, etc. Each gang of coolies is usually in the charge of a kangany who supervises their work, and sees that the 'kanak', or set amount of work, is not only finished by the end of the day, but that the job is done well. The conductor who oversees all works on the division is the planter's right-hand man.

After muster had been taken, I would talk for a few minutes with the conductor about one of the weeding contractors whose field, or contract, was rather too weedy, and then start off at a brisk pace along one of the many paths that led through the tea.

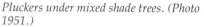

Pluckers under mixed shade trees. (Photo 1951.)

My first stop would have been the plucking field, where the pluckers by then would have taken up their rows, and would be moving slowly across the field in a colourful line, their bright clothes catching the slanting rays of the morning sunshine, making a pretty sight amongst the sea of green tea.

Each plucker carried a large round basket slung on her back, suspended by means of a rope passing around her forehead; each basket would hold 14 lbs of green leaf. The tea bushes are trained to a height of three feet by systematic pruning, and each bush yields a crop of 'flush', and is plucked every seven to ten days. The plucking rounds on an estate are organised so that crop is taken six days a week throughout the whole year. In wet monsoon weather, when the leaf is growing very quickly, plucking goes on seven days a week, with cash plucking on Sundays.

All the pluckers are paid according to the weight of leaf they pick, and although knowing full well what they must do, need constant supervision by the plucking kanganies. Only the young and succulent leaves are required for manufacturing: the tender leaf bud itself, and the next two leaves down (two leaves and

The weighing-up shed – top division. (Photo 1951.)

a bud). If, however, the coarser leaves and stem below are taken and included in the plucker's basket, a poorer quality of tea results. Every single bush is plucked to a level, whether growing on a steep incline or on relatively flat terrain; the top of the bush is known as the 'plucking table', and it is from this flat table that the flush, or young leaf, is picked. This gives a very neat and orderly appearance to the field, and woe betide anyone who leaves a bush with anything but a flat top. In addition, as a plucker moves along her row she must leave each bush clean and tidy; any coarse leaf and stalk found growing up beyond the table of the bush is broken off and thrown away, so too are the unproductive blind shoots ('banji') which have no leaf buds and would merely grow large and coarse whilst at the same time stopping any leaf shoots developing.

Two or three times a day the pluckers have their leaf weighed up, and at such times the kangany, or kanakapulle, will enter the number of pounds of leaf taken against each plucker's name in a small account book that he carries. When the leaf has been weighed, it is then put into mesh coir sacks and transported to the factory, either by lorry along the estate cart roads, or by wire shoot.

I stayed rather longer than I had time for amongst the pluckers, for who would not linger in such an idyllic spot on such a morning. After looking into the baskets of some of the pluckers to see that no coarse leaf or stalk had been included, and having looked over the rows of bushes that had just been plucked, I would move on along a path that would eventually bring me out onto the cart road about half a mile away, near where the road coolies were working.

The path would take me through old Karrupan kangany's weeding contract; he had been working on the estate since he was eleven, as had his father before him. An estate pensioner, he had a five acre block of tea to keep clear of weeds but, as he was in his mid-seventies, his grandsons did most of the work and the bending.

It would be just after 7.30 am when I reached the cart road. Here on one occasion, I found the small gang of road repairers all standing in the middle of the road talking in excited voices. As I arrived one rushed up saying that there was a tic polonga (Russells viper) in one of the road drains: this snake is reputed to be more venomous than the cobra. When resting, it lies curled up in a coil and, it is

Repair work on the estate cart-road. (Photo 1951.)

said, springs from that coiled position at the eyes when attacking. In effect, usually a snake will slide off into the undergrowth or into the tea unless of course it is trodden on, when it will undoubtably strike. This particular one was helped on its way by a few stones, and made a quick departure up the slope above the drain.

On my way to the pruning field I sometimes made a slight detour which would take me through the 94 acre field, where the weeders were half lost to sight bent down amongst the tea. Composed of the older women and very young boys and girls, with an old kangany in charge, the weeding gang was paid a daily wage. Certain parts of the estate however were kept clean by contract weeding, the weeding contractor being paid monthly to look after a certain acreage, as in the case of old Karrupan kangany. This particular field was one of the older ones on the estate, having been planted way back in the 1890s; it had about 2900 bushes per acre, making it quite a task to weed, as the wide spacing of the bushes allowed the sun to penetrate to the ground where the weeds flourish.

Having left the weeders, I would make my way back onto a steep path leading up towards the top of the hill and the highest point on the estate. The view at so early an hour is well worth a photograph, if only to show the steep slopes that daily test the climbing powers of the pluckers. Upon gaining the summit, my attention would be riveted to the opposite hillside – a mile or so across the valley as the crow flies to a patch in the tea from where smoke was rising. Beyond there lay the area where the pruners were at work. In order to reach the pruners I had to take a

zig-zag footpath down the side of the hill to a narrow valley some four hundred feet below along which a small stream rushed over large boulders and rocks. After a steep climb up the other side, I would finally reach the brow of the hill and sunshine again. Upon accustoming my eyes to the glare of the sun and the heat haze falling upon the surrounding hills, I could then see ahead a darker patch in the middle of the light green carpet of tea – the 45 acre field that was being pruned.

Pruning is an extremely hard and backbreaking job, for the whole day is spent in stooping and cutting, nearly always on steep and uneven ground. Pruners receive a higher rate of pay all the year round even when doing other works, as they are the elite of the field workers. The tea bush is pruned every two to four years, according to the elevation at which it grows. After continuous plucking, approximately once every seven days, the bush becomes tired of producing new shoots or flush, and must therefore be pruned to give it fresh vigour. The whole of the top with all its mature leaves is lopped off right down to the main thicker branches below, which are then cut across to a level. This is the general method, although different estates employ different methods of pruning – some prune lightly leaving side branches, some more severely. The pruners are a dedicated group of men who, although under the supervision of an experienced pruning kangany, still take great pride in their work.

Standing amongst the pruners, the sun, now higher in the sky, beats mercilessly down on the exposed earth, a terrific heat comes from the baked ground, but the smell of freshly cut wood sap is most pleasant. Also, there are many patches of shadow in the field as tea needs a certain amount of shade at the hottest time of the day. The shade trees that are most commonly planted between the rows of tea bushes are the albizzia and the dadap, also the quick growing Australian silky oak or grevillea, which is also useful as a wind-break and for timber. The dadap trees are a pretty sight when in flower, their brilliant red petals contrasting against the deep blue sky and the green of the surrounding tea.

I tried my hand for the first time at pruning the odd couple of dozen bushes under the watchful eye of the kangany in the heat of the sun, and I was reduced to the state of a wet rag, with a great deal of honest sweat and blisters on my hand.

There are many other jobs to be done as soon as a field has been pruned; small boys, 'podians', go through removing any moss and ferns that grow around the bole of the bushes. The whole field will receive a special application of manure, after which the ground will be forked everywhere between the bushes; this is followed by the lopping of the shade trees, which provides green manure.

Finally, all the field drains are cleaned out, the valuable top soil that has been washed into them over the preceeding years is dug out and thrown back above each drain, where it is spread around the roots of the bushes. The field is then ready for the next span of its long life. These field works take place throughout the whole estate in strict rotation.

After pruning, the new leaf bursts forth with renewed vigour. The whole field of pruned tea is out of commission for a period of between six and twelve weeks, again depending upon the elevation at which it is grown – sometimes even longer on up-country estates. During this period the new growth is left to develop before tipping; this specialised plucking is carried out during the subsequent plucking rounds by a small gang of the estate's most experienced pluckers. When a field of pruned tea has passed the tipping stage, it is handed back to the main gang of pluckers.

It would be a long way from the pruning field back to the bungalow, but my manager was very particular about having lunch at 1.30 pm if at all possible. By the time I had reached the bungalow my clothes would be wringing wet, and it was pleasant to take a cold shower and down a long ice cold lime juice – made from the fruit of a large tree in the garden – before sitting down to lunch.

The estate bungalow of my day was quite an improvement on the thatched mud and wattle hut of the early planters. In many cases it had electric light provided by a dynamo in the factory; in some bungalows the power came from a small 5HP generating engine housed in a building at the rear of the bungalow compound. Because of the tropical storms, every bungalow also had a lightning conductor sticking up from the roof. The kitchen would have seemed to a European town dweller somewhat old fashioned, and in nearly all cases the cooking was carried out on an open range. The bungalow garden, set against a background of hills and valleys, provided the loveliest of sanctuaries within the estate. Its graceful jacarandas with their heavenly blue flowers, its tulip trees and the massive flamboyant with its scarlet blooms were all a fitting setting for the many exotic birds.

After lunch and a short rest, I again departed for the fields, while H went down to the main office to see to the estate correspondence. Every evening on our return to the bungalow, we would sit down to cold drinks on the verandah before dinner, after which he would generally settle down to read or listen to

Steep slopes daily test the climbing powers of the pluckers. (Photo 1951.)

his gramophone records – and to some of mine – whilst I pushed off to my bedroom for an hour-and-a-half to learn Tamil. I was required to learn twenty new words every day for six days a week, which was easy enough at first, but it became progressively harder and harder to remember the words I had already learned; I felt thankful that I had started learning the language in England and during the voyage out.

Many experiences of that time now stand out in my memory, mainly to do with life on the estate as I spent little time at the club at weekends. I remember how, one hot day, I witnessed the migration of a particular species of butterfly. For hours countless millions of butterflies stretched across the entire landscape in a huge fluttering cloud, painting white the tea and the surrounding valleys and hills; they appeared to be heading in the direction of Adams Peak where, it is said, they go to die.

Pay day and hailstones

Then there was the day – an unusually cold one – when I was in the weighing shed, sitting behind a rickety old table on which I had laid great piles of rupee notes of all denominations, together with a large selection of small coins. A hundred or so coolies were lined up on the cart road immediately in front of me, waiting to be paid. They stood huddled together, shivering in their kamblies (blankets). It had previously been pouring, and the sky was the colour of lead, when, all of a sudden, huge hail stones the size of marbles came crashing down on us, bouncing all over the place. As they hit the tagarams – the corrugated tin roof – above me, the noise was deafening and I was amazed to see the coolies dashing about on the road picking up hail stones and putting them in the folds of their sarongs to take back later to their lines. No-one in the district had seen hail stones for years. The storm did quite a bit of damage to the tea bushes, many of which were left leafless. Although everyone had been drenched to the skin, that was not the end of it. I was on my way back to the bungalow on my motor bike when another heavy hail shower hit me, making it quite impossible to continue. Leaving the bike on the muddy gravel cart road which was now running with water, I jumped down amongst the tea bushes to find shelter under one of the shade trees – but without any success. A change of clothes put matters right when I eventually arrived back at the bungalow.

A cobra bite – the PD's dog dies

I had not long been on the estate when H decided to leave me in charge and go down and spend the weekend in Colombo. It was a hot Sunday afternoon, and after lunch I went to my bedroom to rest. I was lying awake on the bed when I heard a whimpering noise coming from outside the verandah; the next instant, his dog came running through the open doorway and shot under my bed. Presuming that it had come in to find a cool place to lie down, I thought nothing more of it, but after a half minute or so the crying started up again. I swung myself off the bed and looked underneath at what seemed to be a very frightened animal. It was by now shaking and, on picking it up to examine it, I saw a small spot of blood at the top of one of its forelegs. I immediately carried it out to the kitchens and showed the spot to the appu, who thought it was a leech bite, which it might well have been had the dog been down in a damp and shady part of the garden near a small stream.

The poor little dog went into the dining room and lay down under the table shaking all over, and all the while looking as if it was getting worse. I rolled him over on his back, which enabled us to get a better look at the place where the small patch of blood was, and suddenly the appu exclaimed 'Iyo nulla pámbu' which, I well knew, meant 'My God, its a cobra bite'. (It could equally have been the bite of a tic polonga.) A period of about four to six minutes had elapsed since the dog had come into my bedroom and, with probably as many more having passed before it had put in an appearance, it was doomed in any case. But I jumped on my motor bike with the dog on my petrol tank, and set off at top speed for the estate hospital, 1000 feet above us and two miles away. Upon my arrival at the hospital, I stopped my engine and, looking down at the dog, saw that it was dead. It was sad news to have to tell.

It was while I was getting to know the estate and all its boundaries that I discovered a block of jungle along a very steep and rocky part of the estate. As it effectively separated the middle and lower divisions between which I often walked, causing much loss of time, one day I decided to take a short cut through it. As soon as I had left the heat and sunlight of the tea field and scrambled my way over some 50 yards, the cool of the jungle hit me. The tall trees rose to their giddy heights above, while here and there long shafts of sunlight would penetrate, but never reach, the jungle floor. For much of the way down, the slope of land was so steep that I had to lower myself over huge crops of granite rock and boulders by the thick creepers that hung around all the massive trees. I progressed slowly for

The bungalow and garden, with a lovely jacaranda tree in the right foreground of picture. A few weeks after the photograph was taken, the dog died from a snake bite. (Photo 1951.)

Watch out for snakes! (Photo 1952.)

perhaps 200 yards, forever looking ahead for the light that would tell me I had come through.

Soon the steep slope gave way to a more gentle one, and having at last gained more even ground, I rested for a while on a fallen tree trunk. The silence of the jungle, and the complete absence of any form of wild life left me wondering where they all were. I was a complete newcomer, this being my first foray, and I knew nothing of the ways of the jungle, nor did I then realise that, as regular as clockwork, just before noon each day when the sun is at its hottest, there is a painful stillness everywhere as all creatures take refuge from the mid-day heat. The birds were obviously resting in the shade of the topmost branches of the trees, high above the denizens of the forest floor – and yet I had seen none.

Moving on slowly, I became aware of the sound of water coming from a narrow ravine and, doubling back somewhat, came upon a stream. As I approached a small pool, there was a splash as a reptile of some sort swam across to the opposite bank. I had not seen anything like it before, and in my ignorance thought it to be a type of small alligator. It was, as I later found out, a kabragoya, a large lizard or type of iguana of about four feet in length, fierce looking but in fact quite harmless, apart from the fact that its tail can give one quite a crack on the ankles.

At last I came to the boundary of the jungle and there, before me, were the familiar rubber trees of the lower Maousa-galla division of the estate. I felt a little disappointed for, apart from the kabra-goya, I had not seen a single wild animal, snake or bird, but had nevertheless seen some very lovely tree orchids and the exquisite Gloriosa superba, a type of climbing lily with flame red flowers. While walking along under the old rubber trees, close to the jungle boundary, I came upon some old coffee bushes from a bygone age. They were growing out from between several large granite boulders, and were about six feet in height, their shape being more that of stunted trees than of bushes. I arrived back at the bungalow late for lunch that day – my short cut had turned out to be rather a time-consuming one. H had never been through that part of the jungle, and although he had not seen the old coffee trees, he could confirm that coffee had originally been planted on the land that the rubber trees now stood on. The lower division on the estate had originally been opened up as the Maousagalla coffee estate sometime prior to the year 1857.

The Saturday evening bioscope show, and tennis on Sunday

Saturday evenings were often reserved for a 'bioscope show' at the local cinema, after which all those 'in town' would move on a short distance to the club, or drive back to their estates, some of which took a bit of getting to along roads that twisted up the mountain ranges for miles. The fact that the film hardly ever started on time was due to the habit of some of the planters who came from greater distances, of telephoning the cinema earlier in the day to say 'I shall be in this evening, don't start the film until I arrive'. It was therefore not unusual for the audience to be looking at their watches, muttering 'Why are we late today', only to be told by the cinema manger that we were waiting for so and so to arrive. When the film did start, it all too often came to an abrupt stop with a break-down of some sort, and then all the natives would set up a great stamping of feet on the wooden floorboards, accompanied by loud whistling. It was all exacerbated by the vast armies of flees harbouring inside the cane seats. 'Once bitten, twice shy' is the saying, but everyone just put up with

them, although the flees did keep the audience moving about, thereby stopping them from dropping off to sleep. Every Saturday evening the flees had a bumper meal.

Once or twice a month, on Sunday mornings, I would get a lift to the club in H's car; he would spend the morning playing billiards or snooker, while I played tennis. One day we had both left the estate early, he to visit an old friend for the day, and I for the club and a morning's tennis. Unfortunately my motor bike broke down just after I had got on to the PWD road, close to some native buildings. A crowd of Sinhalese soon gathered to watch my efforts at starting the infernal machine. Most Sinhalese, especially those in the planting districts, speak or can at least understand a little Tamil. I had abandoned thoughts of getting to the club that morning, and was on the point of legging it back to the estate when, as luck would have it, a bullock cart appeared around the bend in the road and the driver offered to give me a lift into Matale.

Having left instructions for my motor bike to be pushed back to the estate factory, we set off. We must have made a strange sight as the little covered wagon bumped slowly along the road beneath the trees. There was nothing in the least odd about the look of the Sinhalese driver, but of the passenger sitting next to him one might have thought differently. Dressed in my tennis gear of white shirt, white shorts, white stockings and pumps, I must certainly have looked out of place – nothing like it had been seen since the days of the early pioneer planters, although I do them an injustice, for they had never had the time to play tennis, nor the courts to play on.

Travelling by bullock cart, even for as little as six miles, was an experience not to be missed, but our progress was so slow that I finally arrived at the club in time to have only a single game before returning to the estate, this time in someone else's car.

One day H told me that he was going to underplant a ten acre block of old rubber with cocoa on the lower division. In the Kandy, Matale and Dumbara districts a good deal of cocoa (the chocolate plant, Theobromo cacao) is grown and, as it requires shade, it is quite often the practice to plant it under old rubber trees. Interesting though the work was, it was soon to be overshadowed by the commencement of a new clearing of tea on the top division. A small five acre patch of patana, or grass land, on the top of a hill, surrounded by existing tea, was the location.

Work got under way each day half-an-hour after dawn, when there was quite often a nip in the air. At certain times of the year mist cloaked the valleys below, giving the effect of islands sticking out amidst a sea of white. Everyone enjoys new clearing work, coolies and planters alike, and unlike the pioneering days when jungle was being opened out everywhere at a terrific pace, during my day one was lucky to get the chance of such work, as most of the tea estates had by then been fully developed.

It had been decided to plant up the land at 3'0" by 3'6", that is there were three feet between each plant in its row, while the rows were three foot six inches apart. This would give 4150 plants per acre, but with the cutting of paths and drains, the final number is more like 3500 per acre. The nursery had its full quota of young seedlings that would be ready for lifting at the onset of the monsoon.

A new tea clearing involves complicated planting compared with a rubber clearing. The small hilltop was a wonderful hive of activity. Supervision paths and drains had already been cut, and a large gang of men were busy forking out patches of deeply rooted long grass, while others slashed undergrowth and tended small fires. The conductor, complete with lining compass and aided by a small party of men and boys, worked slowly over the ground with long lining ropes, each marked off with tags of cloth at every three feet. Split pegs, 18 inches long cut from the jungle, were knocked into the ground at each tag to mark the exact position of the hole that was later to be dug for the young tea plants. When the whole of the clearing had been lined and pegged, there were close on 18,000 white pegs standing as straight as soldiers, for leaning pegs were considered slovenly work.

During the following days, work was started on the holing of the clearing. The cutting of approximately 18,000 holes, each 20 inches deep by 12 inches wide at the top and 9 inches at the bottom, soon produced an overall appearance of reddish brown earth everywhere. The filling of the holes with top-soil was carried out at a later date. The whole clearing was then ready for planting when the monsoon came.

My manager seemed to know everyone over a wide area including certain office wallahs in Colombo, and on many a weekend they would arrive for Saturday lunch, leaving the following evening. Although it was good to see new faces, I found such weekends somewhat unsettling as I had much to study and learn, especially the language. Many of the planters had daughters who came out to Ceylon during their holidays, and they and their parents would come to lunch or dinner at weekends. But, at the age of twenty-two, I could honestly say that a tea bush stood more chance with me than a girl! Anyway, I had signed a contract back in England which clearly stated: 'You will not be expected to marry within the first five years of your appointment, and in any case this would only take place with the consent of the company.'

If I had any doubts about my profession in the years that were to come, my contract had also included the following about any termination of employment: 'If, during the first three years of your appointment as Assistant Superintendent, you decide of your own accord to terminate such appointment, then you would understand that you would be expected to refund all payments made to you by way of salary and other emoluments during your period of training, as well as the cost of your outward passage.' The die was cast, and I was happy with it.

Every week H would check my progress in the language. Examinations for young planters were held twice a year at the Queen's Hotel in Kandy, and although one was not expected to sit for the examination before a year to eighteen months, he wanted me to try my luck after only four months on the estate. Whenever exams loom ahead, one is reminded of the candidate who admitted that he did not find the questions difficult, only the answers. Regarding these examinations, it was rumoured that, providing the candidate knew a certain phrase that the examiner would ask, he could sail through with a comfortable pass. What this particular phrase was no one really knew, but it turned up during the oral part, when the examiner asked us all in turn to translate into Tamil 'Your postillion has been struck by lightning' which, you will agree was unfair to say the least – that is, unless one knew the answer. Not being able to impress the examiner at the very start of the proceedings, I had no recourse but to rely on my true knowledge, the lack of which was enough to make me fail at my first attempt.

Time passed all too quickly. My days spent in the hills were indeed happy ones; the surroundings made the life of a planter seem quite unlike work, yet most of the planters were very hard working and conscientious to a degree, working long hours to keep on top of everything. Fortunately the monsoon arrived before I was due to leave the estate, and I was lucky enough to be there for the planting of the five acre new clearing.

Off to the Southern Province

Besides tea, there was a fair amount of cocoa, pepper and rubber around the Matale area, and it was to a rubber estate in the Southern Province that I next found myself journeying, where, as an assistant, I was to be responsible for just under 2000 acres. My earliest childhood recollections were of rubber trees in Malaya, and although the hill districts had a delightful air of peace and grandeur about them, the south of the island was to be rather more wild, with a climate that was more steamy and just as hot.

After goodbyes had been said, I set off on my motor bike for what was to be my longest trip since I had arrived on the island. The journey took no time at all as the PWD roads were then pretty good – in spite of the many cows and the occasional buffalo that wandered along them – and my motor bike went like a rocket.

My new superintendent had written to say that I would be staying with him and his wife at their bungalow for a few days before moving off to my own bungalow a few miles away. I arrived just in time for one of the best old fashioned teas I had had for a long time; his wife was charming and he was a Scotsman; what more could one wish for? The two days were soon over and it was time for me to move on. The bungalow in which I spent my first night alone, apart from the newly engaged cook and Tamil bungalow boy, was situated close to an 1100 acre block of estate jungle, which was just across the valley. As I sat alone that first night with the single kerosene oil lamp casting its bluey white light across the darkened sitting room, I well remember thinking about my tiger – not that there are tigers in Ceylon – and about leopards which, by comparison, did not seem half so bad.

The bungalow was approached by a gravel cart road which wound its way around the hill in a spiral to the top. It was a serenely peaceful place to live, with lovely views of distant hills over which in good weather a heat haze hung, but in the many monsoons that were to come, these same hills provided a dramatic setting for thunderstorms, when the dark sky would be lit by continuous flashes of forked lightning and ear shattering crashes of thunder would echo around the hills and valleys.

A certain proposition is put to me

After settling into his new bungalow, it was not uncommon for a new planter, a 'pootha dore', to get a visit from the father of an attractive Sinhalese village girl, in order that a certain proposition might be made. On estates where a mixed resident labour force of both Tamils and Sinhalese worked, a new arrival might also expect a visit from one of his own kanganies. What the estate labour force did not know about the planter was hardly worth knowing; each estate was a compact and closely knit community of people. The newcomer would soon be sized up by the entire labour force, from the smallest child to the oldest pensioner; all would know what they could or could not expect from the pootha dore.

If the unwary planter had taken a fancy to any of the score of attractive young girls whom he would see working in the fields each day, 'an arrangement' was entered into with the girl's father. Although it was positively taboo to have anything to do with one's own labour, it did of course happen on occasion and could lead to dire complications for the planter. I would say that in my day the greater proportion of planters did not make such arrangements. However, old customs often die hard.

I had been living in my bungalow only a few short months when I received a rather unusual visit from one of my Sinhalese kanganies. I remember the occasion well.

It was an overcast Sunday afternoon towards the end of the south-west monsoon, and I had been planting out a batch of gladioli bulbs in one of the beds in the garden when I became aware of my appu coming across the lawn towards me. I gathered from the drift of his conversation, in Sinhalese mixed with a smattering of Tamil and pidgin English, that one of the kanganies had arrived at the bungalow with two of his daughters and wanted to see me.

Puzzled, I walked to my office at one end of the bungalow and sat down in front of my desk while the appu opened

Graceful casuarina trees lined two sides of the garden. (Photo 1952.)

the office windows and called the man along. The kangany at last hove into sight, followed at a discreet distance by two young, very coy and well decked out maidens. They could not have been more than fifteen or sixteen years of age, and were dressed in their smartest and most colourful saris.

Their father, like most estate Sinhalese, could speak fluent Tamil, and after putting out a big salaam he started off at a very fast pace, all the while looking knowingly at me and his daughters, who were by then standing by his side. After listening patiently for a minute or so, I came to the conclusion that he was asking me if I wanted either of his daughters to come and work in my bungalow which, as things turned out, was quite the wrong impression. Even the most newly arrived pootha dore knew that it was definitely not the form to have a native woman in the home to keep the place tidy; I therefore gave him a curt no. Whereupon my appu, who had been standing behind me listening intently, broke into the rather one sided conversation. Athough understanding very little Tamil, he had of course known what was afoot from the moment the small party arrived; he would in any case have talked to the kangany in their native Sinhalese. Now, in his wisdom and knowledge of the world, he said to me in what was almost his entire repertoire in English, 'Excuse me Sar, Master want Pumble (woman) for bed, is'nt it, Sar please'!

I must have gaped at him for a full ten seconds while the implication of what he had said sunk in. My attitude changed, like the weather often does, and rising from my seat I gave the kangany the

benefit of some of my choicest phrases, ending with the words 'Tura poa, yenude vangala kitta tirumbi varathe' (Go away, don't come near my bungalow again).

Thinking the matter over afterwards, I could not help being impressed with the appu's command of the English language; he had hit the nail on the head most succinctly. It was at times like this that a young planter relied most heavily upon his appu. I pretty soon learnt the Tamil and Sinhalese words for 'bed', just in case I received any more propositions! When I saw the kangany in the field a day or so later he gave me a sly smile; to the native way of thinking it is a very unnatural state of affairs for a young man to be living without a woman. His two daughters lowered their eyes when I came across them in the weeding gang.

The appu was quite old, whilst the bungalow boy was a mere slip of a lad of fifteen. Their quarters were situated at the rear next to the kitchen, and it was they who looked after my simple wants, and kept the home looking shipshape. The only other person was the gardener, and he lived in his lines, coming up daily to work. He generally contrived to be working in some prominent position, cutting a hedge with great gusto whilst I was in the bungalow, and after my departure would move off to the shade of a large breadfruit tree, under which he would squat and chew betel-nut. I soon found it necessary to give him a specific task to accomplish each day.

Once every week the appu used to depart for the whole day to make the 19 mile journey to the nearest bazaar or market town to buy provisions for the following week. The night before leaving, he and I would engage in a quite farcical conversation as I endeavoured to tell him in Tamil and pidgin English – which came quite easily to me – exactly what provisions he was to purchase. His own brand of pidgin English helped me no end as I tried to explain such items as cooking oil, boot laces, red floor polish, and gin and whisky, the last two being understood without much difficulty.

I have a very revealing note in the back of an old 1950 diary which shows the grand extent of my bungalow provisions during my first month there:

1 tin sardines
1 tin corned beef (which I loved, and still do)
2 tins red salmon
1 tin peaches (large)
3 tins beans (large, presumably the baked variety)

It should be pointed out that the stocks held in my larder were merely kept in reserve, in case of dire need. Looking back over the years, I cannot think why I was so lax as to have only three tins of beans, as this was a most cherished item of food. My main working diet was accounted for in the provisions that the appu returned with each week. One item was meat, and this usually used to get pretty high before five days were out as my ice-box was not what it should have been. The situation became a lot better a few months later, when my stocks had risen considerably to include almost everything one could buy in the way of tins, and these were locked away in the larder after I found some strange and unexplained disappearances.

The appu, although working in a kitchen that would make a strong woman faint, would, with little fuss, prepare on an open range an absolutely first class meal. For those readers who may wonder what a first class meal consisted of, let me first explain that a planter's life is a healthy one, his time is lived in the open, walking around the estate, up and down hill under a hot sun or during the monsoon in a torrential downpour, consequently a healthy appetite is normal. So when I tell you that my appu's speciality – lunch or dinner, for which he was known far and wide – was a passable soup made from God knows what, followed by fried chipped potatoes, bangers and beans, with mounds of thick bread and butter, ending with a huge rice pudding, all of which was washed down with copious glasses of water, beer or whisky, you will gather our tastes were simple. He also produced a curry, which was so hot that it kept the 'eye flies' and insects away for miles around. Generally speaking, most bachelors' cooks were not too special and would not have lasted a day in a married planter's bungalow where the lady of the house could keep a sharp eye on things.

My uninvited guest(s)

I used to sit down to dinner at 7.30 every evening and often, as I munched away, a huge rat would come into the dining room; there were others, but I never saw more than one at a time. But one was enough; they were big brutes, probably bandicoots. One evening I thought I would put an end to my uninvited visitor, and told the boy to bring a broom, which was kept handy. Getting up between the first course and the second – this not being the Ritz – I drove the rodent, which had just come in, into a corner of the room where it immediately sat up glaring at me with its flaming pink eyes. I pushed the broom violently forward to trap it in the corner, but it quickly jumped about two feet in the air and landed at my feet. I then acted in much the same way as the Scots do when frantically brushing the ice ahead of a moving curling stone, but rather more vigorously. Whether my bungalow staff had fried rat for supper that night I cannot say. I thought a tame cat about the place would be a good idea, and a few weeks later one was installed. As the rats were as big as the poor cat, I do not know what sort of life the cat had, but at least the rats did not pay any more evening visits. The rat snake, which grows to about five or six feet in length, was also good at catching rats, and one or two of these reptiles were quite useful to have around a bungalow compound as they kept the rat population away and were quite harmless to humans.

My bungalow had no lights, so five or six kerosene lamps were the order of the day; the place was always rather gloomy at night, and if any reading was to be done, the strain on my eyes and the heat from sitting close to the lamp was enough to make them come out of their sockets. Talking of lamps reminds me of the numerous fire-flies that one saw around the garden at night after a sharp shower. There were glow-worms too – repulsive looking fat white grubs of about two inches in length – which gave out a much brighter light than the small fire-flies. Every night the mosquito was the enemy. Accustomed as one becomes to this minute raider and its continual booming hum as it diligently presses home its attack – no matter what odds are against it – the plain fact is, as soon as you cease to hear its deadly hum, it is too late, you know full well that you are about to suffer, or have in fact just been bitten by it.

The bungalow had three bedrooms, a dining room, a sitting room, and an office. The floors were cement finished throughout, highly polished, with coir mats thrown down to make the place look more palacial. The garden consisted of a large lawn surrounded by a low hedge, bordered on one side by a line of five casuarina trees which, when a breeze was blowing, made the most heavenly whistling sound. These are excellent in tropical countries where long periods of drought are experienced. The slope at the rear of the garden accommodated all the fruit trees, which included coconut palms, paw paw, bread fruit, plantain and orange trees, the fruits of which remain green when ripe. There were also about 50 pineapple plants, and every day of the year I had fruit salad, of which I never tired.

The daily ritual – the sound of tom-toms

The life of a young unmarried planter on a tea or rubber estate was by any standards a lonely one, for much of his time was spent in his own company. Each morning I would awake at a little after five to the sound of tom-toms beating down in the darkness of the valley below: da da dum, da da dum – da da dum, da da dum. This morning ritual was carried out by a coolie whose job was to wake the labour force, and this he did by walking up and down outside the lines beating his tom-tom, which never failed to give them – or me, some half a mile away – a rude awakening. I would lie and listen, fascinated by the sound which I shall never forget, and at 5.20 am, just as the first glimmer of light came into the sky, my boy would come to my open door and knock softly, as he knew that I was always awake – how could it be otherwise with the band playing outside! As I washed by the light of a kerosene lamp, my eagerness to start the day would mount, for these were my young days when I was as keen as the sharp edge of a huntsman's knife.

Breakfast usually consisted of two boiled, fried or poached eggs, with toast and butter, followed by a large plate of fruit salad and a cup of tea or two; then I would grab my walking stick and start off down the hill to the muster ground three quarters of a mile away.

Walking along a narrow path that doubled steeply downwards between boulders and tall grass, I was soon soaked with the dew from the ferns and bushes that I had brushed against. Often, before going farther down the hill into the cover of the rubber trees, I would pause to take in the beauty of the unfolding day – the glorious clear colours of the early morning sky coming up over the still dark shapes of the slumbering hills and the buzzing noise all around of the insect life. When at last I had reached the rubber, the tappers would already be arriving with their buckets and knives. During the cool period of the day, the latex from the trees flows most freely and, as each tapper has a block of 250 trees to tap, an early start is advantageous both to the tapper and to the yield of the estate. Any tapper found going late to his or her block is liable to be put to other work, such as weeding. Tappers move silently between the rubber trees, pausing at each one just long enough to open up the cut on the tapping panel, place half a coconut shell under a small spout to collect the dripping latex and then hurry on to the next tree. The more expert tappers would complete the

A Sinhalese tapping 'kangany', his wife also a tapper, and their two children. (Photo 1955.)

tapping of their blocks by about 10.30 am, and would then wait until the latex had finished dripping before going around with their buckets collecting up the latex, after which they proceeded to the weighing up shed at the factory.

It would be almost light by the time I arrived at the muster ground. All the labour force, except the already working tappers, would form up in lines; tools would be distributed among small gangs of men who would then move off to their different jobs. Two large gangs of weeders – comprising older women and young boys and girls – would be sent off to carry on the never-ending battle against weeds and grass.

The normal routine jobs – work on pests and diseases, repairs to roads, bridges and culverts, and manuring – go on throughout the year for six days a week. The actual tapping of the trees is carried out every day of the week, including Sundays, half of the estate being tapped on one day, and the other half the following day. Each tapper therefore has two blocks of trees for tapping on alternate days. A 'wintering period' occurs between January and March depending upon the 'clone' of the trees, and it is then that the trees lose their leaves; but, unlike in temperate zones, they quickly refoliate within a period of three or four weeks. It is during this period that the trees affected are rested, and tapping is stopped completely.

A Sinhalese tapper. (Photo 1953.)

Looking after 1963 acres of rubber – which is equal in area to three square miles – was enough to keep anyone fully occupied. Every day, after visiting the morning muster on any one of the four divisions, not necessarily in any particular order or rotation, I would start off on my rounds, which would be so varied that all parts of the total acreage would be looked at every three or four days.

One day I nearly trod on a tic polonga as I was walking through the rubber. Picking my feet up, as the ground cover crop was about a foot high in places, I was on the point of putting a foot down on a small patch of bare ground, when I saw the snake lying curled around in a circle. I retained sufficient balance to enable me to freeze with my outstretched foot above the snake. Without blinking, or moving an inch, I stayed foot in air looking down at the snake's beady eyes and, after what must have been only seconds but which to me seemed like an age, it slid off into the cover crop.

Little tapping was done during the south-west monsoon, when it poured for a month on end. Branches and whole trees would come crashing down everywhere, and sometimes bridges over the many small rivers on the estate were washed away when these same rivers

Monsoon time. I returned to my car after an hour-and-a-half's heavy rain to find it cut off; the swirling mass of brown water had risen seven feet above the causeway bridge. I took the photograph from the other side of the small river, returning for the car the following morning. (Photo 1956.)

became rushing torrents, sweeping all before them. Roads and culverts became blocked with mud and silt; the monsoon was always an unproductive, but often hectic, period. It was also the time for replanting old, poor yielding rubber, or for planting out any new clearings that there might be.

During this time of year one often picked up a lot of leeches. Many were the days when I arrived back at the bungalow with socks full of blood. The coffee planters had worn leech gaiters around their ankles, but that was in the days when there was an awful lot of untamed jungle around and living conditions were worse in every respect. The land leech is found in damp, low lying regions and is about an inch long. After it has punctured the skin of the leg, it is hardly noticeable under one's sock until after about two hours when its body becomes huge and bloated with blood. It is then about one-and-a-half inches in length and three quarters of an inch thick, and its body hangs heavily against the skin. If one pulls it off before it is ready to depart, it leaves its teeth in the skin and the bite will turn septic. The best way to get rid of them was to brush them off one at a time,

with a piece of lime fruit, or to put a lighted match to them; they would then drop off taking their teeth with them.

There was a part of the estate, between two divisions, which I often went to; in fact it was my favourite walk. A small outcrop of rocky jungle attached to a larger piece of estate jungle stuck out into the rubber, and I used a narrow, usually overgrown path as a short cut. About twice a year I would send a couple of men to cut down the saplings and undergrowth that encroached upon the narrow path, which at times came out into more open patches. The path ran through heavy jungle for some of the way before coming to a small stream, around which there were no overhanging branches, and here the hot sun flooded into the small luxuriant glade.

It was a delightful place, especially around the stream with its surrounding tree ferns; brilliantly-coloured butterflies were always there in scores, drinking from the moisture in the gravel and sand by the water's edge. Exotic birds, too, came to this little paradise earlier in the morning, their long tails trailing behind them. These were the black long-tailed drongos, that flew swiftly and powerfully through the humid dark jungle. More easy to spot was the more spectacular steel blue racket-tailed drongo. I only saw this lovely bird on a few occasions in heavy jungle, flying from branch to branch with a continuous dipping flight; its total length was all of 20 inches, its tail being a good half of that. The Tamils call it 'rettu valam kuruvi', the 'double-tailed

bird', on account of its long forked tail which it carries like a streamer behind as it flies.

After quenching my thirst from the stream, I would often sit watching the butterflies opening and closing their wings as they drank. In the heat of the day around noon, when the sun was directly overhead and the jungle was perfectly still, the only sound in all the world was that of the cascading water as it jumped from pool to pool.

Blasting activities – a close shave

One activity at which I soon became expert was that of blowing up large immovable boulders which curiously enough had the habit of turning up halfway down 'thunder box pits'. These latrine pits, to give them their correct name, were usually sited about 50 yards away from the coolie lines where 50 to 100 souls lived; as the useful working life of just one of these latrine pits was about five years, there was always a new one required to be cut somewhere. On average, one in every four pits dug had an obstruction; naturally if the two diggers came upon a large boulder in the ground only a few feet down, they would start another pit close by, but when a large boulder showed up more than half way down, it often paid to try blasting.

The pits were some three feet square, going down to a depth of 12 feet. If an obstruction were found, digging would be suspended and a special coolie would be sent down to bore an 18 inch deep hole in the rock. This was where I came in, armed with a stick or two of dynamite, a fuse cap, fuse wire, and a box of matches. I would then climb down on a rickety ladder – not the sort that one buys in a shop, but one made from two more or less straight stout branches cut from the jungle, with smaller ones bound between for rungs. At the bottom of the pit all that had to be done was to fix a three foot length of fuse wire tightly into the fuse cap, then fix the fuse cap firmly into the end of the stick of dynamite, lowering the fuse and stick into the 18 inch bore hole in the offending rock, which was then plugged up tight with soil; the fuse was then lit and a fairly quick departure made.

Of the many times I performed this particular feat, there was one occasion when I was extremely lucky to come out safely. I was at the bottom of a pit, about 10 feet down. I had fixed everything, lit the fuse and was on my way up the ladder when one of the rungs broke, and the next instant I found myself at the bottom of the gloomy pit sitting on top of the granite rock with the fuse steadily burning. Down in the confined space deep in the ground I had a choice of either ripping out the diminishing fuse wire and separating it and the fuse cap from the stick of dynamite inside the rock, or of beating a quick retreat up the ladder again. I chose the latter. Luckily, it was one of the lower rungs that had broken, for had it been one of those higher up, I would have fallen further and had less time to act; as it was, I had no sooner gained the top and flung myself away from the opening than the explosion came, sending chunks of granite hurtling up into the sky.

Luck was with me again on another occasion. I was on my way to do a blasting job, and was riding my motor bike along one of the estate roads when, upon going around one particular bend, I ran into a cow – sending both me and my machine skidding into a drain beside the road. The heavy bike fell across my legs, pinning me to the ground for what must have been about twenty seconds until I could extricate myself. I happened to be carrying in my pocket four or five sticks of dynamite, fuse caps, etc, and it was fortunate that the hot exhaust pipe of the motor bike had not lain across that part of me, for had the dynamite come in contact with the exhaust, there would have been a very loud bang indeed.

I had not been long on the estate when the superintendent gave me the good news that a large rubber factory was to be built on one of my divisions. This entailed a lot of extra work, and of course additional labour was required. My camera came out at the beginning of the operation, but unfortunately I have since lost some of the old photographs which would have shown a better sequence of events.

The original lie of the land earmarked for the site of the factory was of a gentle slope, nevertheless the cutting and removal of tons of earth with the inevitable wicker baskets took many weeks, despite the help of a tractor fitted with a grab. I had previously driven an old International back on my uncle's farm near Dalkeith in Scotland, and I could not pass up the opportunity of becoming a tractor driver once again, spending many hours excavating. There is something very exhilerating in being in the midst of 50-80 men and women – not forgetting their bright-

ABOVE
The old smoke-house where the coagulated and rolled sheets of rubber were smoked and cured to a rich golden yellow (seen through clone TJI planted in 1938). Beyond and right is the site of the new factory.

BELOW
A close-up of scaffolding and guy-ropes, with the foreground coolie breaking stone on contract. Gangs of men were detailed off every morning to go to the estate jungle and cut down and transport suitable long, straight trees for use as scaffolding.

eyed little children – all working to one end. A great sense of purpose and achievement.

European engineers from Colombo paid periodic visits to see that all was going as it should, as did my manager on most days. Temporary accommodation was erected to house the skilled native workers from Colombo who were mainly carpenters, stone masons, mechanics and the like, but the bulk of the donkey work was done by the estate coolies.

My working day during this period was, on average, a straight stretch from 6 am until around 3 pm when, having walked the odd ten miles, I returned saturated with sweat to my bungalow for a cold shower, a couple of glasses of lime juice, and lunch. It was on one such day that I sat down, still thirsty as always, and picking up the glass of water on the table, downed the contents in one go before realising that that had been no water. My bungalow boy had got things

TOP LEFT
The old divisional sheet making factory, tool sheds and muster ground along which our stocks of jungle timber were kept for use as required for scaffolding, etc. The coolie lines are beyond.
CENTRE LEFT
Work in progress inside the main tower. (Photo 1952.)
BOTTOM LEFT
East elevation from the muster ground. (Photo 1952.)
RIGHT
West elevation – taking shape. (Photo 1952.)

mixed for once and had somehow poured the contents of a bottle of gin into the water glass. I had a roaring hangover as a result and felt just about as rotten as I have ever done. We all saw the funny side of it later when I told the boy to make it whisky next time, which produced a wide grin on his face: even I can tell the colour of whisky!

After lunch I would leave the bungalow again in time to be at the muster ground and factory building site by 3.30 pm and, having seen to the many requirements for the next day and done some office work, I would finally arrive back at the bungalow between 5 pm and 5.30 pm. This left a pleasant half hour to stroll around the garden before dusk.

On some evenings after dinner, my boy would stand in a darkened corner of the sitting room turning the handle of my old gramophone while I sat by a table close to a kerosene lamp and was bombarded by moths and insects. On some nights I would spend an hour swotting up my Sinhalese. I had passed my Tamil exam at the second attempt, and was therefore entitled to a small increase in salary. Owing to the fact that I had moved to an estate in the Southern Province, where the labour force was both Tamil and Sinhalese, the latter being nearly all villagers, a knowledge of Sinhalese was also necessary. With the help of the conductor who came up to my bungalow two evenings a week, my progress with Sinhalese went sufficiently well for me to take the examination, this time in Colombo, and pass at my first attempt.

On an outlying part of one of my divisions, thousands of flying foxes would come every evening from the nearby jungle to settle on one particular clone of rubber. They always arrived just before dusk and spent the night in the trees, making a low-pitched squeaking noise as they climbed from branch to branch. I believe they were attracted to the sugary

flavour of the leaves, similar to that of the lime tree in England. Although there appeared to be no actual damage to the trees, I put a watcher on, and told him to shoot a few to frighten the rest off; which he did but, after the initial bang, the remainder carried on as if nothing had happened. It was easy to pick them out with the beam of a torch, and a shot usually brought one down. I went up there on a few nights and had a bit of shooting practice. I found that all those that fell to the ground disappeared – the coolies liked to eat them!

Bungalow life – and some light relief

I took great pride in my bungalow and its lovely garden perched on top of the hill. It was so beautifully isolated, with a view of the tops of a vast stretch of rubber trees and jungle over to the distant Ratnapura hills beyond. There was a large block of estate jungle across the valley about three quarters of a mile distant, rising in all its rugged primeval splendour to about 300 feet above the level of my own hill top. Quite often, when the wind was in the right direction, I would hear the deep bark of an elk. I often wondered if there were any leopards there, for sometimes at night the pitiful screams of an animal in mortal pain would come clearly across on the night air. The monkeys, being day feeding animals, go to sleep in the top-most branches of the trees at night, while on the jungle floor below every animal is either out preying upon its

lesser kind or is in turn being preyed upon. By day, troupes of monkeys chattered and crashed through the branches of some of the jungle trees that came up to my garden boundary, and on occasions caused damage to some of the plantain trees behind the kitchen when endeavouring to steal bananas.

One hot Sunday afternoon, my bungalow boy came to say that there were three coolies wanting to see me about a large python that had been seen near their lines. I went round to the small office at the end of the bungalow, where I found them already waiting. One of them immediately told me that his wife had seen the snake when she was going to fetch water from a nearby stream. After a good deal of arguing amongst themselves as to how big the snake actually was – it undoubtably gained a little in size each time with the telling of the story, first from wife to husband and bystanders, and then again from the husband to me – I was finally told that its length was that of two men – tall ones! Not having seen an 11-12 foot python before, I told them that I would go down with them to see the monster. The three men were all pretty excited as we traversed our way downwards in Indian file, and kept telling me that the snake could well take one of their children.

As we drew near the lines, I saw that practically all the occupants were standing along the length of the building watching our approach through the rubber. The woman who had seen the python came forward and, her husband having told her to take me to the spot where she had seen the snake, we set off

towards the stream a short distance away.

In all, a period of about half an hour must have passed since the snake had been seen, allowing for the time taken for the woman to tell her story, then for the small group to reach my bungalow, and for us to arrive at the spot once again. There was no sign of the snake anywhere, and having looked around in a wide radius for a further half hour, I made tracks back to the bungalow, but not before telling all the occupants in the lines to keep their babies and small children from wandering about. I arrived back feeling a good deal disappointed, and sat down to some tea.

It was about an hour later that my boy came to say that they had found and killed the python. As I approached the lines for the second time that afternoon, I saw a large group of men about 100 yards farther on, some armed with stout jungle staves, standing in a circle. As I drew closer, I saw that the long grass in which the snake lay had been flattened while it had been writhing around before its death. It had been killed by rocks and staves. I was quite unprepared for its size, especially its thickness. No one had exaggerated; when the python had been straightened out, it measured nearly 13½ feet. For a python it was by no means large, but its thick, tremendously powerful body would have easily been capable of wrapping itself around a small baby and crushing every bone in its body. Its normal prey is practically anything in the jungle that it can get a hold of, monkey, spotted deer, pig, mouse deer, kabra-goya, and even dogs when it comes within the vicinity of native dwellings. The coolies skinned the snake and brought the skin up to my bungalow, where it was spread out on a long plank of timber, nailed down and salted. When the skin was cured, it was rolled up into a near circle like a swiss roll, and I kept it in a drawer for many a long year before having it made up into three rather attractive wallets.

Sometimes I was incarcerated in the bungalow all day due to the torrential rain. I distinctly remember one particular occasion. Heavy rain had fallen continuously and I passed the time by walking from one room to another watching the storm which, as far as I could tell, appeared to be directly overhead, as the terrific flashes of forked lightning were followed almost immediately by ear shattering crashes of thunder. Torrents of water, coming off the Mangalore tiled roof, fell like a waterfall into the open cement drain that ran all around the bungalow to lead the water away. The lawn itself was a white sheet of water, sizzling under the impact of the deluge upon it. Although there should have been two hours before dusk, the sky had become almost black; I shouted at the top of my voice to the boy to light a couple of kerosene lamps. Moving across to the dining room windows at the rear of the bungalow, I stood watching the water running off the grass in front of me. Immediately in front of the window was a verandah which ran around the whole of the building; it was some five feet wide, formed by the protrusion of the roof. It was while I was standing, face pressed against the window, looking at the grass slope directly in front which was covered by a sheet of running water, that lightning struck at the very spot at which I was looking. A flashing streak hit the ground, accompanied simultaneously by an earth shattering crash of thunder, and the grass slope became in an instant a sheet of flame about a foot or so in height with a radius of about 15 yards. Although about 20 heavy Mangalore tiles above the verandah and dining room were shattered into pieces, unaccountably not a single pane of glass was broken at my windows. The next morning a large circle of the grass slope was found to have been completely scorched.

Sometimes, when a storm had all but passed on its way, and the sky was a mixture of yellow ochre and black, the very stillness of the air seemed ominously charged with electricity. Mist and cloud hung around the brooding jungle tops as the thunder, reverberating from hill to hill, slowly receded. It was then, during the stillness after the storm, that the sound of water could be heard everywhere, rushing and tumbling down steep slopes into the swirling waters of the rivers below.

Readers will long ago have realised that the planter is always on duty, 24 hours a day if need be. For recreation there was always the club – about 19 miles away – where, in pleasant old fashioned surroundings with a billiard room and bar, a very convivial evening could be passed. There was also a tennis court and a squash court nearby. However late one stayed at the club, it was considered by all a sin not to be back on the estate in time for morning muster at 6 am. On one occasion, I can remember leaving the club at the fateful hour of 4.30 in the morning, having arrived there the previous evening at 9 pm. I eventually arrived back on the estate an hour later, as the first glimmer of dawn showed in the sky. Not having enough time to return to my bungalow to change, I elected to drive straight to the muster ground dressed as I was, in my dinner jacket. My arrival at the muster ground to the sound of cock crowing and tom-toms coming from the nearby lines was one of the earliest I had ever achieved. For those of you who are quick enough on the uptake to realize that it does not take one a whole hour to travel 19 miles in a car – even on a remote and jungly road – let me remind you that there were many bends in the road around which one hoped to steer a safe course. It had been a marvellous party.

The cobra and the cricket match

Unlike in the central hill districts, in the Southern Province the estates, whether rubber or tea, were far more isolated and the clubs too were few and far between. Some of the planters took up shooting, but the chief relaxation was to be found either at the club, or in paying visits to each other's bungalows for a meal and a chat, or sometimes for a game of cricket.

As my bungalow lawn was of a fair size and absolutely flat, it was ideal for cricket – not the sort of game one usually thinks of, but one in which the total number of players on the field amounted to no more than five or six; two or three of my friends, the cook, the bungalow boy and the gardener if he could be found. My friends and I would always be either batting, bowling, or keeping wicket, while the servants would act as fielders, which was rather unfair on them. The gear amounted to three stumps, a bat and, as we had no pads, a tennis ball was used.

On one occasion we were all playing on the lawn when the boy gave a loud shout of 'sare pāmbu', which in Tamil means 'rat snake'. We all looked to where he was pointing and saw the snake – some five feet long – slithering along an open drain at the side of the bungalow. I shouted to the boy to go and bring my walking stick, which he did very smartly, while the rest of us stood around watching the snake's progress. With the walking stick gripped firmly in my hand, I hurried over to where the so-called rat snake was and, just as I was lifting the stick in the air, the snake – to everyone's great surprise, and mine in particular – sat up, its hood came out, and it made a lightning strike at my legs. Its quickness of attack had me well beaten and it was pure luck that I was standing just out of its striking range, for that was no rat snake – it was a cobra. My heart missed a beat, and a prickly sensation came over me as I realised how near I had come to being bitten. Most planters in the Southern Province would have killed a few cobras and rat snakes, as there were plenty around, but I had not had such a close shave before.

I am sure that I had never moved backwards so quickly, and it did not get a second chance, but I knew only too well that, had I been standing six inches closer, it would have struck me. Having retreated a few yards from the snake in my initial surprise, I became aware of loud

The cobra slid along the open drain, up onto the verandah and into the bedroom. (Photo 1954.)

shouts of 'nulla pambu' coming from the servants, but by then I did not need telling that it was the 'good snake', as Tamils call the cobra. Knowing that I was dealing with a cobra and not a rat snake, I was a good deal more cautious in my second approach of the snake, which by then had travelled along the cement drain, up onto the verandah, and disappeared into one of the bedrooms. Upon entering the bedroom, I saw that it was slipping about on the highly polished smooth floor, and managed to give it a crack – breaking its back, which immobilised it allowing me to finish it off quite easily.

Snakes will, in practically all cases, slide off when approached, but if accidently trodden on while resting in long grass or cornered or chased, will naturally attack and strike back in defence. I do remember a tale about a cobra that chased a coolie along one of the cart roads for about 30 yards, but have never witnessed such a happening. A cobra, when attacking, can only rear up a third of its length, which restricts its striking range to about 18-20 inches.

The bull-frogs and the frightened nurses

In the cheerful knowledge that, should my friend ever read in print the plain unadulterated facts about his long forgotten past life, he would refrain from contacting his lawyer and would instead reach for a pen in order to call a reunion, I will recount a true story. I think you will agree that it demonstrates to what lengths the appu will go in order to preserve his right to look after the master of the house. Let me tell you the story that came to be known as 'the bullfrogs and the frightened nurses'.

It was my good friend J who was involved. At the time of the incident he was on an estate some 40 miles away, and when I went to stay with him a short while after the frog affair, he told me all about it.

Like myself and most of the younger planters, he was a bachelor. Apparently he had sent an invitation to a couple of charming nurses from the Fraser Nursing Home in Colombo asking them to come and stay on his estate for the weekend. A week or so before their visit, he had told his appu of their intended arrival, and instructed him to get in some of the luxuries enjoyed by those living in the big

city: a tasty joint of ham from the Colombo Cold Storage Company, not to mention Mansion polish, extra soap and wine. He did not, after all, want his establishment to be thought anything other than the Shangri-la he had always imagined it to be. The appu, upon learning of the imminent arrival of two 'Dorasanys' (white women), out of the blue so to speak, laid his own cunning plans.

It should be mentioned at this stage that it is a well known fact that most appus preferred to work for a bachelor, mainly because he would be out in the field all day, whereas a married planter's wife would remain in the bungalow and would therefore make the staff work harder, cleaning and polishing everything in sight.

To return to the story. The astute appu, visualising the possibility of his master marrying one or other of the two young ladies, set his plans in order to thwart any such occurrence. My friend had the most presentable of his two spare bedrooms thoroughly cleaned, whilst the two single beds, under mosquito nets, were laid out with freshly ironed sheets, and there were towels and soap put on the wash-hand basins. Finally, all was made ready, the two nursing sisters arrived and, to cut a long story short, everything went wonderfully well until a couple of hours after dinner, when it was time to turn in for the night. My friend wished his guests a very good night's sleep and departed to his room, while they walked along the verandah porch to their own bedroom on the opposite side of the bungalow. It was about this time that my friend heard a certain amount of noise from the direction of his guests' room, and, upon arriving at the spot where the cries were the loudest, he quickly found the cause. In the bedroom a dozen or so huge frogs were jumping about all over the place making a sort of plopping noise as they landed on the polished cement floor, while the two poor girls stood aghast.

As far as I could gather, the girls, being new to the rigours of estate life, seemed to assume that this was the normal run of things, and that one always had to put up with a few frogs under the beds – needless to say they did not care for the experience overmuch. It had, of course, been the appu's idea to frighten the two white women away, never to return again. The only trouble was, he did overdo it a little – three or four frogs would have been quite enough . . . inside the beds! Probably, some time after dinner and before bedtime the appu had gone

into the bedroom and had emptied a large cardboard box with a dozen of the largest frogs that he had previously found for the occasion. My friend, who was most annoyed at the time, made the appu collect up the frogs and dump them over a steep terrace at the end of the garden. J put the blame squarely on the shoulders of his appu, and that's about all there is to it, except to say that the two white women never visited the estate again; nor did my friend get married for some years, such was his reputation.

For some planters it was a very lonely life. I remember during my time in Ceylon hearing about a young assistant who, during his lonely Sundays, used to go to the boundary of his garden and stand there for hours looking down at the coolies moving about in their lines far below. Perhaps he derived some comfort from seeing other humans close by. Apparently he acted this way for some considerable time before shooting himself.

Then at the other end of the extreme I knew an awfully nice fellow in the Southern Province, who used to chase bats around his bungalow with a tennis racket. I stayed at his bungalow for the night on one occasion and was treated to a performance. Every evening he used to sit reading in his sitting room; all the doors were wide open to the verandah and garden and each night – except during the monsoon – bats would fly into the room, do a circle and then fly out again, whereupon he would throw down his book, jump up, and shout loudly for the boy. When the boy arrived, his master would wait for one of his nocturnal friends to fly in, and would simply point a finger at it, whereupon the boy would run off to return quickly with a tennis racket. My friend would then chase the bat around the room for a few minutes, making swipes at it until he tired of the game. He was honest enought to admit that he had never actually been able to hit a bat. I happened to know that he was a very keen tennis player, otherwise I might have thought differently.

During my first three years in Ceylon I had taken only one week's holiday, when I had ridden around the island along the coast roads, ending up in Jaffna in the north. Apart from being off the estate for the odd day or night, I had made only one trip up-country to play in a hockey match, and one trip with my manager and his wife to a game reserve at Yala in the south of the island. So it was with some excitement that I now contemplated my next change of scenery – a trip to climb Adams Peak.

A visit to Adam's Peak

Although its height of 7363 feet hardly bears mentioning in comparison to many mountains in the Himalayan region and other parts of the world, it is the world's most holy mountain and, as such, must be worthy of a visit. The mountain is venerated by many nationalities, consequently Hindus, Buddhists, Moslems and Christians make their pilgrimages there.

I had for many years glimpsed its conical peak from afar, and having seen my bungalow boy and his family depart one year on their pilgrimage, I resolved to do likewise when I had the chance. This finally came in 1954. As events were to turn out, I could not have picked a better month to go for sheer atmosphere – not so much the more rarified atmosphere to be found at around 7000 feet, but that which is generated by thousands of people on the move with but one goal in mind.

As I wished to see the famous shadow of the peak at sunrise, I decided to base myself at a hotel in Nuwara Eliya, from where I could more easily make the journey to arrive at Laxapana at around midnight. Having arrived at the hotel after a long trip of nearly 200 miles, the very first bunch of people I met told me that they, too, were off to climb the peak that night. Their party was four in number, a nurse, two school-teachers, and a banking type who, like the women, was also up from Colombo. You may imagine how happy I was to be included in their party, as to have been a lone traveller, as I had expected to be, would not have been quite so pleasurable. After a very short sleep we started off in two cars; the banker took the two school-teachers in his own car, while the nurse and I went along in a taxi. We were to be the lead car – 'the cutting edge'. The taxi driver, knowing the way, sped along the dark and continually twisting roads – always flanked by tea or a big drop – at breakneck speed, with the banker hard pressed to hold his position behind us. Our man could not have been a worse driver, but to his credit he did manage to stay on the road; the thing he came nearest to hitting was what looked like a tall grevillea shade tree that was growing in the tea at the edge of the road. I now know the reason why Ceylon drivers drive only as they do – it must be the fault of the examiners! When I bought my first car in Ceylon, I went up to the big city, Colombo, for the day to get my AA driving licence. After I had been into the office and stated my business, a Sinhalese examiner came out with me and we jumped into my car. Before moving off, he assured me that having to drive around the block was a mere formality, and as I looked puzzled for a moment, he quickly added that he would in fact be pleased to pass me without us going an inch, or words to that effect. He could plainly see that I had managed to arrive all in one piece after the odd hundred miles; however, I said that it was quite all right, and shot off smartly, knowing full well that, providing I did not knock anyone over on the pavement, I was home and dry. Our drive was short and sweet; I narrowly missed a couple of cows, and a pi-dog – none of which had any right to be on the race circuit – but managed to keep clear of humans, and did not even put a wheel on the pavement, which, after all, is a novelty to the country man. So you will understand my feelings towards the taxi driver as we hurtled along

Owing to the lack of photographs for my 1954 trip to Adam's Peak, those taken in 1982 are shown.

Our 1982 climb to the summit was made at the very beginning of January, at the start of the pilgrimage season, when there was only a trickle of pilgrims journeying to the summit. Not wishing to see the shadow but only to make the climb, my wife, the photographer and I had started on the pilgrims' path at Laxapana at 5 am, and arrived at the summit two-and-a-half hours later. The photographs were taken at the summit and at different points on the way down.

During the 29 years between the two trips, a big change had come about. Tourists had arrived upon the scene: as January is when Sri Lanka's new industry of tourism is at its height, the Belgians, Germans, French, Dutch, Americans, and Japanese almost outnumbered the true pilgrims. Where previously one had stumbled over boulders and slipped back upon the narrow path which led up the actual cone, today one finds cement and concrete, fashioned into thousands of steps, which are both easy and monotonous to a degree. The once narrow path has been considerably widened and much of the overhanging jungle trees cut down. The flaming torches carried by so many over the years are no longer required, as there are now electric lights from start to finish. There are even loudspeakers along the route up to the summit.

ABOVE
The long winding approach up towards the cone.
TOP RIGHT
Holy Dagoba. Nowadays, electric lights stretch all the way up to the summit.
BELOW
On the way up to the summit, looking back at the white Dagoba.

RIGHT
Where the pilgrims bathe to cleanse themselves before the ascent.
BELOW RIGHT
Buddhist priests and pilgrims look out upon the wonderful scene at 8 am. Despite being only six degrees from the Equator, it is often bitterly cold on the summit at night. (Photos all 1982.)

– they were decidedly of a kindred spirit.

After a couple of hours and many narrow escapes passing through Talawakelle and Dickoya, we reached the final hilltop which led down into the valley of Maskeliya. It was here that we had our first clear view of the Peak at a distance of about five miles. A long chain of moving light made by thousands of flaming torches could clearly be seen, stretching along the approach route up to the cone, spiralling around in a half circle as it reached the summit. We drove on until we eventually came to Laxapana, which was to be our starting point. The time was five minutes to midnight.

Leaving the taxi driver with the cars, our little party soon became engulfed in the stream of pilgrims. Over the first few miles our path lay through tea, and after passing the last of the tea bushes on Dalhousie estate, the path became steeper and we entered the jungle. Having reached the base of the cone, the going became harder and the cold of the night air was no longer noticeable as we warmed to the more serious climbing.

I had brought along a good thick pullover, which I carried together with a couple of bags belonging to two of the women; I cannot remember what on earth was inside them, but one way and another they were beginning to get heavy. As we scrambled upwards over large boulders and up deeply cut steps, we went shoulder to shoulder with pilgrims. We carried no torches of our own, relying on the considerable number that were all about us along the path.

Each family toiled slowly upwards, some leaning on staves cut from the jungle, while others, young and old, their dark eyes flashing in the torchlight, watched patiently as we passed them on the path. Their progress upwards was fairly slow for, unlike us, they were in no hurry and in any case the very old and very young had to be helped, cajoled and, in some cases, carried up the path. Quite a hindrance to those climbing upwards was the fact that equal numbers were returning down from the summit; this caused many blockages along the entire length of the rugged path which led up the cone. To the side of the path was an occasional shed made of bamboo and thatch, and in these the pilgrims would sleep and rest before attempting the final and most trying part of the ascent. Wooden planks to lie on were

Adam's Peak at 7363 ft – from the air. (Photo c1935.)

The shadow of the peak. (Photographed from the summit, c1900.)

their only comfort, but considering the hardships of the long journey, they must indeed have been welcome.

By now everyone in our party was soaked to the skin with sweat from our exertions. Four hours after starting found us at the steepest part just below the summit – we were now on all fours, scrambling up the steep face. For quite some time we had heard the sound of a bell clanging out from the heights above, but now the almost continual noise grew louder. Ahead and above us, near the bell, the steep and narrow path was choked with pilgrims as everyone waited their turn at the bell. Every pilgrim must toll the bell according to the number of times he has made the ascent, and legend has it that no sound will come from the bell when it is tolled by any who are unclean.

At last there was just one Tamil between me and the bell. He took his turn and must have gone on for nearly a full minute, as he tolled it 19 times. How could one follow that? I rung the bell once, which was my due, but nevertheless felt very proud as I did so amongst such a gathering.

As we reached the top, very hot and sweating profusely, an icy wind went through our bones and soon had us all shivering. The two bags that I had carried each produced a jacket of sorts, and within a minute we had all donned our extra clothes. In spite of the coats it was so cold that my teeth were chattering. I wondered how the pilgrims dressed in their flimsy garments could stand it, but they pressed closely together for warmth and comfort. The time was 4.50 am, which left another hour before sunrise.

The highest point on the summit is the shrine itself, ten feet above the terrace, and it is here that the sacred footprint can be seen. Each pilgrim mounts a short flight of steps carrying small offerings of flower buds which, after a prayer, are reverently laid on the ground close to the footprint. If the pilgrim be a Hindu, he sees it as the footprint of the god Siva, if he be Sinhalese, it is the footprint of Buddha, and a Mohammedan sees it as the footprint of Adam. These many religions claim the sanctity of the mountain, and make the pilgrimage to worship the sacred footprint on the summit. The size of the summit terrace around the central rock and shrine is in the region of 70 feet long by 40 feet across.

As far as I could judge, there must have been between 200 and 300 pilgrims on the summit. Two large bonfires had been lit around which many family groups huddled to keep warm; for the rest, some warmth was obtained from the sheer numbers of people standing shoulder to shoulder. We in our small party squatted down against the low parapet wall that surrounds the summit, and much of the icy blast went over the top of us. The bitter cold did not, however, prevent us from looking out upon our grand surroundings.

A thick blanket of white cloud lay beneath us everywhere stretching away in every direction, except that here and there a tall mountain rose, its stark outline showing 2000 or 3000 feet above the sea of clouds. The sky above us was clear and full of stars, while the moon was so full and large that, had it not been for the flickering of the torches all around us, one could easily have read a newspaper by its light. Such a sight could never be forgotten.

As the first glimmerings of dawn broke over the horizon, a great buzz of excitement rose within the multitude. Everyone was by now standing pressed close together on the eastern side of our crowded pinnacle, waiting for the moment when the sun broke over the horizon. A glorious diffused golden glow came slowly over the sky and revealed more clearly the mist-covered valleys below. Having watched the splendour of the sunrise for a very short while, we then made all possible haste around to the other side of the summit – facing west – to look for the famous shadow.

The sun continued to rise and we became aware of a faint but yet none too clear impression of the shadow. I wondered if this was all that we were to see but, as the sun climbed a little higher and its rays lengthened, the impression grew sharper, darker and larger, and in seconds the mighty shadow stood before us. It looked like a distant pyramid floating in the sky – a mirage – one could not honestly say whether it was 10 miles away or 50. As the sun rose still higher, the shadow advanced towards us until we were enveloped by it as it finally merged with its mighty parent – Adam's Peak. The sky was clear, the shadow had vanished.

As we felt the sun's warm rays for the first time, we started off down again. In all our time upon the pilgrims' path, we had not seen another European.

I had not long been back on the estate when I learnt that the company had decided upon the felling and planting of 105 acres of estate jungle situated on one of my divisions. Some 70 acres of this was tall virgin jungle, while the remainder was semi-scrubland, carrying a sparse stand of secondary growth trees.

During the 1950s – unlike the great pioneering years – there was little new clearing work being carried out in Ceylon. Mid and up-country tea estates had been fully developed to their maximum acreages, and in these regions it was rare for any jungle to be opened out for planting with tea. In the Southern Province, the position was slightly different in that there were still new clearings being opened up from estate owned jungle, mainly for planting with rubber. One was indeed fortunate to have the chance of doing this particular work.

The new clearing – hard at work

It had been arranged with a native contractor to fell and clear away all the trees on a 50 acre block of jungle, leaving the balance of 20 acres of jungle and 35 acres of scrubland to be cleared by the estate labour force. The expense of such an operation is great for, whereas it is three years before the tea bush is brought into plucking, it takes seven years before the rubber tree reaches a girth of 21 inches at three feet from the ground and is ready to be tapped.

The contractor and his men had come from a village about 18 miles away, and arrived one morning complete with a ramshackle old lorry and, only a little later, with two elephants which had been ridden all the way. In his 50 acre contract block were many good timber trees which were suitable for furniture making. A large sawing hut was soon erected by his men, and it was to here that most of timber was brought. Once they had started, the men worked seven days a week, except on full moon, or 'poya day', the Sinhalese monthly holiday. It was necessary for two estate watchers, who each carried a gun, to keep an eye on the felling, otherwise some good timber trees would also have disappeared from the adjacent estate-owned jungle; I would also visit the estate jungle which lay close to the contractor's felling area on Sundays and at odd times of the day to see that all was as it should be.

Many of the jungle trees must have been over 150 feet in height, and at ground level their great roots spread in all directions to anchor the lofty giants. Massive trunks rose perfectly straight, without branch or limb, for a full 100 feet to the canopy above, seeking the light in competition with the rest of the forest. The steady click of axes falling upon hard timber and the occasional mutterings and shouts of the coolies when a tree was about to fall went on all day. On some of the forest giants the axes, sharp as they were, bounced back as if they had struck on iron. When felled, the long straight trunks of the very tall trees were cut into more manageable lengths of 20 feet or so, depending upon their girth and weight, and a man would cut a hole in the end of each of these shortened lengths through which a strong chain could be passed to enable the elephants to drag the timber.

There were numerous small villages close to the boundaries of the estate, and from these a good number of Sinhalese would come daily to work on the new clearing; many of their wives and daughters were already employed by the estate, either as ancillary workers or as tappers.

A few weeks after the arrival of the contractor's men, work was started by the estate labour force on the remaining acreage. The estate had just received three Australian 'monkey grubbers', which were going to be used to open out the 20 acres of heavy jungle. Before the monkey grubbers could be used to good effect, the forest floor had to be roughly cleared. A gang of men – all Tamils – worked their way through the jungle, cutting down all the undergrowth and small trees up to a girth of 18 inches; this left the floor of the jungle comparatively clear and open, ready for the monkey grubber men to start their work on the remaining larger trees.

A group of three Tamils worked each machine, which was a simple portable contrivance made of steel with a highly geared winch, carrying on its drum about 200 feet of steel hauser. Prior to winching, the tree's wide lateral roots were exposed and then cut through with an axe; this helped the work, for the tree was then not only more easy to pull over but, when it finally crashed to the ground, the remainder of its root system could be levered and ripped out of the ground. An extra large tree would be selected to which the monkey grubber was anchored at its base, the steel hauser was then run out to the tree that was to be pulled down – the hauser being placed around the tree at about 10 feet from the ground – then the winching would begin with two of the coolies pushing and pulling a lever backwards. The steady click-click as the winching men vigorously moved the lever would only be interrupted by the noise high above of the tree canopy shifting slowly and then smashing its way through the branches of adjacent trees, until it would gradually heel over and fall with a reverberating crash amidst a shower of leaves and broken branches.

Each day I would visit this part of the new clearing and listen to the sound of axes shattering the solitude of the surrounding jungle, occasionally driving out an owl or a group of flying foxes from their slumbers. The smell of resin was pleasant and, as the sun rose higher in the sky and beat down upon the fallen forest, my thoughts would turn to the day when the trees would be dry enough to 'fire'.

Over in the contractor's block of jungle, the distant sound of axes, followed every now and then by the crash of trees, went on all day.

It was while clearing the 35 acres of scrubland that we came upon a small area that had previously been planted with tea. After the land had been cleared of its tallish undergrowth and scattered trees, one could plainly see old supervision paths that had once been traced on the land. The paths were in pretty good condition, and only required cutting out a little. This portion of land had probably been opened out from virgin jungle some 50 or 60 years before, and for one reason or another had been abandoned. It was strange to walk along these forgotten paths in the footsteps of the men who, long ago, had cleared the original jungle, planted tea and tended it. The conductor told me that, according to some of the very old coolies, there had once been a tea estate in that part, as well as a small factory. This news so whetted my appetite that we proceeded to the place the very next day, and found amongst the undergrowth and trees the clearly discernible ruins of the factory.

There were many young clearings on the estate, and on one of these there had been damage to the young rubber trees caused by an elk. This large sambur deer, known as the elk in Ceylon, used to lie up in a good sized block of adjoining jungle throughout the day, coming out at night to go into the rubber clearing and eat the tender bark from some of the rubber trees along the boundary.

On two previous days when I had been making my way through this particular jungle looking for the elk, I had been startled by a large animal which I had not seen but had only heard the crashing of branches as it made off. As it was only active at nights, I put one of the watchers on night duty, telling him to try and shoot the animal. The result can be seen from the photograph on this page.

For the first two or three years I always carried a watch on my wrist while doing my daily rounds but, after continual practice at all times of the day, I taught myself to tell the correct time by merely looking at the sun and shadows or, failing that, by the noise of the birds and insect life – or by the lack of it. I tested myself over a long period, and finding that I was never more than 15 minutes out at any time of the day, gave up wearing a watch. It was not a particularly cleaver feat as all the natives tell the time by looking at the sun, but somehow not to carry the time made me feel a little more free – unlike the city man who lives by his watch.

A big fire – a call at midnight

A few months later I had my first experience of a big fire. We had already successfully set fire to the by then dry 20 acres of felled jungle, with no damage to the adjoining jungle on one side or the estate rubber across a cart road on the other. Now the separate block of 35 acres of scrubland and semi-woodland was to be fired. By dusk the fire had run its course over a good two-thirds of the area, leaving behind smouldering tree trunks and hundreds of small patches of flickering flames which made a pretty sight in the gathering gloom. A pall of smoke rose above the clearing into the evening sky, and the smell of burnt wood was everywhere.

One small area was still burning

The Sinhalese watcher who shot the elk is seen standing fourth from the right. A good sized buck elk weighs in the region of 600 lbs. Elk flesh is coarse and tough, but prized by the natives. (Photo 1956.)

furiously as night fell, and before returning to my bungalow, I saw to it that two good Tamils were left to act as night watchmen. They had instructions to keep an eye on the spread of flames, especially along one particular part of the estate which had a common boundary with a small, native owned, rubber holding, and to let both me and the conductor know if anything untoward should happen.

It was close on midnight when my boy woke me. One of the Tamils had just arrived to say that the flames had jumped across our boundary and were spreading into the next rubber property. As I ran across the drive to the garage, I quickly became aware of an ominous red glow in the sky coming from beyond a large block of jungle that rose high against the skyline. Taking my motorbike, I was soon speeding along under the rubber at breakneck speed, feeling for the very first time in my life that all the cares of the world were upon me. As I drew nearer, my heart grew heavy; I had never seen a sky quite like this before. A deep glow not only filled the sky, but also spread over the whole landscape. When I finally reached the fatal spot, I saw with some relief that the conflagration was mostly on the estate side of the boundary, just within the new clearing itself; nonetheless at half a dozen points the flames had crossed and were spreading through the rubber trees on the other side. Even though these seedling rubber trees – growing amongst thick weeds and bushes – were about 40 years old and on their last legs, the fire had to be stopped, and quickly.

The conductor and a small group of men came towards me as I pulled up, and we immediately set off down the slope below the cart road which led to a small stream. Water was just what was needed, and a fire-break. Being a rubber estate, there was no difficulty in obtaining buckets since every tapper had one to carry the latex. Returning to the road, I told the conductor to jump on the pillion seat and we shot off to the nearest lines to wake the inmates. About 40 men were quickly pressed into service and set off towards the fire, carrying between them about three dozen buckets and axes.

Back at the new clearing, I once again made my way down to the stream and stood looking up the opposite hillside to where the boundary ran. I knew that the men would not arrive for at least another ten minutes and, as I could do nothing without them, I tried to decide where it was best to cut the fire break in the adjacent property leading up the hill. By now the flames had crossed a good length of the boundary and were running through the undergrowth beneath the old rubber trees, setting the trunks of some alight. By the time the men arrived, I had formed a plan. All available hands were put to clearing a seven foot wide fire break all the way up the steepish hillside, about 20 yards inside the adjoining property and some 15 yards ahead of the advancing flames. Amidst a lot of shouting and hullabaloo, they set to furiously slashing the undergrowth and pulling it back. With 30 or more able men thus employed, the fire-break soon extended to the limit of the immediate danger zone, which covered in all about 100 yards along the boundary.

Meanwhile, the remaining men had been carrying their buckets of water up the hill, and were doing the best they could against the advancing flames. As the fire-break was now complete, it was further widened along its entire length. Time passed without our knowing it; the men worked with a strength and fury although they were all very hot, both those carrying water, and those slashing at the undergrowth. I spent my time stumbling up and down the slope, keeping an eye out for any danger points that might break out and generally speeding up the difficult job of the water carriers. During the cutting and slashing of the fire-break, hundreds of small sharp pointed branches were left sticking up from the ground, and these caused many cuts to the ankles and bare feet of the men, lit only in their work by the flames.

Sometime later, the conductor arrived with more men and buckets and thereafter there must have been upwards of 60 buckets of water being thrown down in front of, and along, the entire length of the fire break every four or five minutes. By dawn the boundary area was safe. Notwithstanding the five hour fight, about 80 rubber trees from the adjoining property had been badly scorched.

As daylight came I mustered the men on the cart road. Tired, scratched and bleeding from cuts, they had done a good job. All were to be given a full day's pay. They were a good bunch of men. I, like the coolies, was covered in scratches, cuts and charcoal marks as I made my way back to the bungalow to shave, wash and breakfast. For me the day's work was just beginning.

When I returned to the scene of the night's activities about two hours later, smoke was rising peacefully upwards over the whole of the now blackened land. The first two rows of seedling rubber trees belonging to the smallholding looked a sorry sight. On our side, scores of small subdued pockets of flame smouldered, and a pall of light blue smoke hung over the clearing, drifting slowly into the nearby jungle to disappear amongst the tall lush green leaves. I walked a few paces onto the blackened landscape, and the heat of the ground was such that I quickly beat a hasty retreat back to the road. Everywhere white ash lay thick on the ground, while the blackened stumps of trees still smouldered on. In a couple of days, when the land had cooled, a small gang of axemen would go over the whole area cutting and piling up the partly burnt wood which would be rekindled again. The clearing was then ready for the cutting of cart roads, paths, drains and silt pits, and then for the lining of the ground, pegging and holing.

The first task was that of tracing and cutting cart roads for supervision purposes and, where possible, to connect with an already existing road. It was after the line of the road had been traced, more often than not on a steep slope of land, that, during the subsequent cutting of the road, one would sometimes come upon a massive granite boulder in the very path of the road, unearthed by the road cutting coolies. As with the cutting of latrine pits previously mentioned, a special Tamil would be brought in to bore an 18″ or 24″ hole in the rock, and I would then place my sticks of dynamite and blow the rock apart. If necessary, the 'borer-man', as he was called, would bore further holes and this method would be continued until enough of the rock had been removed to take the road through. I much preferred blasting rock out in an open clearing to going down 'thunder-box pits'; it was much healthier!

In a new clearing at this stage there is always the need for many small gangs of men, whose job is to cut up and roll aside any unburnt tree trunks or root systems that may straddle and hold up the road, path, drain, and silt pit cutting works. As these different works progress, the burnt surface of the forest floor changes; red soil is thrown up everywhere, and the whole clearing takes on a more orderly appearance.

Ravines, down which the water of a thousand monsoons have tumbled, would now be blocked by huge rocks, or choked with half-burnt tree trunks and root systems of fallen trees. These, too, had to be cleared out to afford a free unobstructed passage for the rains. These natural jungle ravines are turned into what are called 'leading drains', and it is into these that all the silt pits and side drains lead. Then, when heavy rain falls as it can only do in the tropics, it does not simply rush down the steep slopes over the cultivation area, but is channelled off, first into silt pits, then into side drains, and finally into the main leading drains. There is no shortage of stone for the building of terraces and the construction of leading drains, for it is found everywhere in the clearing. The Sinhalese stone mason excels at this particular job, and it is always a pleasure to stand and watch the work.

Silt pits, which are used to hold up the valuable top-soil, were unknown in the days of the early pioneers, who knew little about soil conservation; theirs was a big enough fight to merely exist while opening out hundreds of thousands of acres of dense virgin jungle. In later years, when it was seen just how much rich top-soil was washed off the steep slopes down to the rivers below, the cutting of silt pits became standard procedure.

The whole clearing is a scene of wonderful activity when works are in progress: dark glistening bodies cutting silt pits and drains, mumaties poised above heads for a moment before coming down with a crump into the earth, scores of small fires burning all over the clearing, and the constant chink of the stone mason as he hammers, chips and shapes his large stones, while his two helpers wage war with their heavy sledgehammers upon nearby granite boulders. In such surroundings, with smoke climbing slowly upwards into a clear blue sky, it was indeed hard to drag oneself away.

As the different works progressed, the tidying up of the land continued until, at last, cart roads, paths, silt pits, drains, terracing, and planting holes had been cut and, with the filling of the holes, the new clearing was ready for planting when the monsoon came. A nursery had been established earlier and the beds sown with seeds from seedling rubber. When the young seedlings had reached a height of five or six feet, they were 'bud grafted' with buds taken from the branches of high yielding clonal rubber. The young, successfully bud-grafted seedling trees were then cut down to just above the grafted eye-bud, and were then lifted from the nursery as budded stumps and transported to the new clearings for planting out.

It was about this time that I had my first taste of venison. The watcher arrived at my bungalow one day to say that he had shot a deer in the estate jungle. I went off with him and, by the time we had arrived at the spot, two or three coolies had got news of the kill and were standing on the cart road nearby. The deer had been dragged down to the road, and before carrying it away I told the watcher to stand it up for a photograph. It was a full-grown spotted deer.

Illness of any sort had evaded me for five years, but then at last it caught up with me. It happened to be pouring at the time and everyone was soaked through; we were hard at work planting out the budded stumps in a part of the 105 acre clearing. Suddenly an unaccustomed bout of shivering took a hold of me. The atmosphere was by no means cold and yet I continued to shake. I arrived back at the bungalow still shivering, and told the appu and boy to put blankets on the bed and bring me a hot drink and a couple of good old aspirins – the cure for everything. Having dried myself, I crawled into bed and lay there shaking. In spite of the blankets I felt obliged to get out of bed and put on the only two pullovers that I possessed, as well as a thick overcoat that I had brought out from England. It turned out that I had yellow jaundice, and after it had run its natural course I was my old self once again. Having been incarcerated in my bungalow for a few weeks, I was only too happy to be able to escape into the more challenging world outside.

In a few short months I was due for six months leave in the UK. My excitement at the prospect was tempered with the feeling that the future for the British planter in Ceylon was going to be a short one. There were many rumblings going on in the country about the possible nationalization of the predominently British owned estates, and I began to wonder

Spotted deer. (Photo 1956.)

whether I should get out and find a job in England while I was still young enough to make the change.

It was in this frame of mind that I made my way to Colombo and boarded the Orient Line passenger ship *Orion* which, curiously enough, was to take me back to Ceylon again six months later. Despite the clouded horizon, I did go back after all, for a four-and-a-half year tour. But many of the younger planters were beginning to leave the island; the older ones stayed on hoping that things would last out during their remaining days. Was it better to stay on for an unknown number of years, and then have to leave the island and return to the UK at a more difficult age at which to start afresh, or was it better to get out while still young? I chose the latter. Two of my good friends had left a year before me, and I felt that, although I was steering into the unknown, I had made the right if painful decision. After only seven years planting, at the age of 29, I boarded the liner at Colombo on a one way ticket.

Before leaving Ceylon I had bought a property in the south of England where I was to start my own business.

Although the passengers were changing for dinner, I stayed up on deck, leaning against the rail at the stern of the ship. My heart was heavy as the island grew smaller in the distance, until finally I could see it no longer. I turned and walked slowly to my cabin. It was too late to get dressed in time for dinner, and in any case I was in no mood to sit down at table with people I had never seen before; I went to bed with my thoughts. The friends who had come to see me off were now on their way back to their estates; sooner or later they, too, would be forced to make the same decision as I had taken.

After a few very hard years at the outset, the business that I started from scratch is, I am thankful to say, still prospering 28 years later.

(Photo 1982.)

By the mid 1960s only 150 planters remained in Ceylon. The few that were left could see the red light coming, and the steady exodus went on during the years leading up to the nationalization of the estates, which eventually took place in 1975.

The British planter who for close on 150 years had been such a prominent part of the landscape in both India and Ceylon, today exists no more.

Twenty-five years after leaving, I returned to the island of Sri Lanka, as it is now known. In most cases the tea bushes were the same, but the people had changed. And yet they still call their tea 'Ceylon tea'!

Bibliography

Antrobus HA *A History of the Assam Company* (Privately printed by T & A Constable Ltd, Edinburgh 1957)

Antrobus HA *A History of the Jorehaut Tea Company*

Arnold Edwin *Coffee on the Indian hills* (Sampson, Low, Marston 1893)

Baildon S *The tea industry in India 1882*

Baker SW *The rifle and hound* (Longman, Brown & Green 1854)

Baker SW *Eight years in Ceylon* (Longman, Green & Co 1891)

Bald Claud *Indian tea, its culture & manufacture* (Calcutta & Simla 1922)

Blake G *BI centenary 1856-1956*

Bramah E *Tea and Coffee* (Hutchinson & Co 1972)

Bremer JM *Memories of a Ceylon planter's life* (Rivingtons 1930)

Capper John *Sketches of Ceylon in olden times* (Whittingham 1878)

Cave HW *Golden tips* (Sampson, Low, Marston 1900)

Elliot RH *Experiences of a planter in the jungles of Mysore* (Chapman & Hall 1871)

Ferguson J *Ceylon in 1883* (Sampson, Low, Marston 1883)

Forrest DM *A hundred years of Ceylon tea* (Chatto & Windus 1967)

Gordon Cumming CF *Two happy years in Ceylon* (Chatto & Windus 1893)

Griffiths Sir Percival *A History of the Indian tea industry* (Weidenfeld & Nicholson 1967)

Griffiths Sir Percival *A History of the joint steamer companies* (Inchcape & Co Ltd London)

Haeckel E *A visit to Ceylon* (Kegan, Paul and Trench 1883)

Hamilton VH & Fasson SM *Scenes in Ceylon* (Chapman & Hall 1881)

Harler CR *Culture and marketing of tea* (Oxford University Press 1933)

Legge Vincent *The Birds of Ceylon* (Published by author, London 1880)

Lewis JP *A List of inscriptions on tombstones & monuments in Ceylon* (1911)

Lindgren O *The Trials of a planter* (Printed privately, Kalimpong 1933)

MacGregor D *The Tea clippers* (1932)

Maguire E *The Sirocco story* (Davidsons & Company Belfast)

O'Brian *A Series of fifteen views in Ceylon* (Day & Son Lithographers 1864)

Rings *Rings from a chota sahib's pipe* (Calcutta 1901)

Skinner T *Fifty years in Ceylon* (WH Allan 1891)

Still J *The Jungle tide* (William Blackwood & Sons Ltd 1930)

Story H *Hunting and shooting in Ceylon* (Longman, Green & Co 1907)

Sulivan E *The Bungalow and the tent* (Richard Bentley 1854)

Tennent Sir JE *Ceylon: an account of the island* (Longman, Green & Co 1860)

Ukers WH *All about tea* (Tea & Coffee Trade Journal, New York 1935)

Williams H *Ceylon: pearl of the East* (Robert Hale 1950)

Wilson Christine *The Bitter berry* (Hurst & Blackett 1957)

Index

Page numbers in italic refer to illustrations

Map of Ceylon

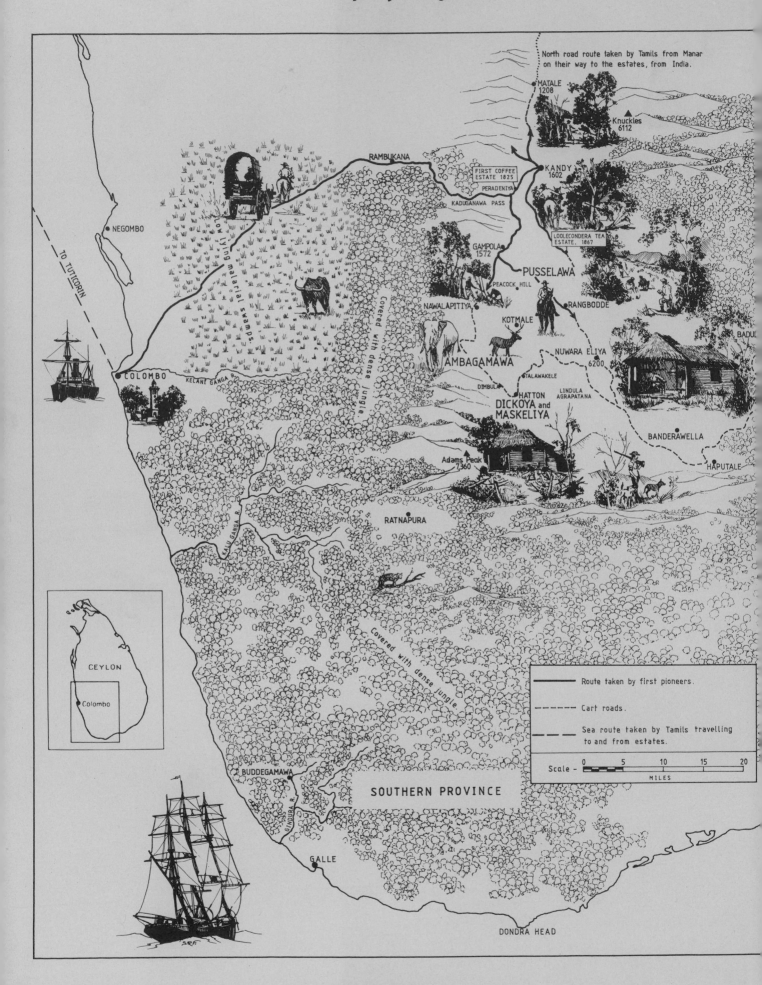

North road route taken by Tamils from Manar on their way to the estates, from India.

MATALE 1208

Knuckles 6112

RAMBUKANA

FIRST COFFEE ESTATE 1825

PERADENIYA

KANDY 1602

KADUGANAWA PASS

LOOLECONDERA TEA ESTATE. 1867

GAMPOLA 1572

PUSSELAWA

PEACOCK HILL

RANGBODDE

NAWALAPITIYA

KOTMALE

BADUI

NUWARA ELIYA 6200

AMBAGAMAWA

TALAWAKELE

DIMBULA

LINDULA AGRAPATANA

HATTON

DICKOYA and MASKELIYA

BANDERAWELLA

HAPUTALE

Adams Peak 7360

RATNAPURA

NEGOMBO

TO TUTICORIN

Low lying malarial swamps.

COLOMBO

KELANI GANGA R.

Covered with dense jungle.

Covered with dense jungle

BUDDEGAMAWA

GINDURA R.

SOUTHERN PROVINCE

MANU GANGA R.

GALLE

DONDRA HEAD

CEYLON

Colombo

	Route taken by first pioneers.
	Cart roads.
	Sea route taken by Tamils travelling to and from estates.

Scale - 0 5 10 15 20
MILES